"Shrinkwrapped describes Michael Grossman's progress as a patient moving from the 'not I' to the 'I am' state. The consciousness he has developed allows him to share his truly rewarding journey with the world."

—Dr. Anneliese Widman, PhD
Author of *When Spirit Takes Over*

"Grossman has spent dozens of years and thousands of dollars talking to shrinks—so we don't have to. 'Just when you know you have to give up on life,' concludes Grossman, 'it turns around and bathes you in its goodness.' Read this; maybe there is enough sunshine to go around!"

—William T. Merkel, PhD, ABPP
Diplomate in Clinical Psychology,
American Board of Professional Psychology
Co-author of *One Family, Two Family, New Family: Stories of Advice for Stepfamilies*

Shrinkwrapped

My First Fifty Years on the Couch

I Michael Grossman

RDR Books
Muskegon, Michigan

Shrinkwrapped

RDR Books
1487 Glen Avenue
Muskegon, MI 49441
phone: 510-595-0595
fax: 510-228-0300
www.rdrbooks.com
email: read@rdrbooks.com

ISBN 978-1-57143-128-8
Library of Congress Control Number: 2009921108

Editing, design and production: Richard Harris
Cover photo: Slobo Mitic

Distributed in the United Kingdom and Europe by
Roundhouse Publishing Ltd., Atlantic Suite, Maritime House,
Basin Road North, Hove, East Sussex BN41 1WR, United Kingdom

Distributed in Canada by
Scholarly Book Services, 127 Portland Street, 3rd Floor,
Toronto, Ontario, Canada M5V 2N4

Printed in the United States of America

Many of the names of characters in this book have been changed
for the sake of confidentiality.

To Susan and Lauren

With thanks to Roger Rapoport, Richard Harris, Ona R. Yufe and Ira Wood. Thanks to the South County Writers Group (Enid Flaherty, Tracy Hart, Ginny Leaper, Camilla Lee, Richard Parker, Jeannie Serpa). And to Martha Murphy, Patti Brickley and Laura Thorne. Thanks to Randy Grossman and Melissa Johnson, and to my sister Jill. Thanks to Dr. Robert N Butler, and Dr. Anneliese Widman. And finally, to "the group."

Contents

"The increased availability and use of psychotherapy has led to more positive attitudes toward mental health care among the general public. Before the 1960s, people often viewed the need for psychotherapy as a sign of personal weakness or a sign that the person was abnormal. Those who received therapy seldom told others about their treatment. Since then the stigma attached to psychotherapy has decreased significantly."

Theories of Psychotherapy and Counseling:
Concepts and Cases,
Richard S. Sharf, B.A., M.A., Ph.D.

". . . [L]oneliness—often connected with fear of intimacy or feelings of rejection, shame, or being unlovable—is familiar to all of us. In fact, most of the work in psychotherapy is directed toward helping clients learn to form more intimate, sustaining, and enduring relationships with others."

Staring at the Sun
Dr. Irvin D. Yalom, M.D.

ONE

Night and Day Differences

THE QUEEN, AS MOM'S FRIENDS CALLED HER, was about to hold court. She studied the long dining room table attentively, unconsciously twisting the emerald clasp that secured her pearls as she scrutinized the preparations.

"Rosa, you ought to know how to position the centerpiece," Mom said. "Emalda, you may bring the caviar out."

The kitchen door swung open, and Josefina arrived holding polished silver Jensen candlestick holders in her brown outstretched arms. Josefina, our short, barrel-shaped Cuban nanny, had impressive staying power and was the only maid who could successfully handle Mom. She'd been with our family for a record five years—prompting Mom to call her "practically a family fixture." Wordlessly, mom pointed an accusing finger at a leaning candle, and Josefina immediately righted it. The rapid shake of Mom's head was a "no" to another maid who, realizing her error, shifted each gold china plate so that the engraved "G" was easily read from seated position. Mom raised a thin crystal water goblet and enjoyed the sustained ring as she tapped it. She held it to the light, then checked the other glasses in succession for water stains.

"Be very careful with them, Maria. Do you have any idea how valuable these are?"

In similar fashion, my younger brother Randy, age three, my sister Jill, age six, and I, a nine-year-old, had been scrubbed for display. Before guests arrived, Mom routinely had Josefina put us to bed and we were expected to stay there until summoned. Inevitably an innocent guest, offering perfunctory conversation, asked how the children were, at which point Mom would feign spontaneity, blossom with delight, and beckon Josefina.

"Josefina, do bring the children to say hello to our guest," she instructed.

That was Josefina's cue to hurry up the curved stairway, pumping her heavy knees against her rigidly starched white uniform like a Tour de France cyclist. She would collect us, lead us down the stairs and parade us in crisp pajamas fresh from the shelves of my father's department store. Guests would greet us with labored smiles, tap our heads, pretend to be thrilled and remark with flat outstretched hands that they'd known us since we were this tall—a comment of equal disinterest to us and the adults. Mom, also disinterested after a moment, signaled Josefina to put us away.

At age nine, I dared break protocol one day by refusing to leave on cue. I made my stand at an afternoon tea party when the sun was high in the western Michigan sky. The usual guests mingled, chatted and obediently admired the three of us kids. But like a freshly popped seltzer bottle, I was fizzing with energy, and I felt that going back to bed was just not acceptable.

"It's early. Why do I have to go to now?" I asked Mom. "Can't I play outside?"

Mother's face darkened, but since several amused guests had turned to watch, she forced a brittle smile.

"Because it's bedtime dear," she said in a razor sweet voice. "And we go to bed at night."

"How can it be night? Look, Mom," I said pulling away from Josefina and going to the window. I pointed to the brilliant midafternoon sun. "It's light out."

Her smile dropped.

"It's-night-time-if-I-say-it's-night-time," she said tapping her foot to each word.

Josefina reclaimed my arm and began pulling me up the stairs, Jill and Randy also in tow.

"But Josefina," I said again pointing to the window. "There's the sun. It's light out."

Josefina continued to march me up the stairs.

"Well isn't it?"

Mom stood scowling at the base of the stairs.

"Well isn't it?" I asked Josefina again.

Josefina said nothing.

"Jill, isn't it light out?" I said turning to my sister.

Jill looked bewildered.

"Josefina?"

Josefina said nothing.

I continued climbing, but tentatively now, less certain the stairs were there to support me.

Maybe my eyes aren't seeing right, I thought, *but it sure looks light out. Yet Mom and Josefina say it definitely isn't.*

Whispering in my ear in her heavy Cuban accent, Josefina said, "*La Señora* she say you go to bed. So you go. Be good boy."

"But Josefina, I tell you it is daytime," I tested a final time.

Josefina raised my covers, and I climbed into bed.

Mom wouldn't lie. So it had to be me.

I lay in bed as the sun arched in its afternoon descent. A shrinking path of light spread across my blanket. I watched the pattern fade until there was no question the sky was black, rendering the issue moot.

As the memory of that afternoon dissolved, I looked up at Dr. Bowen, my therapist of two years. More than anyone, he would understand this latest recollection of Mom's mind-warp tactics.

"So once again Dr. Bowen," I said, "she played with our heads. Both she and Dad did. If a manipulation offered some slight convenience, she didn't care what it did to us. But I can tell you for a nine-year-old, it was pretty confusing."

Dr. Bowen, always sympathetic, set down his session notes and looked at me warmly over his tortoise shell half-glasses.

"This is good, Michael. It's important. Do you see how this fits with your hesitancy to trust? Very useful. Think about it, and let's pick up right here next Friday . . ."

Dr. Bowen rose from his desk and placed his hand on my shoulder, smiling.

I thanked him and left his office.

Knowing how fast a session can fade, how quickly my habit to repress could banish what I'd learned. I replayed the memory until the elevator opened at the lobby floor.

The sun was streaming when I exited his building. At least I think it was.

TWO

By the Roots

MY STORY AND THE ISSUES THAT LED ME INTO TREATMENT began in 1907, thirty-five years before my birth. Starting there slices to the core. Yes, my Midwestern culture impacted me—nobody who grew up in the Bible Belt came away unscathed. But cut to the core, the issues are psychological, rooted in the person who overpowered my family.

My grandfather, Isaac Grossman, founded Grossman's Department Store, the main store in Muskegon, Michigan. He ignored the financial depression of 1907 and opened Grossman's anyway, selling a full line of goods that included clothing, shoes, fur coats, china, jewelry, appliances and furniture. At its high point in the 1950s, Grossman Department Store employed 150 people. The store was big enough to provide a prosperous living for Grandfather Isaac and his eight children, one of whom was my Dad, Isaac's son Herman. Isaac and his store were like a giant octopus that wrapped tentacles around not only Isaac's children, but their children and the children in our family for generations.

Grandfather Isaac was an autocrat, an august figure who dressed the part of the town's leading merchant. Mezzotint photos show him in starched white shirts and suits of fine imported

English wools, in spats and with the black, pearl-handled cane that signaled his approach. He was prominence itself—the man to know in Muskegon, where he held sway over banks and successful politicians.

To reach his office on the department store's fourth floor, you took an old brass cage elevator. Above the pearl call button was a bronze bust of Isaac, depicted as a smiling, kindly patriarch. The sculptor took poetic license and cast Isaac smiling, which it's said he never did. The few remaining old mezzotint pictures emphasize Isaac's stern stare and prominent jaw befitting the demanding family autocrat whose word one didn't challenge. When Isaac needed one of his children in ready-to-wear, that child quickly set aside dreams of taking the Hippocratic oath and quit medical school. If a daughter's fiancé wasn't Jewish or a suitor wasn't from a proper family, Isaac made it clear there would be no wedding.

To give Grandfather Isaac his due, Muskegon looked to its most visible retailer whenever adversity struck, and Isaac didn't disappoint. He and my kindly Grandmother Sadie made sure that families were fed and sheltered when they fell victim to disasters such as house fires and that children of poorer families received needed operations. Grandmother Sadie was a favorite of the local children because she dispensed hard candy and packets of Dentyne gum from her briefcase-sized purse. But Sadie was spacey, frail, and not very present. Isaac was the dynamo.

The proverb says charity begins at home, but in Isaac's case, that's where it ended. When my father and his brothers and sisters heard the tap of Isaac's cane coming up the walk, they froze as all eyes turned to the front door. Isaac's three boys rose immediately when he entered. His five daughters sat in a perplexed trance. The room remained pin-drop silent until each child showed Isaac some sign of deference.

Isaac needed only to glance at a son or daughter to make his will known. A nod sent a child off to do his lessons. A scowl lowered decibels at playtime until, one by one, Isaac molded each eight of his children and quashed any preferences that might interfere with his plans for them.

Isaac's sons adapted adequately to his plans for them. They learned to mimic their father's imperial manners, though they cut lesser figures—more pretentious than charismatic. Still Isaac's boys earned a good living from Grossman's Department Store and they all found a place in Muskegon society.

Isaac's five daughters didn't fare as well. They grew up hysterical, disoriented and fearful. My aunts, like Grandmother Sadie, were sweet and caring to a fault. But they were also flighty, confused, tentative girls who walked hesitantly, as if unsure of their footing. They all shared a most peculiar trait: they fluttered their hands at face level while they talked and they simultaneously blinked their eyes. Though attractive, they were sad, nervous little things. Isaac was able to marry them off to suitable, pliable boys who were eager to marry into a family with money. Four of his daughters never questioned Isaac's choices but the fifth, Harriet, in a moment of unprecedented rebelliousness, told Grandfather Isaac she would never marry the man he selected. Isaac called Harriet to his study for a long, long talk. I never learned what was said, but Harriet emerged from the study with the hysterical look that would become her trademark. She looked exactly that way when she took her wedding vows on the following month.

The long term result of Isaac's total dominance was a family riddled with mental illness for generations. The males especially were prone to volcanic mood swings—the kind that send you from volatile mania to the chill of depression. In modern times their condition might prompt a debate: was its etiology chemical or psychological? Many modern therapists would argue such mood swings are genetic, and offer a prescription for Prozac. And they could support that point of view with statistical proof—the prevalence of mental illness in my family—an incidence so remarkably high that CBS's *60 Minutes* mentioned it in a feature on one of my relatives. Geneticists would insist a chemical imbalance or a chromosomal mishap was at play.

I m not a scientist, but having lived it, my instinct is to disagree. I know firsthand how Grandfather Isaac's shadow spread across our family for generations. I saw how Grandfather Isaac influenced his children, most certainly my father, and my own therapists have underscored his influence. I'm convinced Isaac's influence accounts for what happened to my cousins.

When Isaac's four male grandchildren were born, each of us—my three cousins and I—got a first name beginning with "I." We were not actually called Isaac. That would have been too blatant. Instead my cousins were named Ian, Ira and Irwin. They named me I Michael Grossman. No period—just "I," and it's a curious first name to be sure—given in a Dick and Jane, Mary and Tom era when it wasn't fashionable for first names to be unique as they are today.

Mom said the "I" was a sign of respect, but to me it's the mark of Isaac's influence. Consider the unhappy lives of Ian, Ira and Irwin. Each one of them suffered from powerful, manic-depressive mood swings—as I myself did—with the result that not one my cousins sustained a relationship with a woman. Ian, Ira and Irwin never married. Each of them had to be institutionalized and each died prematurely, the oldest living only into his fifties.

California police found Cousin Ian dead on the park bench he frequented. Cousin Ira used drugs until his weakened heart gave out. Muskegon locals tell me that Cousin Irwin would sit on a street curb at night in a heated exchange with himself. Irwin lived the longest. In his fifties, doctors found a malignant tumor on his neck, but Irwin refused treatment and died two years later. Police estimated he'd been dead a week when they found the body.

Of the four cousins, I am the only survivor. I'm in my mid sixties, married and I have a child. I am the only cousin to cast off the painful depression we all felt. My better fortune wasn't happenstance. I was saved by secrets I discovered in my therapy and if there was any luck involved, it was my good fortune in stumbling across the most unusual mix of therapies and therapists. The caring therapists—and some of them did not care—helped me pull myself from the kind of bone-deep freeze my poor cousins never escaped.

The first step to avoid their fate was the hardest because I had to accept that I needed therapy, and then I had to go into it willingly. I had to get past the popular bias against getting treatment, and I had to look at my idealized view of my parents. It was obvious to my therapists, but as a boy I fought the suggestion for years that everything wasn't perfect in Camelot.

THREE

The Vise

MUSKEGON, MICHIGAN, IS IN THE HEART OF THE BIBLE BELT, and when I grew up it was a land in which people gossiped about scandalous church attendance rather than celebrity overdoses. I didn't attend church at all. I was Jewish, which didn't exactly bring out the welcome wagon. Our local country club posted "NO JEWS ALLOWED" signs and I recall asking Mom more than once why class mates called us "dirty Jews " when Josefina made me shower daily.

In Grandfather Isaac's day, Muskegon was a logging town with a perfect natural seaport and miles of sandy beaches fronting Lake Michigan. It attracted both commerce and tourists until myopic town management made sure Muskegon's own industry became its chief export. Businesses scurried to relocate south after the town fathers levied heavy taxes on them and the powerful unions presented their onerous demands. By the 1970s most of the factories had left Muskegon and the once-prosperous city led Michigan in state unemployment.

Despite high unemployment and weak economic times, Grossman's Department store continued to flourish in the forties and fifties. My father and his seven siblings, equal stockholders after Isaac died, continue to make a comfortable living at the store. Isaac's influence on the family—from dress styles to morals—continued undiminished even after his death. Isaac's sons, grandchildren and many sons-in-law modeled themselves after him for generations.

My Uncle Ralph, Isaac's son-in-law and Cousin Irwin's father, adopted Isaac's imperious demeanor as soon as Ralph married Isaac's daughter Francis. Except for my father, Ralph is my best proof that it was Isaac, not run-amuck genes, that molded our family. What Ralph did to my cousin Irwin one night had origins in Isaac's imperious ways.

Uncle Ralph, an obstetrician, achieved minor acclaim in the 1950s by introducing hypnosis in the delivery room as a chemical-free alternative to anesthetics. Uncle Ralph was also our family doctor, and I can still picture him in his white coat, listening to my chest through his cold stethoscope. He'd puff cigar smoke in my face and tell me in a droning nasal voice of his contributions to modern medicine. I listened longer than I wanted to, to words I didn't comprehend and chapter-by-chapter outlines of his new book that he said would revolutionize delivery-room procedures. He might actually have become famous had hypnosis ever become a popular obstetric option. It infuriated Uncle Ralph that it never did.

Uncle Ralph was so much like the picture I'd formed of Grandfather Isaac that I almost sensed Isaac's ghost hovering whenever Uncle Ralph was around. I sensed Isaac coming through Ralph because of what happened the night Cousin Irwin had his Bar Mitzvah party—fifteen years *after* Isaac's death.

Irwin's Bar Mitzvah celebration took place at Uncle Ralph's country-club-like estate on acres of precisely trimmed grass. There were strings of lights in the trees, waiters offering silver trays of hors d'oeuvres and violin music drifting from the antebellum-style, columned porch of the main house. About a hundred guests shook hands with Irwin, handed him Bar Mitzvah presents and said what a fine job he'd done reading his Hebrew. Irwin beamed.

I was standing next to Uncle Ralph when Irwin came up.

"Gee Dad, isn't it wonderful? All these people came to my Bar Mitzvah party," said Irwin.

"No one is here for you," said Uncle Ralph. "These are my friends. Who do you even know?"

Irwin's eyes clouded and he left.

I believe my cousin endured similar cuts from his father for all of his short lifetime. But I don't believe Irwin had any idea how vulnerable he was to them. Irwin assumed it was his nature to be morose and had no idea how precariously his tender mind teetered.

I was luckier. Early on I sensed something was amiss because of my mood swings. I can recall when I first started to worry. At age seven, I was in the living room watching a new invention called television. We owned one of the first sets, a Motorola, and I sat beneath the wooden console that towered above me, gawking for hours at moving pictures on a ten inch black-and-white screen.

What got me thinking about my own mental stability was a television drama about a troubled child. "Mentally disturbed" was the term the announcer used. The show opened with a boy staring blankly out his bedroom window. You could hear his parents bickering in another room, but the boy ignored them. Clearly his mind was elsewhere. To dramatize his emotional state, the cameraman crudely cycled the lens focus from clear to fuzzy, clear to fuzzy. As if we might have missed the point, the announcer, sounding like he was in an echo chamber, said the boy's mind had "taken flight."

Early in the show, when the boy fell into a cloudy mental state, he could snap back to reality at will. But he was drawn to his internal world, and its pull steadily increased. It got ever harder for him to return to reality. In the show's last scene, with the boy's mother standing over him, it was painfully obvious that his mind was no longer there. The announcer explained that the boy was trying to return, and the viewer could see wrinkled determination on his brow. But his mind was now imprisoned permanently. The boy could only rock and stare. As the mother shook him, the camera moved in for a close-up on his blank eyes. He didn't even blink. As a final dramatization that he was gone for good, the camera turned his eyes into static, and then the static expanded full-screen.

The show gave me the willies because I identified with that boy. When I felt depressed, my own mind repeatedly drifted to a Walter Mitty world where I could fly or beat down bullies or become invisible and know everyone's secrets. How many times had I wondered what would happen if I couldn't return from my daydream?

Yet I also knew I wasn't completely like the disturbed boy. Sometimes my daydreams were fun, especially the ones that gave me superpowers and let me fly while bullets ricocheted harmlessly off me. To test my secret flying skill, I'd tie one of Mom's good guest towels round my neck and run headlong at the couch shouting *"S-u-p-e-r-m-a-n."* I knew I couldn't really fly even before I got the wind knocked out of me.

But, again like the boy, painful moods came over me frequently, unexpectedly and always in the same way. In the beginning, the mood shift was barely perceptible. Then my thoughts started to speed up until they went so fast they wrenched control from me. All I could do was watch helplessly while darting from one thought to another, each with only the thinnest of connections. I'd get tangled in an endless, streaming sentence:

Maybe that's why my allowance wasn't in the sugar dish . . . sugar is so fattening . . . which is why the guy at school called me a fat, Jew pig—though he's as fat as I am . . . but girls really like him while they hate my looks . . . maybe 'cause of my glasses . . . which I'll take off if I ever get to kiss Judy Maslow . . . but I won't 'cause she winces when I approach . . . just like Dad's face wrinkled when he warned what he'd do if I didn't get my homework done tonight . . . and now he's late getting home so he'll be in one of his black moods . . .

My mind pinballed from one subject to another, without pause, without purpose, without rest, in a streaming dialog I could not halt. Thoughts gathered mass and crashed past my saturation point, and all I could do was hold on and pray for it to end. When my exhausted brain did finally slow, I knew only too well what was coming next—the second half. The attacks usually jumped from mania to depression, although sometimes they came on in the reverse pattern. Sometimes I'd have half an attack—racing thoughts only or only depression. No matter which type, mania or depression, once an attack started, nothing could stop it.

The slow-motion half of a vise attack tightened in steps, like a wrench on a nut, locking me ever tighter in its paralytic, grip. In this depressed state, my body felt unable to generate the spark needed to pass commands from one nerve to the next, let alone send the signal past a thousand synapses. That lack of spark didn't matter because the signal would find a brain that wasn't receiving.

Feet dead. Arms don't lift. Nothing's working. No energy left. Who cares? Why bother? Never ends. Dumb me. God make it be over.

I called them my "vise" attacks because no matter which phase of their onslaught—the brain-ripping hyperactivity or the numbing depression—my head stayed in its grip until I had no fight left. Sometimes I found myself in the vise for no apparent reason. Other times a classmate's "fatso" or "dirty Jew" triggered an attack. Most vise attacks sucked my energy in a smooth progression, as if someone was lowering a dimmer switch. But some came in an instant, as fast as the flick of a switch. The speed of onset wasn't terribly important because even if I saw it coming, all I could do was watch. It was a freight train heading down the track, a behemoth growing bigger while I stood locked on its headlight. I knew it was useless to try to get off the track. I had tried that a hundred times before.

After a vise attack, I felt exhausted, flattened and frightened by my thoughts.

I was insane, wasn't I? I was losing hold, wasn't I?

Afterward I would spend my afternoons in bed, sadly watching cloud shapes out my window. I'd dissolve with the clouds from one shape into another, turning from a knight on a horse to an elephant to a crocodile's mouth to a swooping pterodactyl. Mom would stick her head in and tell me to get outside and play. I'd transform into the next shape.

One attack scared me so badly that the recollection still makes me shiver. I was walking home from school, careful not to step on any cracks in the sidewalk. My mind was bulging with thoughts—speedy and racing from subject to subject. The walk home took me past a green hedgerow that ran the full block and towered two feet above my head. As I walked, I happened to glance inside the hedge, and my eyes fixed on three intersecting branches. I began to trace the branches, following one to its intersection with the next. I grew intensely absorbed. There were so many branches it was hard to know which one to follow. Suddenly, in a terrifying flash, I felt my whole body was lifting off the sidewalk, that some powerful force was taking me inside the hedge.

In my imagination—and it felt very real—the world outside the hedge disappeared. Even though I was still walking down the side-walk, it felt as if my entire consciousness—my mind—was trapped in the hedge. Frantically, I traced the branch I'd been following to the next forked junction and then to the next, scrambling to find an exit. My mind was searing from the intensity of my drive to escape. Then, as if my thoughts had exploded and scattered, I was tracing not one but tens of branches at once. I traced so hard and so rapidly that I feared the speed surely would rip my mind apart. I scanned back and forth, up and down, mentally tracing even the hundreds of jagged leaves in my desperate hunt for an exit.

If only I could stop my mind from crashing though the hedge like a trapped animal, I thought.

Still split in two—physically walking down the block with my consciousness trapped in the vegetation—I pleaded with God to blow me out of the hedge. The way I pictured it, I would get thrown from the hedge and would land in the nearby street just as a car was coming. I didn't care that the car would hit me. At least the thundering in my head would stop.

By the time I reached the street corner, the terrifying daymare was over.

After that the vise attacks came more frequently, but I developed a set of tactics to handle them. When under attack, it was best if I could sit in a quiet room with minimal stimulation. That wasn't always possible. If under a vise attack when other kids were around, I'd come up with some pretense to get away. But falling under attack when adults were around was the hardest of all. Then I had to ride out the attack while pretending that nothing was happening. I had two special tricks for that situation. I would divide my mind in two. I sent half of my thoughts deep inside to wait for the vise to let up. The other half did the torturous work of entertaining, and I would gossip about school or make up jokes for the adults. I pretended to be very interested in whatever they had to say in hopes of distracting them from what I was dealing with.

"Really, so your husband is cutting the lawn this afternoon. Wow the whole lawn. He likes gardening doesn't he? But he has a really hot day for it," I'd say hoping the teacher couldn't see the gloom that was pulling me down.

Does anyone give a hoot about your smelly old husband and your lawn, the hidden half of my mind thought. *Please just leave, and soon.*

"Say, did you hear what Harry Truman said when a reporter probed about rumors that he was indecisive?" I asked. 'So are you indecisive?' The reporter asked Truman, who replied, 'Well, yes and no.'"

I winked at my teacher.

"Now I have another one for you . . ."

Isn't she ever going to leave? She has bad BO, and I have to smell it and it makes me sick when I'm already feeling awful, noted my subterranean half.

It was critical that I, not the adults, control the conversation. If I lost control, they could dominate me, and I might take in their vibes. Because when I was depressed, I was hypersensitive and especially susceptible to adult energy. The vise made me hyperreceptive and porous. That was fine if the adult was kindly, but not all of them were. Some had judgmental natures. You know the type—the know-it-alls who have glib, positively certain answers for every life issue. That kind was eager to break me, their energy would sour me the way someone else's bad breath spoils your own. Dealing with them amidst a vise attack knocked me off balance. And the more insane I felt, the harder the vise clamped.

I needed help—someone to turn to. But whom could I trust? What if I chose the wrong person?

FOUR

"Shrink"

IN THE SPRING OF 1949 my fourth grade teacher, Mrs. Melba, asked Mom to come for a little chat. They whispered at Mrs. Melba's desk, lowering their eyes when I looked up from crayoning. I caught occasional snatches. "Rebellious . . ." "angry . . ." "distant for an eight year old . . ." Mom conceded I was a little moody, but she disagreed with Mrs. Melba that there was anything more than that wrong with me. After all, she said, the kid isn't pulling wings off butterflies or lighting fires.

I would never hurt a butterfly.

But I started a fire in the field by our house. I raked leaves into a pile to burn, and since it was windy I cleared a wide safety circle before lighting the pile. But the wind scattered sparks, and the leaves beyond my pile curled black and burst into flames. I tried to beat the fire out with my rake, but it spread quickly. I was swinging wildly while trying to act nonchalant when a neighbor passed by. She could see I'd lost control of the flames and called the fire department. It must have been a slow fire day, because every truck in town arrived with sirens blaring and lights flashing. Burley men in black vinyl slickers dragged thick hoses across the yard while neighbors pitched in with buckets of water. I sneaked off to the house and hid in a closet. I lay in the dark closet for hours, pretending I had the power to be invisible, until Dad got home and pulled me out.

My teachers said the fire proved that I needed help, and finally Mom gave in. It was decided that I would get psychotherapy, a radical notion in those days, especially in a small Midwestern town. "Getting shrunk," the lay term for analysis, meant you were plumb crazy, and it was a desperate measure. But it was also considered cutting-edge, and if Mom was anything, she was receptive to a fashion. She scheduled an appointment with Dr. Anne Cronick, the town's only trained psychoanalyst.

Dr. Cronick actually lived just down the dirt road from us. She was more than a neighbor. Her son Chuck was my best friend, and I played at their house daily after school. I never liked Chuck's mom. Her mouth looked like she was sucking a sourball, and her eyes, magnified by wire-rimmed glasses that pinched the end of her nose, had a candle snuff's power to smother me. She treated Chuck and me as if our role in life was to track in dirt.

Fortunately, my therapy with Dr. Cronick was not at Chuck's house. Dr. Cronick had an office downtown, so I could hide the news that I was in therapy. Chuck never knew, and that was one humiliation I was spared.

At three, the appointed hour, Dr. Cronick greeted Mom and me. I'd never seen Dr. Cronick in a white smock before. She led me to her office, sat in a heavy maroon morris chair and folded her arms impatiently. I sat at a child's red desk that was way too small for my eight year old frame. My shins extended above the desktop like Lucy in a *Peanuts* comic strip. Dr. Cronick handed me balsa wood and glue and told me to build model airplanes—while she peppered me with questions.

"Anything you say is our secret," she assured me, cracking her face powder with a smile that exposed yellowing teeth.

This is a stupid waste of time, I thought. *I don't like building models, and I surely hate her.*

But I clenched my jaw and said, "Oh sure."

What if therapists can see my thoughts the way Uncle Ralph's X-ray machine shows my bones? She'll know that I hate her, I thought.

Dr. Cronick's interrogation continued while I glued balsa wood and grunted answers—"S'pose so" or "Naah" and an occasional belligerent "Says who." She repeatedly eyed a thin gold wrist-watch that was too small for her fat arm. At precisely ten to the hour she stopped each session and swept her hand imperiously toward the door the way you'd swat off a fly.

After three months of this, our sessions mysteriously ended. One day when it was time to leave for my appointment, Mom didn't tell me to get my coat. I was not going to remind her.

Good deal, I figured.

Mom forgot again the following week and the week after that and in fact she never mentioned therapy with Dr. Cronick again.

Years later Mom confided that Dr. Cronick had told her not to bring me anymore.

"You're wasting good money," Dr. Cronick had said.

During months of therapy, I discovered that Mom, not Dr. Cronick, could read my mind and knew all my secrets. She knew I'd stolen cookies from the school cafeteria and about the dirty magazine under the Anderson kids' bed and how we rolled cigarettes using tea for tobacco.

She shocked me repeatedly. "Mom, how did you know?"

"Don't ever try to fool me. I have a magic flashlight that can see your thoughts," she said.

After that I tried to control my thoughts when Mom was around, concentrating hard to avoid my secrets. Fortunately her power was short-lived and ended about the time I stopped seeing Dr. Cronick.

Years later my sister Jill mentioned, "You did know mom was also Dr. Cronick's patient while you were going?"

After my ill-fated sessions with Dr. Cronick, Mom no longer talked about getting me "help." My teachers still pressed, but Mom dropped the subject. I was thankful Chuck never found out and prayed that no one else, especially my classmates would ever know.

In the 1940s, if they made you get therapy, you didn't tell anyone. If word got out, mothers would hurry their kids inside when they saw you coming. People didn't even want an adult around who'd had therapy. In a small town getting shrunk was as bad as being Jewish. And on that score, one kid actually searched my scalp for the horns he heard all Jews have.

FIVE

Herman

WHEN GRANDFATHER ISAAC DIED IN 1941, my father Herman took over Grossman's Department Store. Everyone in Muskegon knew Herman Grossman, son of Isaac, and people said Dad filled Isaac's shoes well. He was important enough that the traffic cop put away his ticket pad when he leaned in and saw it was Dad, and the mayor asked for Dad's blessing to run for reelection.

"Pillar of the community, your Dad is," people said to me.

"Did you know your father hired western Michigan's first Negro salesman?" They said. "That he helped Gerald Ford get elected to Congress?"

He must have done something for Congressman Ford, because years later a scroll arrived declaring Mom's birthday, October 24, Roz Grossman Day. The thick parchment had a red wax seal by the signature, which read: *Gerald Ford, President of the United States.*

Despite an imposing facade, Herman was a hesitant man. After all, he was born of Isaac, who left all his children lacking in confidence. Herman graduated high school with honors, but he was an anxious student who found it hard to concentrate. After graduation, Herman tried to enlist in the Air Force but was rejected due to high blood pressure. He was admitted to Harvard, but the exam pressure was too much for him, and he flunked out. He did better at the University of Michigan and attended law school at the University of Chicago. But in his second year of law school, Isaac summoned Dad home when he needed to fill a vacancy in the furniture department. Dad would have preferred to finish law school, but he knew when Isaac summoned, you came.

Isaac died in 1941, and as directed by his will, the department store stock was divided equally among his children. The brothers and sisters elected Herman president, but eight siblings with equal stock and voting rights was a recipe for chaos. Predictably, the store became a battleground, ripe with hurt egos, shifting alliances, plots and counterplots. Over time Herman purchased a majority of the store's stock from his brothers and sisters, but the buyback came with plenty of injured feelings and strained relations.

Herman considered himself exceedingly lucky when he was introduced to Rosalind Morgan on a blind date. He never recovered from his good fortune. He couldn't fathom why the sought-after Ohio state beauty queen runner-up accepted a second date with him and then a third. Herman assumed he wasn't much of a looker, and surely his disposition was erratic. So it was a happy surprise that Rosalind, a woman with a jewelry tray full of fraternity pins, continued to date him—among others. Herman proposed to Rosalind a year later, and to his even greater surprise Rosalind accepted, disappointing a more likely suitor, the heir to a Pennsylvania steel fortune. Rosalind said she loved the steel baron's parents but found the boy insufferably dull. Rosalind told her girlfriends she found Herman exciting. Herman, she said, was a real character.

Indeed, Herman had moments of charming eccentricity and flair despite his lack of confidence. He dressed well, choosing quality, cutting edge fashions that made bolder statements than the conservative Isaac had made. As an early audiophile, Herman bought top-of-the-line high fidelity equipment for his oasis, a music room where he stacked half a dozen Macintosh amplifiers, preamps and tuners in chrome cases with ebony trim and oversized steel dials. I liked to look in the back to see the silver tubes that glowed pink in comforting rows.

Dad also spent a lot on jewelry for Mom. On many a night he would present her with a pearl, a diamond, an emerald or a black opal. There'd be an apology for his latest outburst as he placed the bauble on Mom, who for the moment was pleased. I was trained to stand with my sister Jill and my brother Randy and admire Mom's latest acquisition. Mom would nod her approval, a sign that Dad had been forgiven for his latest outburst. For the moment.

We kids had even more reason to be wary of Dad's temper. Dad might be playing the Dukes of Dixieland, striking the counter with his forefingers like drum sticks, when he'd notice a light left on in a room or a neglected chore.

"I told you to cut the lawn. Is there some reason why you didn't? Are you wounded or is your leg broken? Or do I have a son who's a goddamned idiot that can't follow instructions?"

A smarter son would have promised to cut the lawn immediately or at least would lay low until the fury passed. But at around age eight, something shifted in me. I tired of being obedient and trying to be perfect, since I didn't get much when I was. So I turned defiant and angry, which felt better than my compliant behavior. I began to egg Dad on and couldn't stop myself from pushing him as near to his volatile brink as I could. I tested constantly. It was like a dance routine. I'd wisecrack. He'd get into my face, and I'd step back. Then he'd pull back, so I'd taunt until again he returned face-to-face. Each time he drew near, I'd gauge how close to blowing he was. If his eyes turned dark and his forehead pulsed, it was time to retreat. But as frightening as the dance was, it made me feel like Dad's equal—like I had some control over this volcanic presence who was, by the way, the man charged with feeding and sheltering me. If only I'd known when enough was enough.

When the volcano blew and Dad went after one of us kids, Mom acted oblivious. But she took Dad on unhesitatingly the day he shook his fist in her face. Mom pulled his fist down and called him a lunatic, warning that if he ever, ever threatened her again they were finished. She warned Dad to get "help," and she scared him so that on that very spot he swore he'd go for therapy immediately. After that there was never a question who was really in power.

Mom didn't want Dad to see Dr. Cronick. It was easier to keep quiet if he saw an out-of-town therapist. To accommodate her, once a week for two years, Dad drove to Chicago, and there, on the couch of Dr. Anton Barenholtz, he listed the shortcomings he promised Mom he would discuss.

When Dad was home, Rosalind helped him expand on his list. It was clear to Mom that anything wrong with their relationship must be Dad's fault, and Dad, insecure to start with, never doubted Rosalind's assertions.

But unlike Rosalind, Dad desperately wanted to work on his shortcomings, and he was determined to better himself. Despite the depth of his insecurity, or perhaps because of it, he was determined to scrutinize every aspect of his character. He would systematically work on himself the way a cabinetmaker repeatedly sands an unfinished board. He had his handwritten list of personal goals. Today he'd work on his temper, tomorrow on being more charitable and the next day on being the most ethical person he knew how to be. He'd study each subject, pacing as he read aloud appropriate famous quotes. He reserved Sundays to work on his vocabulary by reading the dictionary. He'd write unfamiliar words on scraps of paper and then try to use them in sentences. He subscribed to a humor newsletter, memorized the jokes, and practiced reading the punch lines aloud again and again. When guests didn't laugh at a new joke, Mom would roll her eyes, and Dad, humiliated, would return to his study to practice his delivery.

He fared better as an amateur actor, taking the leading role in several local Muskegon Civic Theatre productions including *The Man Who Came to Dinner* and *Inherit the Wind,* where he played the role of Henry Drummond. Local critics said he could have been a professional, that he'd missed his calling, and the production did well enough to draw audience members from as far away as Detroit.

Rosalind was as insecure as Herman, but she had the confidence of knowing she controlled Dad. The two had an unwritten pact. When in doubt, it was time to second guess Herman. Nor were Mom's instructions to Herman limited to his personal life. She also felt it was her calling to help him run his department store. Dad hired and fired managers based on Mom's nagging assessments. Weak department heads were smart enough to know their fate hung on their ability to flatter Mom, who made sure Herman promoted her sycophants. Stronger managers whose sole interest was the good of the store quickly fell to Mom's persistent ax.

In the fall of 1969 the union struck Grossman's. It wasn't the first time. Muskegon business owners generally knew enough to appease the unions and avoid wage strikes. Over the years Dad had handled the unions rather well. But when the unions struck Grossman's that fall, Mom decided she would show Dad how to humble them. Imperiously she summoned the union chiefs to a meeting, but she grew angry when they showed her little deference. Dad's instinct was to settle, and he negotiated an acceptable compromise—a reasonable wage increase. But Mom had other ideas.

"Are you going to let those union bastards push you around, Herman?" said Mom. "Just who do they think they are? You show them you have balls."

Herman wasn't sure about his manhood, so to prove himself, he let the strike occur. It dragged on for months. Early in 1970, Grossman's Department Store went belly-up.

Mom told Dad she was proud of him. Dad reminded her that they were broke.

Even though he was president of the temple, every Christmas Dad insisted on being Santa for a day. He sat in the gold throne in the third-floor toy department, and kids lined up, sat in his lap, whispered in his ear and had their photo taken. Dad kissed each child awkwardly, usually so hard they would cry. Bewildered by the response, he handed the tearful child back to their equally confused mother.

Children everywhere were fair game for Dad's kisses. Even when he walked the streets of London or Brussels, he couldn't resist sweeping up a passing infant, raising it high in the air, kissing it, and shouting, "I lubbbs de little children." It happened too quickly for the astounded parent to stop him, and parents were less cautious in those days. But Dad wasn't able to bring home that playfulness. At home, his model was Isaac's stern countenance and autocratic cautions. I can imagine the father telling his son, "Herman, parenting is a deadly serious business. The parent's duty is to raise diligent, moral community leaders and good Jews. Frivolity has no place in the rearing of a child. And don't expect to guide them with words alone. Sometimes a thick paddle says what you really mean."

Isaac's warning left Herman plagued by fears that he was a poor parent, and he didn't hesitate to express them out loud to us.

"You kids will amount to nothing," he worried. "You are rude to your teachers. Your grades are mediocre. Michael, you are not adjusting. Randy, you think I don't know about the change you took from my dresser? Jill, you got a D in math. You kids lack goals. You shirk from chores and ignore your homework. You watch TV when you should read a good book. It's my fault. I've failed to instill a sound morality in you. But how have I gone so wrong?"

Adhering to a dead patriarch's standards and egged on by Rosalind, who made sure Dad knew of all our misdemeanors, the frustration often proved too much and the volcanic Herman had to blow.

Dad would head to his study and return with the thick black, leather barber strap wrapped around his fist and he'd take us to our bedroom for a dose of what we deserved. The strap wasn't that bad. Far worse was his painful remorse when he finished. He fell completely apart and put his hands to his head and shook and wept. Seeing that was terrifying. We'd ignore our stinging fannies or bruised arms and rush to assure him that we hardly hurt at all.

SIX

Rosalind and Josefina

ROSALIND, MY MOTHER, WAS BORN IN 1916 into a wealthy Cleveland family that lived in one of the gilded Victorians that made Shaker Heights famous. Her father, my grandfather Morris Morgan, built the impressive mansion, flying in stonecutters from Rome to sculpt its façade. Grandfather Morris had invented a part for a railroad switch, then invested his royalties in the stock market and became a multi-millionaire. A brilliant but cautious man, Morris had his doubts about the stock market in the late 1920s. Nothing rises forever, and the market was moving too fast, he thought. So as a precaution, Grandfather Morris set aside a million dollars in a separate bank account. That was huge money in those days, and it would certainly insure his family's safety should his market instinct prove prophetic.

Unknown to Grandfather Morris, my grandmother, Sarah, received a tip on a sure stock and secretly withdrew his safety-net fund to buy it. When the crash of '29 came, Morris was not one of the men out on a building ledge, because he knew he still had his million dollars. Or so he thought, until Sarah broke down in tears and confessed they were flat broke. Mom and my grandparents had to leave their mansion and move to a drab, one-room rental apartment over a dry cleaner in a rough Cleveland suburb. For a year Morris didn't speak to Sarah, though they stayed married. Mom was thirteen at the time, and she couldn't understand why the family had to leave their home in Shaker Heights or why she was withdrawn from her private school and had to leave her friends.

It took Mom a decade to regain the status she'd lost, but in 1941, by marrying my father Herman, she was welcomed as the newest member of Grandfather Isaac's powerful family. Like most who lived through the Great Depression, Mom always feared the return of bad economic times. To compensate, she surrounded herself with symbols of prosperity—art and other handsome, expensive objects. Comforted by the jewelry my father bought her, Mom often wore diamonds even to casual events.

"Simple but elegant," she would say, modeling a new necklace in her mirror. Marriage also meant that Mom could replenish her wardrobe and hire servants, which helped reestablish her sense of importance. Her imperious manners disguised her underlying fear, old memories of the little girl from Ohio who'd lost her home and been dragged from her school. Even as a child, I occasionally saw Mom's little girl look break through from beneath her polished social poise. In rare moments when she dropped that mask, I saw a secret sadness in her eyes—for example, when we walked along the lake behind our house and she didn't know I was looking, or in unguarded moments when I caught her looking fearfully out the dining room window. Her daydreams always ended with a startled look of surprise and a quick tightening of her face as her trademark imperious look returned.

Her arrogance cloaked powerful needs she could neither expose nor meet. But unlike Dad, who could have moments when he revealed himself to the point of masochism, Mom was too insecure to allow much introspection. She couldn't own her sadness or allow herself to see it, let alone show that vulnerability to friends, so she perfected her own ways of avoiding it. First she would stay in constant motion, always keeping a step ahead of her despair. But when it threatened to get ahead of her, when her emptiness rose like water to near neck level, when it threatened to drown Mom in dejection, that was her cue to travel. My dad was smart enough to write the check and let her go. She'd hurry off and board a flight to somewhere and roam the world. Like a bubble, she'd float into our lives and then burst away. My sister Jill, brother Randy and I would stand in front of our house, hand in hand with a cook or nurse, and wave goodbye, watching Mom's suitcase-laden car leave a dust trail down the road. The picture the word "mother" conjures up for me is a woman's rear sandwiched between two suitcases.

As a teenager, my sister Jill, my confidant in all matters family, wondered aloud what would happen if the day came when Mom was physically unable to run any more. The first hint of the answer came after Mom returned from a tour of India. Her traveling companion confided that Mom paid a famous guru to read her fortune. She described Mom sitting lotus-style while the guru spilled bones from a sack and studied them. His face grew troubled, then ashen, and he arose, refused to complete the reading and returned Mom's payment. "I will not speak of your ending," he said, looking fearfully at Mom, and then he left.

My sister and I wondered for years what the guru had seen. What was so terrible? Would Mom die in a plane crash? Or be burned in a fire? I had to wait until my late fifties for an answer. I believe what the guru saw was Mom's Alzheimer's—the neurological ransacking of her mind that occurred in her eighties, twenty years after my father had died. Mom's short term memory stopped functioning.

After the parent-children battles that are so common among baby boomers, Jill, Randy and I finally succeeded in getting her into a facility for the severely memory impaired. But then Mom was trapped since she could no longer travel. When the sadness bubbled up and started to overpower her, she couldn't dart away to lose herself among the classic portraits at the Louvre but instead had to stare at a wrinkled, sallow reflection of herself in the bathroom mirror. As Alzheimer's deepened to dementia, the demons she'd successfully escaped finally had their way with her. She sat in her apartment with the shades drawn, her mental acuity fading, and worse, she was fully aware that it was happening.

She would tap fingers to forehead repeatedly. "You have no idea," she would say, "no conception of what it's like to lose your memory."

Despite efforts to cheer her, she would lay in her nightgown in her darkened room and stare expressionless at the television. As the dementia progressed, she wrote angry notes on yellow stick-up slips and pasted them on the bathroom walls, in dresser drawers and throughout the pages of her books.

"My friends could care less about me," she wrote.

"My children hate me," she scribbled.

Yet face to face, Mom feigned delight whenever we visited.

"I couldn't ask for better kids," she'd say smiling beatifically.

"How can I ever thank you?" she'd say to friends until they left the room.

The staff at her memory unit adored her. She would work them like the guests at former parties. Even memory impaired, she could still do it. She put her arm around each attendant to confide he or she was her very favorite.

As a young woman, Mom developed the ingratiating social habit of expressing a strong interest in the subjects of interest to others. This came naturally for her, because in fact she had a natural curiosity, especially if the subject at hand was a work of modern art, the stock market or politics. About the only subject of little interest to her was child rearing. She delegated that chore to the stream of nannies that arrived at our home, cared for us a while and then moved on. Nannies saw that we ate, left for school and went to bed at age-appropriate times in accord with the bedtime chart Mom had ripped from an in-flight magazine. Most of our nannies were Cubans, the result of Mom's frequent visits to Havana to see old friends. In 1947, Mom returned from one such trip to Havana accompanied by the woman who became a kind of half-nanny, half-second-mother to my sister, my brother and me.

We'd been told to expect Mom back from Cuba that day, and I

looked up from my Tinker-toy construction to see her burst through the front door with the woman she introduced only as Josefina, who was 5 feet 2 inches and two hundred pounds of Cuban energy packaged barrel-shape. In no time at all Josefina was omnipresent, materializing out of air to remind Mom of Jill's doctor's appointment or to trail me and gather the dirty clothes I mindlessly tossed down the hall. Over the fifteen years that Josefina stayed with our family, she mothered Jill, Randy and me, keeping us presentable and out of trouble. The kitchen was a command post for Mom, but it was Josefina who was actually the master at the ovens and range. The pots on our stainless steel Thermador range constantly bubbled with fried *plátanos* or *arroz con pollo*, Budweiser-sautéed chicken with yellow rice, onions and green olives, served with *frijoles negros*.

But mostly, Josefina was our safety net, the placid core in the center of our hurricane. She was adroit at handling Mom and Dad. Her surgically timed questions to "Señor Herman" distracted Dad when his reddening complexion warned the volcano was active. She waited for us after school, and if I came home mud-caked, unlike Mom, who'd be annoyed, Josefina figured, well, that's what little boys did and cheerfully washed the spots I missed on backs of my arms.

Jill, Randy and I understood her blend of English and Spanish, but many others could not, especially when she spoke like a machine gun.

Intelligible or not, she was a force. A policeman once pulled her over in her '52 Chevy to explain she was doing sixty in a forty-five zone. Josefina, not accustomed to holding back, indignantly insisted her old '52 couldn't even do sixty, but her Spanglish explanation mystified the officer. Attempting to be courteous, he smiled and handed her a speeding ticket. Josefina assumed he was patronizing her, got out of the car eye-popping mad and went face-to-face with the officer, declaring she'd see him in court.

A couple of weeks later her Spanglish similarly bewildered the local judge presiding at her hearing. "Señor Judge, this *no es* possible, *esta* ticket. You see my car she is old old old Chevy *que* can go *no más que* maybe fifty, not what he say—sixty," she scowled at the hapless policeman. "No is possible Señor Judge Sir because she is old-old-old."

"But the officer had you on radar."

"Then the radar *está* broken, Señor Judge, because my Chevy no can go *más que* fifty."

I'm told Josefina delivered this plea in her white maid's uniform, flailing her robust brown arms in every direction. Her black eyes danced in full thyroid explosion until an incongruent curtsy to the Judge suggested she had completed the first of many arguments she'd prepared.

The non-air-conditioned courtroom was sweltering, and clearly Josefina had prepared more to say. The judge looked at the policemen, who shrugged in agreement, and then leaned over the bench.

"Mrs. Guerrero, since this is your first offense, I'll let it go, but please watch your speed."

Josefina smiled coquettishly at the Judge, giving the policeman a look of frigid indignation, somehow delivering both expressions simultaneously while bowing away from the bench.

So it was that we had two mothers, and in a session years later the therapist remarked how critical it was that we'd had our Cuban one as a counterpoint. Josefina was a firewall, a barrier between me and my father's volcanic temper, there to distract while I tiptoed behind the unpredictable giant. She offered a whispered guidance that suggested a detour around his rage, and trusting her taught me that not all adults were as volatile as my parents.

She wasn't my sole supporter, but she was my most powerful non-professional ally. She lacked even a high school education, yet I often wonder—as one therapist did aloud—if what I learned from Josefina wasn't as powerful as any insight that came to me on the couch. She clearly cared for us, and her caring reminded my sister, brother and me that we were more than possessions to be pulled from a drawer.

She was water in the dry season, which was about to become arid.

SEVEN

Dog House

IN 1954 DAD BUILT MOM A HOME. Frank Lloyd Wright did the original design, but he was not allowed to finish his work. I heard Mr. Wright and Mom arguing over the blueprints.

"Interesting, Frank, but where is my laundry room?" Mom asked.

"Frank Lloyd Wright homes don't have laundry rooms," said Wright.

"No no, Frank," Mom said. "This isn't Frank Lloyd Wright's home. It is my home. It's a Roz Grossman home and it will have a laundry room."

Wright was unbending so Mom fired the great architect, replacing him with another from Chicago. He added a laundry room to Wright's original drawings and the home was built. Pictures of the finished project appeared in upscale architectural magazines. The local Muskegon papers thought it newsworthy that Mom refused to let the builders cut down a massive oak tree that stood in the center of the lot. Wright's solution was to build a central atrium around the tree. Initially it delighted Mom that the house with the tree in the middle was the talk of Muskegon, but she quickly tired of explaining why she had wanted to keep the tree and placed a sign at its base:

THIS TREE IS FOR OUR DOG

It would have been funnier if we still had our dog.

I had gotten him when I was four. Dad had come home one night carrying a portable cage. Out had waddled the purebred german shepherd puppy, who had unsteadily passed by the adults and headed directly for me. He'd licked my face, and his scratchy tongue had made me squeal out the sound "Sirette." I have no idea where it came from or what it meant, but that's what we named him. Sirette.

Wherever I went, Sirette went. Summer afternoons he stood guard when the nanny put me outside in my white playpen. If a stranger came near, Sirette raised his ears and growled and the person quickly retreated. We lived in the woods then, in the small village of Montague, Michigan, on White Lake. With no nearby neighbors, Sirette was my sole playmate. My dog and I were inseparable until I had to start kindergarten, and then Sirette waited all day at the front door for my return.

In 1954 Mom and Dad said we were moving to a new home they were building in Muskegon. We were told the house was quite modern, being built by a famous architect, and that the new house had a tree in the middle, just for Sirette. But when moving day came, I couldn't find my dog. I looked everywhere, searching all his usual spots, combing the nearby woods, calling and calling for him.

"Sirette can't come to the new home." Mom said finally. "There's not enough land for him, so I gave him to your uncle, where he'll have a more space to roam."

"I don't understand," I pleaded. "Sirette has to come. I'm not going without him. You said the tree was for him."

It made no sense. All I wanted was Sirette, and I wasn't leaving without him. But Dad angrily put me in the car though I pounded on the windows the whole way calling for Sirette.

I never got to say goodbye. For a while I called my uncle, who said Sirette was doing fine and held the phone to the dog's ear for me.

Six months later mom announced that Dad was bringing home a new dog.

"Why can't we have Sirette?" I asked.

"The answer is *no*!" said Mom stamping her foot.

The new dog turned out to be two Springer Spaniel puppies. My sister Jill got Missy and I got Madam. Though she was no Sirette, Madam was playful and lickey. But something terrible happened. Mom insisted that the dogs had to stay in the garage when Jill and I were at school. But Mom forgot about Missy and Madam when she backed her car out one day, and she ran over Madam. The local vet said Madam might live, but she'd need a thick brace-like wire through her leg. I couldn't look at Madam's brace. It was too awful. Jill said she would take care of Madam for me.

Madam didn't make it, and soon afterward Missy mysteriously disappeared. One night Jill called Missy to dinner, but she didn't come. Jill kept calling, but rather than help, Mom got increasingly agitated and angrily told Jill that deer hunters probably shot Missy. I didn't believe it was hunters—especially after our local vet called to say how sorry he was about Missy.

Danny the Doberman followed, but he too had to go. Mom said it was because Danny got his dirty paws on the hall curtains. Then came Peanuts and Popcorn. But again Mom forgot to look in the garage so Peanuts suffered Madam's fate.

I loved each of those dogs, and Jill did too, but we felt increasingly afraid to become attached. They came and went too quickly, and Mom took their departure so lightly. I wondered how she could be so careless. How hard is it to look around when you back the car out? I can tell you this. I stayed far away from the garage when Mom went for her car.

My nightmares began about that time. I remember one especially since it kept recurring. I was in bed staring out the window at a huge tree silhouetted in black against a twilight sky and full moon. Perched on the black branches was the Wicked Witch of the West from the movie *The Wizard of Oz*. For me she was such a frightening movie character that when she came on screen I had to turn backward in my seat. The witch out my window, like the wicked witch in the movie, wore a black cape and had the same greenish face and maroon lips. Her red eyes bore into mine. I wanted to turn away but was riveted. The witch laughed at me and tried to melt me with the hatred in her eyes. They burned into me, but I was locked onto their glare. I watched as the witch's face changed. Sector by sector it morphed into a real person. I awoke in a cold sweat. The face on the branch was Mom.

EIGHT

The Red Sea

DAD LIKED TO TALK ABOUT MORAL IMPROVEMENT. He frequently lectured on the subject at League of Woman's Voters meetings, and to the Shriners, Hadassah and our temple congregation. But his three children received the bulk of his lectures. When Dad was of a mind to pontificate, he held forth in his study behind his desk wearing thick, black Buddy Holly glasses and blowing Cuban cigar smoke that smelled like tar. He'd swivel around in his leather Eames chair, punctuating with his hands, emphasizing by clearing his throat.

Dad's words became muffled background static as I daydreamed of casting for brilliant sunfish.

The specific subjects varied, but his underlying theme was always our moral betterment. Dad, a devout Jew, occasionally lectured on the emphasis our Jewish heritage placed on morals, explaining that he learned this as a boy when he regularly accompanied Grandfather Isaac to temple. After Isaac died, Dad continued to attend Friday night services, adding Saturday morning temple prayer as well. His piousness was rewarded with the temple presidency, and I was told I had to support Dad's reign by attending services too. Mom and I never shared Dad's enthusiasm for temple, but Mom was smart enough to pick her battles and to acquiesce on all things Jewish. I wasn't so smart.

One night in the spring of 1954 Dad came into my bedroom to remind me I'd be thirteen soon.

"Are you planning to have a Bar Mitzvah?" He asked.

It wasn't a question.

Begrudgingly I went to my first Hebrew lesson with Dr. Morris Rubin, a short bald man with a Yiddish accent, never seen without his red bow tie. I picture him wearing it in the shower.

Dr. Rubin explained that my Bar Mitzvah preparation included writing a speech about a prominent Jew. He picked Chaim Weitzman for me.

"You see, Micchhael," he said extending the "cchh" as if clearing his throat, "Weitzman was a great Zionist and von of deeh founders of Israel," said Dr. Rubin.

Why do Yiddish people sound like they have cheese in their mouths? I thought, trying to distract myself from thoughts of Chiam Weitzman.

"So we vill start now vit the alphabet then," said Dr. Rubin.

How bad could Hebrew study be? I thought, figuring nothing could be worse than public school.

Torah study was hands down duller. At least the English alphabet had relevance. So when it was time to go, I often went fishing, skipping about half my Hebrew classes. I had a plan. Rather than take the trouble of learning Hebrew, I could fake my required Torah reading by memorizing the Hebrew sounds like lyrics to a foreign song. You don't need to know how to read the Hebrew alphabet to sing *Hava Nagila*. I would have pulled it off if Dr. Rubin hadn't called Dad after I missed my fifth lesson.

I was in bed when Dad came into my bedroom.

"Either you are having a Bar Mitzvah or you are not," Dad said. "It's okay with me if you're the one to break generations of family Jewish tradition. But if you choose to have it, God damn it you will learn Hebrew, Michael."

"I'll think about it," I said defiantly.

"That you will," Dad said, "and I'll wait for your answer all night if I have to," said Dad, pulling up a chair to my bed and staring at me with burning eyes.

I can win this battle of wills, I thought. *Dad looks determined but I had a will of steel. I'd outlast him.*

So I lay in bed, twiddling my thumbs as visibly as possible. Dad stared at me without blinking. An hour passed and he showed no sign of tiring.

I can outlast him, I thought.

Another hour passed and the man wasn't even blinking. I was growing tired and wanted to get rid of him.

"Okay. I promise to learn the Hebrew and write the speech," I said.

When Dr. Rubin told Dad the draft of my Chaim Weitzman speech was unacceptable, Dad hired a ghostwriter to repair it. The ghostwriter used every word in the long vocabulary list Dad handed him. That everyone said they weren't the words of a thirteen-year-old wasn't the point as far as he was concerned. The words would remind the congregation who the father was.

The Bar Mitzvah took place six months later. As I'd secretly planned, I memorized the Hebrew sounds, only pretending I could follow the lines of Hebrew with a Torah pointer. Seeing the approving faces of my relatives in the audience, I gloated on my way down from the podium. I knew I could pull off the sham.

According to Jewish tradition, as a Bar Mitzvah I was now a man. I liked that but knew it was a mixed blessing. Now Dad dragged me with him to services on Friday nights. I felt like a jack-in-the box sitting with him in the pew. My eyes would close while the rabbi droned on, until I'd slump and Dad would elbow me awake.

To be fair, one year the rabbi did give a sermon that didn't put me to sleep. I remember his tale about a little boy who attended High Holy Day services in ancient times. The boy sat in the balcony with his mother, since back then they separated the women and children from the men. The rabbi in the tale began the service when suddenly the little boy took a toy whistle from his pocket, stood up, and blew the whistle with all his might. Outraged, the temple elders rose to surround him with their white and blue prayer shawls flapping.

"Wicked boy," they scolded, and they descended on his mother as well.

But the old rabbi interrupted them.

"Enough," he said powerfully. "Leave the boy alone. Be seated," he instructed his congregation.

When the chamber fell silent, the rabbi spoke.

"Do you not see? The little boy did something wonderful, not a bad thing. The boy was so filled with Sabbath joy that his heart overflowed, and the only way for him to express his love was by blowing his whistle, which he did with all the spirit his tiny soul could muster."

I liked that story, and I easily identified with the little boy. The way I saw it, I was a lot like him. The elders in my temple didn't get me either. I was called a "wise guy," rebellious and disruptive, and they were partly right. I could never resist mocking feigned piety when I saw it, though much of my satire was rage seeking any excuse to vent.

In earlier days I had tried to be the obedient child. I'd tried until it was clear that accommoding Mom and Dad was a dangerous tactic. Bowing to Dad's temper or accepting Mom's manipulations inevitably left me feeling the loss of even more of myself. And there were no rewards. They took my accommodation not as a plea for love but as a grant of permission to have a bigger bite of me, a white flag that signaled that they had crushed me into compliance. The only thing keeping me intact was my iron will and unyielding resolve that I wouldn't be molded in the image of my father and of Grandfather Isaac.

I received unintended support from an unlikely source one Sunday morning when, after sermon, the rabbi chatted with the kids in my class. He made an excellent point.

"Good Jews," he advised, "think for themselves. They question everything. Never, ever believe something just because someone important says it's true. God gave you a brain of your own. Use it. Decide for yourself and do as the Talmudic scholars did: Challenge everything."

The rabbi made sense. People lie, and how do you know what to believe if you don't question them? My literary hero Holden Caulfield said much the same thing in *Catcher in the Rye*. Weren't the phonies Holden hated nothing more than authorities who preferred to bend a child to their will rather than acknowledge his or her individuality?

That following Sunday I took my seat in the temple's filled pews. The rabbi, high above us on the podium, began his sermon. He spoke about Moses and how, many centuries ago, our Jewish ancestors were slaves in the land of Egypt.

But God wanted his children to be free, said the rabbi, so God called his servant Moses to him and outlined *His* plan to free the Jews. God instructed Moses to ask the pharaoh repeatedly to let the Jews go free, and each time the pharaoh refused, God unleashed a new plague on the Egyptians. God brought draught and locusts and famine and frogs. Finally God sent the angel of death to kill the firstborn child in every Egyptian family. That was enough for the pharaoh, who threw up his hands and told Moses to take the Jews and go free. Moses hurried the children of Israel out of town and quickly they reached the shores of the Red Sea.

"But how would they pass?" asked the rabbi rhetorically. "Moses held his arms out, and miraculously, the Red Sea parted and formed a land path. The children of Israel walked through the Red Sea to the land of milk, honey and freedom.

Hold on a minute, I thought.

I raised my hand.

"Put your hand down," warned a heavy man seated next to me.

But I kept waving until it was impossible for the rabbi to ignore me any longer.

"Michael it is not our practice to interrupt the Sabbath sermon," said the rabbi. "So what is it?"

My father, seated several rows ahead, turned and stared at me in shock.

"Rabbi," I said, "the part about Moses parting the sea?"

"Yes, Michael," said the rabbi, "Moses spread out his arms and the Red Sea parted to form a land path to freedom for the children of Israel."

"A path just popped out of the water, huh, Rabbi?" I asked. "Just popped up...?"

"Yes, Michael, we Jews believe in miracles, and God's miracle parted the waters for our people."

"Give me a break!" I said defiantly.

Dad turned white.

The part of my psyche that lives in fantasyland held the unreasonable hope that the rabbi would remember his story of the boy with the whistle. That ungrounded part of me pictured the rabbi standing like Moses with outstretched arms to calm the angry elders now surrounding me. He would explain I was doing what all Jews should do: questioning authority.

But the rabbi clearly approved when the sweaty fat man next to me arose, bug-eyed with anger, and led me by my earlobe out the sanctuary doors.

I'd have to wait for later therapy to fully understand the appeal that "question authority" had for me. I had little impulse control and found it impossible to pass on a chance to tweak any authority who wasn't making sense and who was keeping me away from my friends and a Sunday of play.

I felt proud when my temple classmates slapped me on the back and said how cool I was to take on the rabbi. But I knew there was nothing noble about it. I wasn't questioning authority so much as taking an impulsive shot at Judaism and at my dad, giving both the metaphoric finger. I was not allowed to return to temple, and that was great with me. And Dad angrily grounded me for two months—not so great. I knew I had to pay a price. The two months went by quickly and Sunday school wasn't real school.

Real school was public school where I was about to learn the real cost of playing the angry clown. There were repercussions coming I would never forget.

NINE

St. Louie Blues

THE PUBLIC SCHOOL I ATTENDED held fifth, sixth and seventh grade classes in a single room. Our teacher, Mrs. Wishman, moved among rows organized by grades, alternately helping her students with their lessons. At the end of the last class before summer break, Mrs. Wishman beckoned me up front to her desk. The other fifth graders were filing out of the classroom, but the sixth and seventh graders remained seated and the big kids watched attentively while I shuffled up the aisle. Mrs. Wishman put a hand on my shoulder in a kindly fashion while the big kids smirked.

"Michael, we've talked about how much you clowned around this year," she said. "You didn't get your work done."

I shrugged my shoulders. The kids in class loved my clowning, especially my monster face contortions. It seemed worth it at the time.

"I can't advance you to sixth grade," she said softly.

"I don't care." I said, but not defiantly since she was being nice.

"I think you do care," she said gently "I'm going to talk to your parents. Maybe we can get you some help."

Help. There was that word again. Red-faced, I left the room to meet Mom out front for my ride home. How in the world would I tell her that I flunked? Worse, what would Dad do when he found out? My stomach tightened as I imagined their response.

I could count on Mom to turn on me. She'd shrug her shoulders and say, "I give up on him, Herman. I completely give up."

But Dad would pull me by the arm to the garage, where he'd roll me across the floor with his boot the way a lumberjack rolls a log. He'd be spitting expletives that never formed a sentence. Between Mom running over my dogs there and Dad's temper, the garage wasn't my favorite spot in the house. The first few times, the cement floor was freezer cold, dirty and rough as sandpaper wherever it touched my skin. But I learned to let my mind float, sometimes thinking about Lake Michigan's stormy winds when the freezing snow blew so fiercely it numbed my cheeks. When he'd had enough, Dad took me to his study with his big desk and his smelly cigars and pipe rack. Behind smoke clouds he would talk to me about failure and how hard he worked to keep me in clothes. Then he'd just stare out the window and not look at me.

I'd wait and let his words became muffled background knowing Dad's tirades couldn't last forever.

Flunking fifth grade gave my teachers new reasons to press Mom to get me "help" despite the failure of earlier attempts through Dr. Cronick.

They asked Mom in for a parent-teacher meeting which Mom described years later:

"The boy needs 'help,'" argued Mrs. Wishman.

"Nonsense," argued Mom. "He's just a boy being a boy."

"Well this is a boy being a boy who can't pass fifth grade. We think it's more than that," said the high school assistant principal. "Surely we all agree that he's quite capable, Mrs. Grossman."

"He's quite capable," Mom repeated, feeling immensely relieved. "All my kids are."

It was now clear to Mom that no one suggested my problem was a genetically low IQ. That possibility dispensed with, Mom was suddenly more amenable.

"I suppose professional help couldn't hurt," she conceded.

I told Mom and Dad I didn't need help, reminding them that my visits to Dr. Cronick had wasted everyone's time. Dad said it wasn't my choice, so soon thereafter Mom drove me to a weary, paint-chipped building in the older part of downtown Muskegon. The sign on the lawn was shaped like a feather. It read: CHILD GUIDANCE CENTER, A RED FEATHER AGENCY. A steep and unlit wooden stairwell led up one flight to a reception area, where a man who introduced himself as Dr. Neumann VanDervort met us. He looked like a barbershop singer, with wavy white hair parted down the middle and a bulbous red nose above his smile. His eyes were blue but unlike Dr. Cronick's blue eyes—they were kindly. Dr. VanDervort shook my hand warmly and sat Mom down in the waiting room while we went to his office.

Dr. VanDervort held up a series of black and white paintings and asked me what I saw in each one. I said a blindfolded fourth grader could do better by spilling ink on a paper.

"But do you see any figures in the pictures?" Asked Dr. VanDervort.

"I suppose this one could be a butterfly and that one a man on a horse," I said, pointing.

Next he gave me crayons and asked me to draw a house. Though houses typically have angled roofs, our ultra-modern house had a flat roof, and I drew it that way, mostly to make his senseless assignment less boring. My flat roof proved terribly interesting to Dr. VanDervort, as did the stick figures of a family he had me draw. He invited his colleagues in to see them. The three of them passed them around—nodding in apparent agreement.

When his colleagues left, Dr. VanDervort asked Mom to join us. He gave me a book to read while the two of them debated my fate. I thumbed pages but listened intently.

"The drawings show significant depression," said Dr. VanDervort, "and suggest considerable underlying rage."

He pointed to my stick figure family.

"Notice the eyes. Mrs. Grossman, may I be candid?" Asked Dr. VanDervort pausing for permission.

"Of course you can," Mom said sanctimoniously. "Everyone knows you don't have to pull any punches with me. And please call me Rosalind."

I doubt that all the store managers you fired for disagreeing would think you wanted straight talk, I thought.

"I believe Michael's home life is a significant contributing factor, Rosalind," the doctor said.

Mom nodded, "Yes, yes. Herman's temper. I knew it—I knew it would come to this. I told him so repeatedly."

Didn't take her long to throw Dad under the bus, I thought.

"Well, if that is the issue," continued Dr. VanDervort, following Mom's cue, "then you need to get Michael away from his father. Removed from his present environment. I suggest that you send Michael away to school."

"To where?" Mom asked, surprised.

"I'll help you find a good school," said Dr. VanDervort.

No way am I leaving home, I thought. *I'm not one of the family dogs. You can't just run me over because I flunked fifth grade. I didn't rob a bank or kill anyone. Surely Mom won't go along with this*?

Mom phoned Dad, talking with sweeping hand gestures and sighing dramatically for Dr. VanDervort's benefit. Soon Dad arrived, out of breath and clearly upset. He paced up and down the doctor's office, pounding his fist in his palm.

"I will not send my own child away from home," he declared. "What would that say about me? That I failed as a father. I won't have it."

I felt bad for Dad. I could see he was really bothered by what I'd done. Flunking fifth grade was pretty bad, I guess, but why did they have to send me away? I wouldn't go. I'd refuse to go.

Before long both Mom and Dad said that I had to go and that I could throw tantrums all I wanted but it wouldn't change a thing. It didn't. In the fall of 1953, Mom and I boarded a Capital Airlines flight bound for St. Louis, Missouri, and the school Dr. VanDervort had recommended.

The DC3 had two enormous engines. A stewardess in a blue uniform with a matching military-style cap brought me a soda, Planters Peanuts and a set of silver wings.

A blast of humid air hit when the door opened and we debarked in St. Louis. The airport terminal, no bigger than the Muskegon Airport, was a small white wood-slat building with a Coke machine and four bathrooms—two *Whites Only* and two marked *Colored*.

We took a cab to the home where I'd be boarding while I attended school and pulled into the driveway of a huge, multi-story white house with a sign on the lawn that read POTTER HOUSE. It was the house pictured in the brochure Mom had showed me on the plane which promised, "Potter House was created to provide a supportive, therapeutic setting for children." Mom repeated her favorite line, "Potter House caters to children of privilege whose parents can afford the finest support available."

Twelve kids boarded at Potter House. I was the youngest. I remember Cathy Snider, whose dad owned the whole SpeedStar Gas Station chain. Everyone whispered "the whole." Joel Fried had brown glasses, wavy hair and a bad skin condition and used a plastic pocket protector in his blue madras shirts. The owners of Potter House permitted Joel to bring his beautiful, longhaired dog Smoky. I loved Smoky, and Joel said I could pet him any time. But when Joel got upset, a daily occurrence, he would scream and Smoky would run and shake in the corner.

Potter House had high, wood beamed ceilings and a massive, curved staircase that led up to three floors of bedrooms. As the youngest boarder, I was assigned the only bedroom on the fourth floor, so I only saw the other kids at meals or when I went down a flight to the bathroom.

Like all Michigan kids, I loved cars. I cut car pictures out of magazines and taped them on my walls. I spent hours putting up pictures of Detroit's newest models. Chevy had just introduced a fiberglass sports car called the Corvette, and Studebaker rolled out the Golden Hawk with fins like an airplane and a brushed metal dash. Packard's Caribbean convertible looked like a Chris Craft with tires.

The other contents of my small room were a chair, a night stand, and an electric alarm clock so I wouldn't be late for school again after they called to complain about my tardiness. The room was hot year-round, so even in the winter I lay on top of the covers, sweating in a T-shirt. I was terribly lonely, and I missed home. My room at Potter House wasn't like my own room. I was used to my own room. St. Louis didn't have beaches like ours at Lake Muskegon, and I wondered if my best friend Chuck fished the lake on the log raft we'd built.

I rode my bike the two miles from Potter House to the Whitbury Academy, the private day school I attended. Whitbury also distributed a thick paper brochure, and theirs boasted of a one-teacher-per-student ratio. They got the first half of the equation right—the one teacher part. All my classes had one teacher for lots of students. I didn't see any difference from public school back home. So why couldn't I just go to school back home?

On our arrival the first day, we were ushered into a library-like, oak-walled office and introduced to the headmaster, Mr. Finius Monahan. He handed Mom a white folder bordered in gold leaf and titled,

WHITBURY ACADEMY'S CUSTOM TAILORED ACADEMIC PLAN FOR STUDENT I MICHAEL GROSSMAN

The plan outlined the fifth grade courses I needed to repeat plus those required so I could complete sixth grade in the same academic year.

I quickly came to hate stuffy old Whitbury Academy, and it became my greatest pleasure to disrupt class whenever I could. I mimicked the teachers when they turned to face the blackboard and gave intentionally goofy answers that made my classmates howl. I got sent to Headmaster Monahan a lot, and clearly he didn't like me much.

I did learn to name the fifty state capitals. I only memorized them because I liked Mr. Cuppilow, the one teacher who befriended me. He looked like he'd been plucked out of an antique picture frame. Even in St. Louis's sweltering summer humidity, he wore a gray wool sweater that buttoned down the middle, achieving symmetry and near perfect alignment with the part down the middle of his hair. Nostril hair created a misplaced moustache on his beak-like nose. He wasn't much to look at, but Mr. Cuppilow was the nicest of teachers. I liked the game he created to challenge me to match states to their capitals while he pretended he was a quiz show host.

When we reached Rhode Island on his list, I always said, "For Little Rhody it's Providence."

I liked to call it "Little Rhody" because Mr. Cuppilow had said the entire state was only 48 miles long. The joke never failed to get the desired response. The first time I said it, Mr. Cuppilow threw back his head and burst into a long laugh that became a train of shorter snorts.

That year I also learned what attracted guys to girls, information most surely not provided by Academy's uptight instructors. My extracurricular instructor for that lesson was eleventh grader Mary, whose straight, golden hair reached her trim waist. She wore tight red cashmere sweaters stretched over what we guys called her "bust." Actually, in Mary's case, our term was "gargantuan busts." Mary was sexy, but as an eleventh grader, she was out of my league.

My buddies and I routinely spent recess bouncing a ball off the school's garage and catching it on the fly. One day I threw wild, and the ball sailed completely over the garage. When I ran around the building to retrieve it, there was Mary with a twelfth grader named Fred, both tight against the wall. Mary was grinding her head around in Fred's face while Fred's hand moved up and down the front of her sweater. They paused when they saw me.

Mary giggled. "Come over here," she said smiling slyly.

I did. She took my hand and slid it up her bust, and then she winked. My jaw dropped, and Fred laughed at the look on my face. It happened so fast that I was stunned. But afterward, night after night I'd lie in bed thinking of Mary and reviewing that moment. I loved Mary. Only Mary. I was lonely, and Mary was the answer. I wished I was her boyfriend instead of Fred. Whenever Mary saw me at school after that day, she gave me her sly wink.

I finally found a friend at school. Jimmy Palermo lived with his aunt in St. Louis and took the trolley to school. He attended Whitfield on a special city program for kids who'd gotten in trouble, but he never said what for. Though he didn't know a thing about fishing, it was good to have a friend again. After classes we took the trolley downtown to the big department stores. Jimmy showed me what to do. Anyone watching would see me pick up an item from the counter, look it over and put it back, while my other hand shipped a duplicate up my coat sleeve. It wasn't my favorite thing to do, but Jimmy liked it, and he was my friend.

Riding home after school one day, I parked my bike in front of a neighborhood grocery store and entered. I didn't need anything and don't even know why I stopped, but suddenly on impulse I grabbed a quart-sized glass bottle of Coke and tried to shove it in my jeans pocket. Only the neck fit in and I left the store with most of the bottle visibly hanging out my jeans pocket. I'd reached my bike when the counter lady stuck her head out the screen door and demanded I come back. I debated. All I had to do was to ride away. But I was too scared so I returned. She eyed the quart bottle hanging out my jeans.

"You hungry?" she asked.

"No."

"So why are you stealing?" she asked.

I shrugged, really getting scared now.

"I want to know why," she demanded.

My mind raced, and I said the first thing I could make up. "Well you see, I never took anything before. But I want to join this gang at school, see. And they have an initiation. You have to steal something."

How did I come up with this stuff, I wondered.

The counter lady asked where I lived. I was so frightened that I gave her my real address, and she let me go. I felt sick to my stomach and vowed I would never steal again. I didn't know why I did in the first place.

The following morning Headmaster Finius Monahan's assistant beckoned me out of class. Headmaster Finius Monahan was sitting behind his desk, hands clasped, one hand restraining the fingers of the other. Clearly he wished they were around my neck.

"Where do you get off telling people that the Whitbury Academy trains you to steal," he said.

I turned pale.

"I . . . I never said school said that," I assured him, trying to be brave.

His cold stare persisted.

"All I said was . . ."

He interrupted, "Your parents have been called and you, Grossman, are outta here."

I had no bravado left. I began to cry. "I never said school told me to steal. I said I did it to join a gang,"

"I can't wait to be rid of you," Finius Monahan thundered back.

"Please Mr. Monahan. Please give me another chance," I whined.

Monahan pointed to the door.

That night I lay I bed and worried about how to handle Dad. What words would set him off the least? He could lecture me on the eighth commandment all he wanted, and I would listen without a peep as he reminded me how much it cost him to send me to Potter House.

I lucked out. Dad couldn't go to St. Louis, so only Mom attended the academy's hearing. Mom and I sat at the long conference table with my teachers as Headmaster Finius Monahan summarized my crimes. When he finished, he called for a show of hands as my teachers voted rather enthusiastically to send me home. Except for the lone holdout—Mr. Cuppilow. For a sweet old guy, he was stronger than I imagined. He stood up to Finius Monahan and argued with the other teachers, insisting I was worth a second chance. He stuck up for me so firmly that after much debate, the others reluctantly agreed to let me finish out the year—with certain provisos: Mr. Cuppilow made it clear I had to behave in all my classes and that I'd be suspended immediately if there was one more stealing incident.

Trembling, I promised never to steal again.

Mr. Cuppilow repeated that there must be no more antics in my classes.

I promised that I would behave in every class and that—as he also requested—I would not play with Jimmy Palermo anymore, though in a whisper I tried to say that stealing was my own fault, not Jimmy's.

With the fear of god in me, I behaved for the rest of the year.

When the term ended, Mom flew to St. Louis for a final meeting with Headmaster Finius Monahan, who was all smiles as he energetically shook her hand. Headmaster Monahan produced pages of test scores and charts for Mom, confirming what a great job Whitbury had done to prepare me, and a letter certifying my completion of two school years in one.

"He can start seventh grade in the fall," said Headmaster Finius Monahan, adding *"back home."* He rose from his desk to shake Mom's hand again.

I was surprised. I'd never taken a single test at Whitbury, so where did Headmaster Finius Monahan get all those charts and the test scores he showed Mom? I'd learned nothing all year, not a thing except the state capitals. I was about to ask just what tests they were talking about, but I thought better of it. If Mom was fooled, well, it didn't really hurt anyone. I was going home which is all that really mattered. But what a bunch of bull.

Home at last. It was all I could think about. I'd see Chuck, and we'd take the raft out, and finally I'd see Jill and Randy and Josefina, and I'd get to sleep in my very own bed again.

But the plane Mom put me on wasn't going home. The ticket read "Portland, Maine."

"Summer camp," Mom announced, "you're going to love it."

Camp Ironwood was on Sebego Lake, Maine's second-largest. The camp was okay. It just wasn't home. I learned to shoot arrows and to take white, black, green and yellow plastic cords and braid them into a square lanyard. A hurricane passed over camp one afternoon, and I was amazed that winds could bend big trees like twigs. I ate a Japanese food called sukiyaki and saw a blue flying saucer pass over the mountain at the end of Sebago Lake. My bunkmate swore he saw it too.

When summer ended, the camp director called me into his office to tell me I'd had a really good summer. I was calming down, he said, and he complimented me for coming a long way in so short a time. Unlike Headmaster Finius Monahan's phony report, he really meant it. For the first time ever I had good news for Mom and Dad, and I couldn't wait to tell them as I boarded the plane for Michigan.

Mom wasn't home when I returned.

"She's visiting her friends in Cuba," Josefina explained.

She returned a week later and was in her bathroom when I went to tell her the good news. She was sitting before her big lighted mirror carefully penciling her eyes, opening her mouth as if somehow that steadied her hand. I told her what the director said about how much progress I'd made at camp.

"He said I'm really growing up, Mom," I said.

"Yeah, I'll just bet," she said.

In the fall I started seventh grade. That was the age when most kids began to date. In the 1950s we learned about sex much later than kids today do. TV sex was minimally suggestive so guys turned to *Playboy* and got an idealized anatomy lesson. I never saw a porn movie until I was an adult.

I had a lot of buddies, but I wasn't popular with girls. For one thing, I wore "Huskies," the Levis euphemism for jeans for a fat kid. I also wore glasses, so some kids called me "four eyes." Dating was a self-conscious torture. I hadn't a clue what to say to a girl. But since my buddies dated, I had to or I'd look like a "fruit."

My first date was with Connie Riley.

"She's got some reputation," said my friend Chuck. "I saw Connie through the window doing it with some guy on her living room floor."

"You're kidding," I said.

I asked Connie out to a movie, but I was too young to drive, so Mom had to take us. I was surprised how easy it was to talk to Connie. But each time I spoke to her, Mom's face appeared in the rearview mirror watching us. It was so embarrassing we finally rode in silence.

Afterward, Mom asked me what I saw in Connie.

"She's nice," I said.

"Is she really your type?" Mom asked.

I shrugged. I'd thought she was, but now I wasn't sure.

"You can do better," said Mom. "Trust me, you can."

"I don't have to see her again," I said.

Mom smiled.

But Mom asked the same questions about whomever I dated, always insisting that I could do better. She didn't understand that the girls in my school weren't exactly dying to date a four-eyes kid in huskies.

I wasn't entirely displeased that Mom said I could do better. Mom was beautiful, with shoulder-length hair that tossed when she walked or turned her head. People asked if she'd been a model. So it was flattering when she ran her fingers over my cheek, cradled my face, and said I was her "little man."

But what I couldn't understand was why Mom's fondness for me dissolved the minute Dad got home. As soon as the grinding of the garage door motor signaled his return, Mom would drop her hand from my cheek, cease gently stroking my hair and, to my utter shock, start to scold me. I never knew what hit me even though I should have—it happened nightly. One moment she would be so sweet; a second later she'd be circling Dad to say how bad I was, even before the man had time to hang his hat. Worse, I didn't know what I'd done wrong.

"Herman, do you have any idea what this kid pulled today?" she said.

Dad didn't care about some minor infraction. But Mom drilled away at him, persisting until Dad, beat from a long day at work, couldn't take it anymore.

"You damn idiot," he'd shout, pounding the table and then heading for me.

Like a whirlwind he'd shake me, but when he finished, he always felt bad about it and skulked off to his study. As if nothing had transpired, Mom would wave her hand like a wand, and I'd be transformed again into her special confidant.

"See how out of control he is, Michael? Just like I told you," she'd whisper and put her arm around my shoulder, adding, "I know you won't ever be like that will you, my little man?"

It was so confusing. White was black, then back to white again. Was I her little man or her bad kid? Did she even like me? The ground beneath me kept falling away.

Lying in bed I made a nightly resolve never to believe her again. But she was my Mom and I needed my Mom so I could never quite resist when the next night she'd pull up to me and cradle my cheeks. Eyes closed, I'd dive head-first into the empty pool again.

My relationship with Mom was like a visit to the carnival house of mirrors. You know with certainty that the warped mirrors will distort the way things look, but who can resist looking again? Or was it more like finding myself trapped in a revolving door that had no exit? I'd push the glass in front of me, trying to go faster so I could reach Mom in the partition ahead of me, though any fool could see I would never catch her. Did Mom want me to catch her?

And what did she mean when she whispered her little man was the man she trusted most? Did Dad know she said that? Were they glad I was back home and did they ever talk of sending me away again? That question in particular haunted me. I had to know their plans for me, and I made a terrible mess of things because I tried to find out.

TEN

The Fall

I'd been back from St. Louis a year, and I never wanted to leave home again. I studied enough to pass seventh grade safely and stayed out of trouble.

One thing that made school difficult was that the vise attacks were back. Two in particular held me so powerfully and paralyzed me so totally that I felt pulled underwater, riddled with fear they wouldn't end. Would I have to spend all eternity in this state? I had to hide the attacks from my parents and teachers least they send me for "help", the excuse they used to send me away. So when the vise clamped tightened and the numbing paralysis came on, or when my mind raced wildly, I locked on my habitual jaw-straining smile or employed the other mannerisms I knew would disguise my actual state of mind.

I couldn't stop worrying that my parents had a plan for me that would take me away from home again. A memory flashed of my hot, sad little room on the fourth floor of Potter House. I didn't ever want to be that lonely again. Didn't they want me home? Did they talk behind closed doors of sending me away again?

A serendipitous game of one-on-one basketball led to a plan—

a way to test Mom and Dad so I would know how they felt, so I could get out of the limbo I was in. My basketball opponent mentioned that he was going away to a college prep school. I didn't want to go to college or ever leave home again. But now I knew how to test my parents. I worked out every detail even down to how the conversation with them would go. I would tell my parents about my friend's plans and wonder aloud if I should attend prep school too.

"I couldn't bear to have you leave home again," Dad would say.

"You can prepare for college just as well at home," Mom would say. "And in no time at all you'll be a grown man. I want to enjoy you while I can," she'd sigh and smile at me.

"I'd miss you too much," Mom would say.

And Dad would add, "We wouldn't be a family if you left, son."

I tested them that very night, telling them about my friend and casually wondering aloud if I shouldn't go to prep school too. I paused, waiting for the conversation to proceed as scripted.

"Good idea," said Mom. "There may still be time to enroll you for this fall."

"I know the Dean of Men at Lake Forest Academy," said Dad. "He owes me a favor."

My teachers lobbied for a military school, but Mom and Dad sent me to Lake Forest Academy in Illinois, a non-military, "normal" prep school. Calling it a normal school was an exaggeration. No girls went there, and the curriculum was unchanged from the Academy's founding in the 1857. Many of my classes were irrelevant, a waste of time. I hated that they were mandatory and was quick to state my opposition. I especially disliked Latin.

"Why would anyone study Latin these days?" I wondered aloud in class.

Professor Mathais turned and looked at me curiously.

"Well, how many people speak Latin these days?" I asked him. "When was the last time the fast food attendant asked in Latin if you wanted fries with your Coke?"

Professor Mathais liked me, so I got away with it, which was a good thing because he made life difficult for students he didn't like. He didn't like my friend Jim Carburry. Once when he asked Jim to conjugate a Latin verb and he tried but stumbled, Professor Mathais called on me. Luckily I got it right. Professor Mathais turned back to Jim, smirking with exaggerated drama, and said in a highly pompous voice, "You see, my dear Mr. Carburry, how very simple it is . . . simple, my dear Mr. Carburry, even as you."

The class howled with laughter, except for poor Jim, who sunk even lower in his seat. I didn't think it was funny either.

I balked at having to take Music and Art Appreciation until I met the professor, Phillip Trevor. Professor Trevor was not like Professor Mathais or any of the other Academy teachers. He was more like my old St. Louis instructor, Professor Cuppilow. Professor Trevor invited me to his apartment. I didn't know why he liked me, but I relished the time I spent there. His apartment was the antithesis of my stark, cold, ultra-modern home in Muskegon with its institutional, black concrete floors. His floors were dark cherry planks that provided a soothing atmosphere, as did the Persian rugs and tall mahogany cabinets with antiques. Copies of famous paintings hung on the walls next to his collection of handsome woven tapestries.

Mrs. Trevor always greeted me with the warmest smile and then fluttered from room to room while the professor and I sat on a heavily stuffed couch and talked. The Trevors always insisted I stay for dinner, as I hoped they would because Mrs. Trevor's thick stews with big chunks of meat and potatoes were a welcome alternative to the cafeteria's chipped beef on toast, which we guys called "shit on a shingle."

I could talk comfortably to Professor Trevor when he asked me about dorm life and my other classes. Talking to him was like talking to a friend—as long as I was careful not to drop even a hint about my vise attacks. That was too risky. Being sent away to prep school was one thing, but sent off to a loony bin would be quite another. After dinner we leafed through oversized art books, and Professor Trevor explained what was unique about each master's style. He nodded approvingly when I commented too.

Despite the Trevors, dorm life was bleak. I had acquaintances but I wasn't close to anyone and I had to be careful with "the guys," I knew how vicious they could be if they thought you weren't cool. They were friendly to me because I could pull off acting cool—though it was exhausting to pretend to be tough and to nervously crack sex jokes. I felt bad for kids like Jim Carburry, who couldn't pull it off. The quiet ones had it rough. The guys called Carburry a four-eyed faggot, which got a big laugh. But Jim wasn't gay, and I wore glasses too. No one back then was openly gay. Carburry was just a shy kid who wasn't a jock.

Though the academy wasn't military, life at an all-boys school had a military toughness, a cruelty that flowed from the lack of balance between male and female energies. There was little variety in the roles that were acceptable if you wanted to get along with minimal hassle in the dorms. By now the vise attacks came with weekly regularity. Acting cool, playing the role for the guys for anything longer than a brief hallway exchange, threw me off balance, and was often a prelude to a vise attack. The attacks were the most intense when, instead of rebelling, I felt defeated. That's when my anger, having no alternate release, turned inward. I felt sullen, often for days at a time—like a scuba diver, belted in weights, moving in slow, aquatic motions. When my spirit dropped to that gloomier place in some lower region of my psyche, I knew the fastest way through the despair was to wait it out in bed. But sometimes doing so extended the vise attack when, as I lay for hours, I compared myself to Dad.

Dad was important. Dad was powerful. Who was I? Everyone back home knew Dad. Nobody knew me. Dad got into Harvard. I was barely getting by in prep school.

What if each generation following my powerful Grandfather Isaac produced lesser men?, I wondered. *Would it help if I made myself physically stronger?*

I resolved to build up my body and try out for academy sports teams. I ran track, lifted weights and played football. Though I lettered in track, I was no good at football. It made no sense to me to smash an opposing lineman, my own teammate, in a practice that wasn't a real game. So the coach benched me for the season, and I didn't second-guess his decision. Fourth quarter of the final game that season, out of charity the coach put me in. I was wired to show Coach what I could do in a real game. At the hike I cracked into my opposing lineman so hard I knocked him crashing to the ground, clearing a wide hole for our halfback to run through. We scored the only touchdown of the day on that play. Or we would have if the referees hadn't called it back. Someone on our team jumped before the snap. The referee called out my jersey number.

My hostility was never far from the surface, and it grew as the year progressed, building pressure to the point where it seeped out when I didn't want it to. I started taunting upperclassmen bullies with the sarcasm I once reserved for my teachers. My taunts merely annoyed my professors but the bullies wanted to fight. I'd confront much bigger guys if they picked on me or on a fellow student, and I'd wise off to them, leading them just to the edge of the fight, provoking them just as I used to toy with Dad. But before it came to blows, I'd walk away, enduring their cries of "chicken" and their clucking taunts.

I backed down because I'd been afraid to fight since I was eight years old. That was when Dad announced I should know how to box.

"Real men box," he said. "Learn to defend yourself."

"Not interested," I said with Dad towering over me.

Dad led me to the garage and laced me into a pair of his red Everlast boxing gloves, which extended to my elbows. I turned pale when Dad grunted and started dancing around me, sweating and taking light jabs.

What frightened me was the uncertainly. I feared that Dad would forget he was boxing a child as he jabbed at me in his trance. Never in full control anyway, how much would it take for Dad to hit me as hard as he hit the sand-filled punching bag that hung by a steel chain from the garage ceiling? The bag weighed a hundred pounds, yet it bent and whooshed as each punch landed.

That picture—Dad's fist denting the heavy sandbag—flashed each time I weaseled out of a fight at the academy, until one afternoon when I couldn't retreat

My roommate at Lake Forest Academy was Robert Swerg, a dorky kid with an acne peppered face, but a nice roommate who was some kind of math whiz. I was grateful when he helped me with my algebra. His mom regularly sent him baked goods, and Robert invited me to take a brownie from his steamer trunk whenever I wanted one. I was doing just that one afternoon when a friend of Robert's stuck his head in our room.

"Ah-hah!" He said, assuming he'd caught me stealing from Robert.

He made such a fuss that the other guys on our floor came running down the hall with Robert among them. They told Robert I'd been caught red-handed taking a brownie from his steamer trunk. I waited for Robert to explain that I had his permission to do so, but for reasons I still don't know, Robert stood mute. The guys said the two of us had to fight—that a fight was the only way to settle the score, so they marched us down to the men's room.

There is no way to get out of this, I thought as Robert and I stood surrounded by the guys.

The familiar image of Dad's punching bag flickered, and, as if psychic, I saw what was coming. I pictured myself lying facedown, motionless on the dirty, urine-pungent bathroom floor. I'd have given anything to get out of there.

Robert put up his fists, so I raised mine. Robert threw a punch but swung wide as I moved to avoid it. I shifted my weight between my front and back legs, dancing around as I did. Robert's second punch missed, as did a third. My dance was working. But I concentrated so hard on my footwork that I forgot to keep both fists up. Robert saw the opening, swung and connected with my jaw. Something cracked in my mouth. My front tooth wrenched backwards. My warm blood tasted salty.

The fight was over, and Robert had won, but I was pleased. Fighting wasn't bad at all. It wasn't the life-or-death moment I'd feared since I was eight. I was alive, still standing and actually quite comfortable. No pain. The guys treated the gap in my front teeth as a sign of my manliness.

As I left the bathroom, I flashed back to Dad coming at me, snorting, sweating, with that bull-angry look in his eyes. I was just eight, and that was a curious thing.

How brave do you have to be to scare a kid of eight? Did Dad enjoy scaring me?

Little did I know the day was coming when I'd get the answer.

ELEVEN

Kake Walk

I ASSUMED I'D BE DONE WITH THE LEARNING PHASE OF MY LIFE when I completed high school the following year, 1959. However, my parents had other plans for me. I was going to college.

Mom provided the list of colleges I was to apply to. She picked top-rated liberal arts colleges like Brandeis, Antioch and Oberlin. These were admirable choices, my teachers noted, but they diplomatically suggested that with my C+ average and abysmal SATs, I'd be wise to send at least one application to what they called a "safety" school. Mom said I didn't need a safety school, but at my teachers' urging, I sent off an application to the University of Vermont. Mom made appointments with admissions counselors at Brandeis, Antioch and Oberlin but said we needn't bother to visit the University of Vermont.

My admissions interviews were not exactly models of the way it's done.

"He's a flower just starting to bloom," Mom told the Antioch admissions counselor, explaining away my low grade point average.

I shrunk in my seat. The counselor looked the other way.

At one point in the interview he asked me why I wanted Antioch

College. I hadn't a clue why, knew nothing about the place and hadn't even opened the fat Antioch catalog envelope when it arrived in the mail. I had to answer him, and fortunately I remembered that my classmate, Wally Frankleman, said Antioch was the first college to experiment with co-ed dorms. Wally wanted to live in a dorm with his girlfriend.

"Well," I said trying to sound thoughtful, "you have co-ed dorms."

"So?" asked the admissions counselor.

"Well, don't you find separation of the sexes artificial?" I asked, thrilled with my intelligence.

The counselor gave me a curious look.

Well, I thought, *there's still Brandeis University.*

But I didn't fare any better at the Brandeis meeting when the admission counselor asked what I'd liked about Lake Forest Academy. I was stumped for an answer, since there wasn't much I did like. My mind raced during the awkward silence.

"They encourage you to think for yourself," I finally said, again delighted with myself.

"For example . . . ?" he asked.

I didn't expect a follow-up.

"Well . . ." I said groping, "well . . . if you thought a professor was wrong, well you could go on strike and not do your homework."

He stood and wished me well.

In the fall of 1960 I arrived at The University of Vermont, known by the acronym--UVM. Those initials made no sense to me since any Michigander knows UVM is the University of Michigan. I accused them of plagiarism, but my academic advisor explained the initials came from the college's Latin name, *Universitas Veridis Montis* (University of the Green Mountains; the name *Vermont* itself also comes from the Latin for Green Mountains.).

Even at my "safety school" things got off to a shaky start. They gave the 900 incoming freshman a spelling test, and I got lowest score. But it was insignificant compared to confrontations I began to have with UVM's Dean of Men.

To get to the University of Vermont from Michigan, Mom and Dad drove east across the provincial routes in Canada, then down into Burlington. Along the way, Dad bought two cases of Crown Royal, his favorite scotch, which was cheaper in Canada. Each bottle came handsomely packaged in a fake leather-bound book.

We arrived in Burlington late at night and headed straight to our hotel. In the morning we discovered that our red Ford station wagon was missing from the hotel's parking lot. We hadn't unpacked the car, so the thieves got most of our personal belongings. Mom took me to buy new clothes, and then she and Dad hopped a plane back to Michigan.

A week later the pay phone at the dorm rang, and the guys hollered out my name.

"Dean Craven here," said an important sounding voice when I answered the phone. "Dean of Men. The Burlington police found your station wagon abandoned in the woods. They want you at the precinct to identify it. I'll pick you up in front of your dorm in twenty minutes."

At the police station I confirmed that the red station wagon was indeed my family's car. A Vermont state trooper in a Mounties-style hat started to unload its contents. Box by box he asked me to confirm that each one was mine. Clearly, all the contents belong to us, but I went along with presumed police procedure and nodded "yes" to each box he showed me. Finally he removed the last two boxes from in the rear of the wagon, and when I nodded "yes." perfunctorily, the dean and the trooper looked cunningly at each other.

"These are yours?" he asked again.

"Everything you've shown me is ours," I said. "It's our Ford wagon with our Michigan license plate."

"So you were planning to sneak liquor onto campus, Grossman?" said Dean Craven moving aggressively into my face.

I hadn't a clue what he was talking about and I told him so.

Feverishly Dean Craven tore open the box and removed a leather book, opening it like he'd discovered the secret to alchemy. He waved the bottle of Crown Royal in my face.

"You know the rules about liquor on campus!"

"Sir, that's not mine. That's my dad's." I said.

"Oh I'm sure your dad hides his scotch in leather-bound books," said Dean Craven sarcastically.

"No really sir. They're Dad's. That's how they come packaged," I said weakly.

The dean was making me feel like I really was guilty.

"If I catch you with a drop of booze on campus you'll be out this fast," said Dean Craven, snapping his fingers.

We drove back to my dorm in sullen silence.

Why didn't I tell Dean Craven to call Dad? It occurred to me as he drove down the road from my dorm. *Well, let a little time pass and Dean Craven will forget all about it.*

But a month later I was back in his spotlight. It wasn't Dad's scotch this time but my politics.

In the summer of 1960, my freshman year, UVM administrators announced a new set of rules governing students who lived off campus. The onerous restrictions were the talk of campus and were apparently motivated by the University's desire to expand its academic role to that of parent, chaplain and the morals police. Before a student could rent an off-campus apartment, the University had to approve of its layout. It couldn't, for example, have a private stairway since that would make it easier for a boy to sneak a girl up to his room. Students disapproved of the new rules, of course, arguing that the university's role ought to be to teach and nothing more. I, like all freshman, had to live in a dorm, but the off-campus issue offered me an irresistible platform. I attended a big campus rally, cheered the speakers and shouted my own insults at the administration through a megaphone. My waving fist and my TEACH DON'T PREACH sign attracted a reporter from ABC-TV News who interviewed me, camera rolling.

The following day the dorm pay phone rang. Dean Craven was calling me again.

"Michael, I am sure this can't be true," his voice boomed with its usual dramatic excess, "but my associates insist you were on TV last night urging students to throw stones through the Waterman windows?"

The dean's office was in the Waterman Administration Building.

"I said it," I replied, puffed up with bravado, "and I meant every word of it."

"My office in fifteen minutes, Grossman!" demanded the dean.

I received a second warning, but that wasn't the last straw.

Most of UVM's administrators, like Dean Craven, were determined to crack down on students, and in fairness, the University had to do something. Endowments were declining, surely due in part to UVM's reputation as a party school, a campus of fraternities that held classes as an afterthought. There was more than a little truth to this. At UVM the fraternities and the administration shared almost equal power. Even Kake Walk, UVM's famous annual winter festival, was jointly administered.

Kake Walk was a full week of parties curiously honoring America's Southern slave heritage. White males danced the same "cake walk" that plantation slaves once performed. The master would instruct his slaves to dance for his guests, and the slave who performed the funniest dance earned a piece of cake. The university chose to honor this tradition by having white males come to Kake Walk in black face paint, with lips painted wide red and with white minstrel-style makeup around the eyes. The look was intended to portray an animated, presumably happy-go-lucky "darkie."

Few on campus thought it bizarre that a state-supported college nestled in the Green Mountains of Vermont celebrated this tawdry tradition of the American South. Annually for 61 years, UVM faculty and students lined up to watch Kake Walk minstrel shows, hear Southern music, eat Southern foods and munch watermelon dished by faculty members from ice-filled, galvanized trash cans. In 1963, against a background of Confederate flags, UVM students danced Southern jigs as Martin Luther King marched on Washington, and again the following year when he won the Nobel Peace Prize. In fact, the University of Vermont held Kake Walk for sixty-one years before they noticed that on other American campuses, faculty and students were fighting for the civil rights of African Americans.

The Kake Walk festivities reflected a social insensitivity that dominated the UVM campus, especially its fraternity houses. When pledge time came around, I had little interest in joining. Ironically, the fraternities found me desirable—for the most peculiar of reasons. They liked the role I routinely played to camouflage my intense social discomfort. After years of vise attacks, I'd learned to hide every sign of despondency with the role I now assumed as an automatic response. Even those who knew me would describe a comic, rebellious personality with no reference to the turbulent, depressed character that was closer to my real nature. I would tell jokes and improvise dialog on the spot—falling into a satirical monologue anytime I wasn't alone. Instantly I'd become Mr. Master of Ceremonies. Classmates thought I was funny, and the coolest guys in the dorm let me tag along with them. I was conflicted about my act, exhausted by the effort, but my need for acceptance overruled the competing need to be alone and wait out my sadness.

Years later, after many therapy sessions dealing with my heightened social discomfort, I came to better understand my drive to be accepted. The need to be thought of as cool, part of the in crowd, came to me generationally, originating with Grandfather Isaac, who exhibited the twentieth- century equivalent of the modern need to be chosen from the waiting line for admission into a hot nightclub. Losers failed to gain entrance. The relatives who helped me fill in my picture of Isaac explained he would suffer no losers among his children. He didn't permit my aunts to sit on the dance sidelines, though any fool could see they were painfully shy. Isaac not only insisted that his hypersensitive daughters attend dances; he arranged their dates. He demanded they go on class outings and persuaded classmates who were employees at his store to nominate his daughters for student offices. Should a son fail to secure a prominent position in community leadership, Isaac made no effort to hide his contempt. Little wonder that Dad was tormented by his need for esteem.

Though I couldn't yet articulate the reason, I knew in my gut how ashamed Dad would be if he thought I wasn't popular. So I hung out with the right guys, even joining them at fraternity pledge parties although I had no interest in going.

Each fraternity boasted how different it was, though all pledge parties were cookie-cutter affairs. A six foot or taller brother greeted us to lead us down a hallway lined by overconfident upperclassmen who aggressively pumped our hands. Was the whole world running for office? The long hallway routinely led to a central room with high ceilings, flags, trophies and varsity letters on the walls. Upon entering, the brothers moved in on us the way dogs sniff one another. Juniors and seniors wearing turtlenecks and tweedy sports coats with elbow patches handed us goblets of spiked punch and started to grill us. I handled their scrutiny the way I handled every social emergency. Somewhere inside me, panic tripped the switch that threw me into the manic state that locked the grin on my face. I would concentrate intensely, trying to fill each painful, everlasting second of acoustically magnified air time. Typically, I would launch into a glib if frenzied diatribe against the university administration, especially Dean Craven. I pushed through my shyness to keep the act going, improvising as my social panic drove me for more material.

Let me end my act on a high note and get out of here before the brothers see through me, I prayed.

It was only a matter of time before they would see through me. They'd discover that the guy they thought was funny was actually a shy, anti-social, angry nerd who wouldn't fit in.

Yet the brothers never figured me out. House after house, fraternity upperclassmen urged me to stay a while longer. The more harshly I ridiculed the administration, the more they delighted in it. As they laughed harder and harder, I felt smaller and smaller, as if growing less visible by the minute. My brain stretched, frantically hunting for material—anything to say that would keep the performance going.

I became aware I was splitting in two. Half of my consciousness was exposed on stage, while the other half was hiding, cloaked within. The exposed half pleaded to escape.

Is this what happened to my Cousin Ian, I wondered, while comparing Dean Craven to an ostrich. *Mom called last week to tell me about his tragic experience. It seems Ian, also acutely socially uncomfortable, was standing among the guests at a party last week, when everyone noticed he was talking to himself—only to himself. They reported that his eyes seemed to look through everyone. People at the party weren't sure what to do, so they called my aunt who came and took Ian home.*

The fraternity houses I visited invited me to pledge. They actually recruited me like sports scouts after an athlete. I told the guys at the dorm I wasn't sure if I should join any fraternity, but they said I'd be crazy not to and, as usual, I went along with them. I couldn't tell them what was really going on, and I figured it wouldn't much matter if I did join. It was only a matter of time before my new fraternity brothers would discover that their hotshot comedian was deeply depressed and hostile. That wouldn't amuse them at all.

TWELVE

The Circular File

UVM's college newspaper, the *Vermont Cynic*, announced a writing contest. Anyone could submit an article, and first prize was your own editorial column. I showed a fraternity brother a few things I'd written and he encouraged me to enter. To my surprise, I won. I titled my weekly column *The Circular File*. Predictably, my pieces were diatribes—sarcastic indictments of UVM campus life. My favorite target was the Reserve Officers Training Corps, better known by its acronym, ROTC. UVM was a land grant college, and by law every able-bodied male was mandated to take two years of ROTC.

ROTC was a natural satirical target. ROTC drills looked more like a bunch of boys playing with toy guns than like men training to become manly soldiers. The fact that the teenage students who became ROTC officers took it so seriously only egged me on further.

I satirized ROTC through a series of imaginary letters written home by a farm boy who had enrolled at UVM to study math, science and history. He couldn't understand how ROTC fit into his college curriculum. An especially concrete fellow, the young farm boy was baffled when the ROTC officers shouted orders at him.

"They keep telling me to 'Dress Right,'" he complained in a letter home, "but they choose my outfit, not me. I don't even like green. They shout 'About Face' but never tell me what about my looks is bothering them."

ROTC officers, especially if they were members of the elite Pershing Rifles Club, considered my slapstick columns heresy—a life-threatening attack on their cherished institution. These were the guys with heavy acne whose hearts fluttered around scrambled eggs on a hat visor. They were fanatical, attending extra credit drills to practice twirling rifles the way a cheerleader spins a baton, not that that skill wasn't critical in case war should break out in Vermont.

The officers took revenge for my columns by citing me with demerits at the mandatory Friday drills. They wrote me up for shoes that weren't spit-shined or brass that didn't gleam, and since I got the demerits whether I shined them or not, after a while I didn't bother.

When my columns on ROTC persisted, the officers marshaled for further action. They executed their plan to get me the day ROTC held its practice parade drill, an assembly of the whole battalion in the stadium-sized field house. It was a day of preparation for the big ROTC pay-off—the parade ROTC officers lived for, when the Governor of Vermont saluted the passing troops from the stands.

I stood at attention in the front row of my company.

"Today," the student commanding officer shouted through a megaphone, "we will teach you to stack arms. You stack three rifles together teepee-style like this," he said demonstrating.

This is typical of ROTC planning, I thought. *Stacking arms was the one skill that would not be on display at next week's parade.*

An officer approached on my left and shoved a second rifle into my chest.

"Hold this," he ordered.

I was now standing at attention with a rifle on both sides.

A second officer approached.

"What the hell are you doing with two rifles, maggot?" he demanded.

"Sir . . ." I began to explain.

"Shut up, maggot dog," he snapped.

A third officer approached—Major Eagleton himself. Now all three were shouting in my face, demanding to know why I held two rifles. They became increasingly belligerent while I, ever the unruffled soldier, looked crisply ahead without blinking. I took their abuse about a minute and then, I surprised them by breaking ranks. Mimicking a Nazi gait, I marched ten steps forward, shoving through the three of them as I did. In front of the full battalion, I executed a smart about face. At full attention I saluted Major Eagleton and, booming at the top of my lungs, yelled, "Major Eagleton, sir!"

The two other companies stopped marching and turned to look, and the field house fell silent. All heads faced my way.

"I do understand, sir, that God chose his least endowed creatures to be ROTC officers, sir. I understand, sir, your difficulty distinguishing between a single as opposed to two rifles. It is indeed a difficult count, sir. But sir, since a soldier should only have one, sir, I suggest you take this rifle," I released the rifle held on my right hand, "or this!" I let go of the rifle in my left hand, sending both rifles crashing loudly at Major Eagleton's feet. "Take either or both, Major Eagleton, sir, and go fuck yourself with them. Sir."

The field house roared with cheers.

When the natural flesh color returned to Major Eagleton's face, all he could say was, "That . . . that . . . that just cost you five demerits, G-G-G-Grossman."

If one skipped drill entirely, the worse you could get was three demerits. A demerit meant an hour's work sweeping floors and filing papers, and if you didn't work them off, ROTC could subtract a point for each demerit from your overall college grade point average. Enough demerits could actually prevent you from graduating.

When drill ended, and after Major Eagleton had finished writing me up, I headed my Chevy back to the dorm, driving up the dirt road that led from the field house. In the distance I recognized the Third Reich gait of Major Eagleton, goose-stepping around a mud puddle. I pulled just past him, stopped, backed my Chevy into the puddle and floored it. In my rear view mirror I watched the mud drip off the black visor of Eagleton's hat, plopping in brown dabs to spread over his twice-pressed olive coat.

I received an additional ten demerits, but it was worth it. My only regret is that ROTC sent Dean Craven notice of their punishment.

While I enjoyed spoofing ROTC, my columns on the faculty encountered a disapproving and more powerful audience. Many professors felt that I'd attacked their ivory province with the then-uncommon suggestion that students ought to grade the faculty. I argued that students should have a hand in determining curriculum. I urged that tenure be dropped and that faculty departments should be profit centers, paying their way through grants, sales of intellectual property and consulting services.

Then I took on Professor Caswell.

There were good literature professors at UVM, but since "good-better-best" invites comparison—one teacher had to be the dullest and most irrelevant of them all. In 1962 that distinction fell to Professor Earnest Caswell. The word on campus was that if he were not tenured, he wouldn't be around.

I had English with Professor Caswell, and it was even worse than I'd been warned. He was killing the great masters. I had to listen in pain while he mangled classics with irrelevant comments. He would no longer call on me after I'd disagreed with him in class several times, so I decided to address my concerns more publicly in my next *Circular File*.

My article described Professor Caswell as the English department's most brilliant educator, notable especially for his heightened sense of the tertiary.

"Tell me," I asked rhetorically, "who among the faculty can identify minutia like Professor Caswell?" I accurately described a typical Caswell exam question: "How many total characters are there in the book?" To get the correct answer you had to include an aunt who never appears in the book but is mentioned once offhandedly by the protagonist.

"Professor Caswell is a man," I wrote, "who gets us past the vagaries traditionally associated with literary analysis—distractions like questions of theme, symbol or characterization. Caswell avoids subjectivity, bypasses it, by going straight for literary certainty with his factual approach to the classics. He might, for example, require us to identify the brand of whiskey the protagonist drank or the color of the hero's boyhood bicycle—and these are irrefutable facts. In this manner, Caswell frees literature from the uncertainties of interpretation, displeasing vagaries associated with the softer sciences. Thanks to Professor Caswell, literature is finally quantifiable like mathematics and is as factual as history."

I went to Professor Caswell's class the day after the article appeared. When I entered the noisy classroom, everyone hushed instantly and watched from their seats. Professor Caswell, in a stained double-breasted blue suit—all the style when he'd purchased it thirty years earlier—stood next to his desk. He was seething.

"Grossman, since you know everything, I see no need for you to attend my class," he said pointing to the door.

I went to the English Department and explained that I needed the English class credits, that what I'd done was not illegal and was legitimate free speech, and that Caswell had no right to remove me from a class I'd paid for in full. Professor Caswell was summoned and he repeatedly insisted he would not suffer me in his class. The head of the English department was called in to decide. He had to support his professor, but it was clear from a few things he said that he didn't think much of him. His Solomon-like solution was to permit Caswell to keep me out of his class, but, over strenuous objections, Professor Caswell had to give me the final exam. Since Caswell wasn't completely oblivious to how he was regarded by his chairman, he didn't dare flunk me when I did well on his exam.

My columns in the *Vermont Cynic* were not without their smug self-righteousness, but they were glimpses of a rudimentary set of values forming beneath my belligerence and comic mask; that besides these defensive shields, automatically deployed, was something more organic—a sense that natively looked for kindness, admired sincerity and felt that all my classmates deserved respect. I felt compelled to take on professors who cared about neither their subjects nor their students, and it wasn't just my compulsive venting. Besides the pool of hostility that always seeped, there was also sincerity, a more adult version of the boy in temple who could not quietly accept that Moses parted the Red Sea. That part wasn't angry so much as it sought logic, fairness and an environment that promoted a communal goodwill.

But I didn't understand yet how to separate that natural goodwill from my subterranean hostility. I had not yet learned to distinguish the legitimate from the innocent targets of my rage. So hostility and goodwill came out together, inseparably interwoven and simultaneously expressed. The mixed-message presentation made it easy for the targets of my satire to notice only my anger and respond angrily in kind. My hostile presentations overshadowed my purer intentions and received only the continued disapproval of the faculty. I failed to show them the student who wanted excellence in class, who wanted passionately to learn, who thrived on an excited faculty and an involved student body. Since that part of me lay under my invisibility cloak, I became increasingly isolated, hungrier, groping blindly along an unlit labyrinth for a path to their understanding if not their praise. But I'd created an unappealing self-portrait. The face I held up for my teachers to admire was distorted because I didn't have the skills. So they scorned much of what I showed them, and my depression deepened.

Further isolating me was my distrust of their authority, which I coupled with an intense yet secret shyness. I was too uncomfortable to talk to professors after class or visit in their offices, though I, not they, had erected the barrier. After class, I'd watch intently as fellow students went up to talk to the professor. Whatever their intentions—and oh, was I suspicious—the students were self-assured enough to visit them, and clearly their professors enjoyed the exchanges. While I badly wanted the contact, I couldn't make myself approach. I'd get lost following an unending trail of obsessive motive analysis and along the way I ripped to shreds my yearning to reach out. What would I do, I worried, if my oversensitive antenna detected that a professor believed I was there to pander to him? I couldn't risk that misinterpretation. No, I would stay in my seat, jaw clenched, even as I fantasized that one professor—like old Mr. Trevor—would see something in me.

THIRTEEN

Napoleonic Notions

I STARTED COLLEGE AS A FRESHMAN AND A VIRGIN. In the 1960s there were lots of freshman virgins reading *Playboys* in the dorm bathroom stalls. Naiveté was still possible, and sexual intercourse was still shrouded in mystery. What separated the men from the boys was the line dividing those who had "done it" from those who still hadn't.

I didn't discuss sex with an adult. I would never be comfortable talking about it to my high-minded dad, or to a rabbi or a school teacher. Sex never came up in my early therapy, as if the rules of the couch permitted every subject but sex. I'm sure my therapists were as uncomfortable with the subject as I was.

The guys and I, on the other hand, spoke of little else, and while our sexual knowledge wasn't anatomically correct, it was closer to the truth than our tales of conquest. Secretly, I wondered what it felt like to do it, a thought I had on more than one occasion—for example if I passed a pretty girl . . . or in the shower . . . laying in bed . . . at a movie . . . or breathing . . .

One Saturday afternoon a group of dorm friends asked me to drive them to Montreal, where at seventeen we could legally drink.

Montreal was a four hour ride from Burlington, and we jumped into my '53 Plymouth and headed northeast.

I was fully into my Mr. Master of Ceremonies persona, and because only a nerd admitted he was a virgin, I spent the drive time bragging about what a stud I was and how I was going to get laid the minute I hit Montreal. Actually, the term of art was that I would "fuck my brains out."

Montreal was bitter cold in the winter, and we could barely feel any warm air coming from the Plymouth's anemic heater, so we stopped to warm up at the first bar on the outskirts of the city. Old men speaking French sat at wood tables drinking beers and watching hockey on TV. If someone made a goal, they would jump up, pound the table and scream, *"Sacré Bleu."*

One of the guys left the bar and returned a few minutes later.

"Grossman," he said, "we found a cabby who knows where you can get laid."

"Gee," I said, "that's great, 'cause I could sure use another piece of ass . . . but, ah, I don't have my wallet."

"No problem," they said. "We've got money."

"Well . . . well, but I don't have any money back at the dorm either," I fumbled. "Flat broke this month."

"No problem," he said. "You drove. It's on us."

I hadn't expected this and I couldn't think of any way out. I concluded a simple "thanks but no thanks" wouldn't fly after all my bragging, so I followed them to the cab like a dead man walking to the chamber. The cabby drove down alleys lined with dirty snow and finally stopped in front of an apartment building missing most of its paint. One of the awning arms was off its mount.

"In there," the cabbie gestured.

I held onto the cab door an extra moment, breathing heavily before I started in. Afterward, the guys told me the cabby said I must have needed it real bad.

As I approached, a girl came out of the building and passed me under the awning. Her hair was in a beehive, and she wore a shawl around her shoulders. A heavy, bald man in a yellowing white shirt stuck his head out the door, calling the girl back by whistling through two fingers. He pointed first at me, then to her.

"Fourteen dollars US. I get seven. She gets seven."

The girl was young, thin and okay looking, although one of her eyes didn't track perfectly. I followed her down a dimly lit hall to a bedroom where a lamp with a lone bulb and no shade was the only light. In faint light I could make out two old dressers, the kind you'd buy at a yard sale. There were no pictures, and the bed had no sheets or pillows—only a white bedspread turned gray from use. The girl shut the door and removed several bobby pins from her hair, which fell to hide her face. Mechanically she shoved her skirt down. There were no panties, just her pussy, which looked like a Mohawk haircut against anemic skin. With her sweater still on, she flopped back on the bed, facing me like a counter waitress. I took my clothes off, but I wasn't sure what I should do next. After an awkward pause I shrugged my shoulders and requested instructions. She beckoned me on top of her and I climbed on, unsure how to fit, figuring my legs must parallel hers like two wishbones. To my surprise she slid me *between* her legs, a novel position and quite unexpected.

"What should I do next?" I asked with escalating urgency.

She reached me, moving her fingers up and down.

"Tell me when you want to puuuttt it in," she said in French-thick English.

"Now. *Now. NOW!*" I screamed.

I pumped twice.

At a calculated cost of seven dollars a stroke, I became a man in more than Jewish eyes. Almost immediately the girl hopped out of bed, pulled her skirt up in three zigzag movements and left.

I didn't ask if I was any good.

Back at the bar the guys patted me on the back, but I wasn't listening. Half of me was really disappointed, while the other half busily obsessed about the syphilis I'd just contracted. I imagined that a tick-like snake was at that very moment overwhelming the good cells, sucking out the healthy pink and filling each with poison muck. Little bacteria snakes were oozing from organ to organ, advancing for my brain.

Someone told a joke about a lame Irishman, but I never made it to the punch line. I was thinking of my Cousin Irwin. What if the lump on his neck wasn't cancer? What if it was syphilis contracted one night after he tended bar. I pictured him staggering home unsteadily, falling into bed with a stranger for a clumsy session with another drunk.

Maybe that's why Irwin refused treatment, I thought. *Maybe he wanted to hide his disease?*

I left the bar in search of a drug store, returning with a bottle of rubbing alcohol. Back in the men's room I poured alcohol over my privates and thought of Napoleon. I knew about Napoleon's syphilis. They didn't have penicillin, so Napoleon went stark raving mad. It didn't matter that he was a brilliant military strategist. He was crushed by the same bug creeping up my spine.

The next day back at the dorm, the guilt about what I'd done, my moral self-disgust became fully obsessive. I paced in agony all day Sunday. At precisely 9:00 a.m. Monday morning I dialed the first physician I found in the yellow pages. I told Dr. Adams I had to see him urgently, and I arrived an hour early for my appointment. I took a chair in his waiting room under a gold-framed picture of Jesus and rehearsed what I'd say. I prayed Dr. Adams would joke man-to-man about the whole thing, but the Jesus picture should have tipped me off. Dr. Adams waved an indignant finger in my face. He embarked on a stern hellfire lecture about what the Bible said lay ahead for me and about the woes of whoring. I was thinking he wouldn't give me the penicillin I wanted, but he finally did. I felt the bacteria dying seconds after he finished the injection.

So I was no longer a virgin, but it wasn't the sex of my dreams. I'd expected the Fourth of July but got Yom Kippur. It wasn't worth the biblical torment, and when a vise attack came on that evening, I welcomed the distraction that sent me hurling down the shoot.

Many years later, after difficult therapy sessions on the subject, I would better understand the origins of my powerful sexual guilt. Besides the obvious influence of Bible Belt mores, I would discover that my guilt was fed by constant comparisons. I placed my self-image, tainted by my misadventures, alongside a picture, accepted by a naïve boy, of my father and Grandfather Isaac—a portrait depicting them as the epitome of moral righteousness. Naturally I suffered by comparison. How could I not? I judged myself a core degenerate, and how quickly that conclusion added to my self-hatred. I disgusted myself, and my self-disapproval was a constant drip that collected in an internal reservoir. Years would pass before I looked into that pit and dismissed my moral shortcomings as a boy's natural sexual curiosity. I wasn't perfect, but a firing squad was overkill. One thing that helped profoundly in dealing with my guilt was my discovery later in group therapy that to a one every member was plagued by a similar self-loathing. Seeing that helped me understand that I was no more a black creature of the pit than I was a white angel. I was a human being—which meant that I carried attributes of both. If only I'd known that when I returned in guilty despair from Montreal. But it was a gift I hadn't yet received.

The vise attack that followed Montreal lifted after a few days in bed pretending I had the flu. When I felt strong enough to face people again, I shaved, dressed and headed off to class. Dean Craven was coming down the steps of the Waterman Building as I passed.

"Grossman," he beckoned.

"Yes sir," I turned to him.

"I hear you're becoming quite the international traveler."

"Traveler, sir?" I said.

"I hear you're fond of Montreal—of all things French," he said dripping with sarcasm. "At least that's what Dr. Adams tells me."

He paused for dramatic emphasis.

"You do understand, don't you Grossman, how very close to dismissal you are? Yes?" Dean Craven raised his eyebrows, his face graver than usual. He didn't wait for a reply but turned and walked away. There was no medical confidentiality in those days, and I learned later that Dean Craven kept Dr. Adams' letter in a file he was building on me. He was fully prepared for the last straw—which came in the fall of my sophomore year.

FOURTEEN

Dean Craven's Revenge

I PICKED CHERRIES DURING THE SUMMER BREAK OF 1961, working on a farm in Hart, Michigan. It was the hardest work I'd done—tougher than supposedly more rigorous jobs like shoveling wet cement, carrying construction plywood on my back or toting mortar to masons. When you pick cherries you move up and down the ladder all day, balanced on a high rung, with your arms stretching into the branches. You grab as many cherries as possible and set them in a bucket tied to the ladder. The sun hammers you, and by the end of the day you're so caked with orchard dust that you have to shower it off in layers. Tough as it was, I'd take picking cherries to what was coming.

Before I left college for summer break, my fraternity brothers nominated me for the position of student representative to Freshman Orientation Week. They continued to think of me as Mr. Master of Ceremonies. I asked them to run someone else, but they assumed my protests were false modesty. Our house had the votes, I was elected, and I attended the faculty planning meetings. My assignment was to return to campus a week early next September and run the campus tours offered to the freshman and their families.

That was the plan, but it wasn't what happened.

The trouble was that picking cherries in the hot orchard left me with time on my hands to obsess about Freshman Orientation Week. Running the tours meant that I'd start my sophomore year under a piercing spotlight, scrutinized by the faculty, the administration, by my fraternity brothers and by hoards of overprotective parents. I'd be on stage a whole week, facing every manner of crazed parent. I had a lot of time to imagine the social interactions. Some of the dads would be palatable, others would be obnoxious—the "when I was in school . . ." experts who wouldn't let me finish my sentences. The freshmen would expect me to be a confident, model upperclassman. While my teams were giving tours, the faculty would hand me contradictory assignments, and I was never very tactful when their requests were clearly stupid. My fraternity brothers had expectations too. They expected me to scout for "our kind" of pledge prospects and invite them to visit the house.

As I carried buckets of Michigan sour cherries to the central bins, I grew more and more agitated about the fall. I dreaded having to power up, smile wide and become Mr. Master of Ceremonies again. I dreaded it in my bones.

When falling leaves signaled that it was time to return to Burlington, a familiar angst crept over me. At first, as I packed, mindlessly stuffing my clothes in an old army surplus duffle bag, I didn't feel the strands of invisible cord encircling my chest. But my attention was drawn to them as they tightened their hold. I lay down and let the cords secrete a viscous layer that oozed and hardened as it rolled me into a brittle cocoon. My psyche clung on the brink of a vise attack as long as it could. But I couldn't hold it off forever, and when I did let go, I dropped, toppling head-over-heels, spiraling down into an unlit hole, crashing through layer after layer of outstretched sheets of a sticky morass. This was a different vise attack, more powerful even than the one at the hedgerow. It was a pit with many false bottoms. I fell helplessly to the first bottom, but when I thought I was done falling, it collapsed, and I fell through a second bottom, then a third. When the fall ended for real, I lay paralyzed. I tried to move but couldn't. My mind transmitted, sending instructions to my legs to swing out of bed, but nothing happened. I concentrated harder, sending more deliberate signals to my legs, but a suction of unfathomable force restrained them.

As I lay immobilized in bed, I received an incessant tom-tom beat of notices that it was urgent that I leave. I needed to get up, to achieve motion, but the longer I lay there, the more I felt my paralysis would never end. Was there an alternative? If I could I get to the pills in Mom's cabinet, was there something I could take to void this? To void everything? No one was around. Everyone was out of town. No one would know for days.

I must phone school and let them know I haven't left yet. I can tell them I have a bad flu.

But I couldn't move.

The room's complete darkness was a comfort, that and the relief I felt from its stillness, void of sound or stimulation. The dimmest light or a sound as soft as a dropped pin—scattered my stability like a pool table break. I lay motionless while the morning became the afternoon and dusk turned to night. I lay paralyzed until the sunrise brought the morning—for four days.

At last I felt the vise attack slowly lifting, unwinding like a dusty mummy's wrap to allow the return of movement and sensation. In time I was able to get up, got dressed, shave and eat. I threw my duffle bag in the car and headed north to Canada, then east to Vermont. Winter had come early to Canada, and it was already snowing. The odometer ticked off the miles while I thought about the angry reception awaiting me. I wanted to turn back.

I will do anything to avoid them, I thought. *I can't face them. I'll down a bottle of aspirin at the next motel. Or how about a tube? I could run it from the tailpipe into the car. But who am I kidding. I don't have the guts.*

My headlights did their best to penetrate the locust swarm of snow. Ice-clumps formed on the wipers, and their swing-click-slap mesmerized me. The ice traced a semicircular path, and the buildup obstructed my view. I twisted the radio dial, hoping for a station, but got only static. Occasionally I'd pass through a small town but everything was closed. I watched the red needle on the gas gage slip from a quarter to an eighth to *E* and then below.

If I run out of gas on those isolated roads, I'll have no heater, and it is ten degrees below, I thought. *What is it like, freezing to death? Don't you just go to sleep? Is that how it was for Cousin Ian the night he died on his park bench? Did he just fall asleep and fade into eternity?*

I slapped my cheeks to shake off the drowsiness.

At the next village I saw a parked patrol car with smoke coming from its tailpipe, so I stopped and tapped on the ice-fogged window. The window lowered, and I faced an officer with a Mounties hat. He said he would wake someone who'd sell me gas. I thanked him profusely, refueled and headed back into the night.

A red-eyed sun rose over Burlington as I pulled into the dorm parking lot.

Freshman Orientation Week was over and everyone was furious with me.

"You're a fuck-up," said my fraternity brothers.

I was really frightened, but I didn't let on. I swelled my chest and laughed.

"Good one, huh," I said, like it was all a big gag.

Nobody was laughing, and I heard Dean Craven was looking for me. I dodged his calls. I'd screwed up badly, and I'd embarrassed my fraternity brothers. I'd disappointed the faculty and let the new freshmen down. For a month I was persona non grata and my brothers hardly spoke to me. It was just as well, since I couldn't explain what had happened. What would I say?

"Gee, guys, I would have come, but I went nuts and couldn't move."

I formally apologized to them all.

While I was fully prepared to accept their continued scorn, people's anger at me subsided as my sophomore year progressed. Life got easier, but it still wasn't much fun. I disliked the UVM mindset, the stay-cool, party mentality in a school in which Kake Walk, which should have been a bad joke, was an annual high point. I found little passion in my classrooms, but rather a what-do-I-need-to-do-to-get-by approach, and most instructors accommodated that mind-set with exams that rewarded rote memorizing over learning. UVM was for students who made and spit back lists. It wasn't the campus to find stimulating conceptual discourse. Maybe all colleges were like that. I was a sophomore, what did I know? But hoping that some were not, I decided to transfer out for my junior year.

By the middle of my sophomore year, I was an honors student with good enough grades for a transfer. That fact surprised no one more than it did me, because I'd nearly flunked out as a first term freshman. I'd kidded myself into thinking I was doing okay, and then my first mid-term grades arrived: F, F F and a C-.

My faculty advisor called me in, looking thoroughly bored during the meeting.

"I'm clear and I assume you are too Michael that you aren't college material. A lot of boys aren't." he said. "Nothing to be ashamed of. Maybe a vocational school."

"So I'm kicked out?" I asked.

"Not officially. Officially you have the rest of the quarter to bring your grades up," he said. "But let's be realistic. Four Fs and a C-minus?"

I flashed back to Ms. Wishman, pulling me on her lap to whisper that I'd flunked fifth grade. Never again. I wouldn't let it happen. I'd alter every aspect of life before I'd flunk out. And that's exactly what I did.

To avoid dorm distractions, I all but moved myself into the library. Morning, noon and night, weekdays and weekends, month after month I burrowed, hunched over my books, in the library stacks. My back hunched into a painful C-shape. My yellow highlighter moved methodically across my text books, across and down, line after line, underscoring blocks of text. When the latest James Bond movie was showing in town, I was at the library memorizing the periodic table of the elements. When The Platters played at the UVM auditorium, I was studying the ten metatarsals and twenty-eight phalanges that make up the thirty-eight foot bones. The night of the annual school dance, I flipped quiz cards reviewing the progress of the Axis powers as they advanced during WWII. My friends no longer asked if I'd go with them, though they knew where to find me. I was in the stacks shifting from one sore cheek to the other on an unforgiving wooden chair.

I had a problem retaining material. I'd review a lesson carefully but immediately forget it. I wasn't stupid, so something else was at play. I didn't have a lot of childhood memories, almost none before seven. When repression is that powerful, you block globally, and you can't pick and choose what you forget. So the difference between endomorph and ectomorph and the date of the Battle of Gettysburg get scooped along with childhood memories into a net of thwarted recall.

The first review of my textbook material was like seeing it for the first time. I had to read, re-read, underline and re-read again. I'd number the key points, read paragraphs aloud and memorize mnemonics. But I ended my first college term with Cs and a B, very much to the surprise of my academic advisor, who repeatedly looked back at his report to verify my grades. My performance continued to rise, and soon I made Dean's list. His good one, that is.

"I'd like to transfer out," I said to my advisor in the middle of my sophomore year, "to the University of Michigan—the real UVM. It's a good school, and it's near home."

"Your grades are good enough," he said. "Did you send them an application?"

I'd spoken to an admissions counselor from the University of Michigan who reviewed my application and said I would almost certainly be accepted. But Dean Craven learned of my application when, as a matter of form, the University of Michigan admissions requested copies of my transcripts.

They received the transcripts but also a copy of Dean Craven's folder on me with a strongly worded letter warning that I was a troublemaker. The admissions department sent me a rejection letter, and the admissions counselor wouldn't take my calls. I didn't blame Dean Craven. I had let the university down.

But when I applied to Michigan State University, I had my transcripts sent immediately, and received an acceptance letter before Dean Craven could intervene.

FIFTEEN

Guilt Trip

I WANTED TO GET IN TOP PHYSICAL SHAPE before I started Michigan State University as a junior in the fall of 1962. I hoped I'd like MSU and find campus life more stimulating, but I was realistic about my expectations. I didn't expect a new college to change my state of mind, and I had no illusions about my vise attacks. I knew they would follow me. But it occurred that building up my body was a way to fight the thick lethargy that often accompanied their attacks. So I began lifting weights and jogging. Chuck and I found construction jobs for the summer, which built my abs. We shoveled wet cement, carried 6-by-4-foot sheets of plywood on our backs and lugged cinder blocks to the masons for $3.25 an hour—the most money I'd ever earned.

I didn't date much that summer. To overcome my anxiety with girls meant that I'd have to pump up Mr. Master of Ceremonies, and that seemed like more trouble than it was worth. I was satisfied with the company of the centerfold girl in each month's *Adam* magazine. They revealed more, though were lower-class than *Playboy*'s centerfolds.

It was the summer of my best friend Chuck's macho stage. The son of two psychiatrists, his mom effete and his stepdad effeminate, Chuck was desperate to fit in with the burly laborers at the construction site where we worked. Chuck grunted a lot that summer and talked in short, staccato tones with a kind of make-my-day Clint Eastwood bravado. He walked with a pack of Camels rolled up in his T-shirt sleeve, always coolly tapping the half-open pack on the table until a single Camel slid out. He mastered the art of lighting his Zippo by scraping the flint wheel up the leg of his Levis like a gunslinger—fastest flame in town.

One night near summer's end, Chuck and I went to Hick's Restaurant, famous for pizza-sized hamburgers.

"Town's a bore. Wanna go somewhere," he said coolly in his best John Wayne. "How-bout Texas or Florida or Mexico."

"Mexico," I replied.

"'Kay," Chuck said. "Lotta women."

We left two half-finished hamburgers on our plates and jumped in my '56 Chevy. The plan was to go home, get cash and clothes and meet in half an hour.

Chuck returned with a duffel bag, removing a Luger from the bag.

"What the hell are you doing with that?" I asked. "How'd you get a gun?"

Chuck hid the pistol above the radio under up the car's dash.

"Protection," he said gruffly. "Ya never know."

I opened a tattered AAA map, and we drove south for a couple of days, passing through Mexican customs at the border town of Piedras Negras. Wrecked cars and broken bottles were scattered along streets that smelled of urine. Piedras Negras got its start as a coal-mining center, but nobody came for coal anymore. Now they came for booze and girls. The dusty streets offered a checkerboard of shops with silver bracelets and leather belts hanging from tattered awnings. There were saddle stores, tequila bars and squalid brothels with dark-haired women who stood out front and promised how good it would be.

Chuck and I swung through the old-west-style doors of the El Matador Bar. We downed tequila shots, smoked Camels and looked at the wall paintings of matadors riding naked women. Chuck went over to the bar and started talking to a pretty girl. She was young, maybe twenty, with dark reddish-brunette hair. I wanted to approach one of the girls too, but I didn't have the nerve, so I stayed on my stool. I tried to look extra manly so no one would think I was gay. I chain smoked until Chuck came back with his arm around the girl and a cigarette dangling from his mouth.

"Let's blow this joint," he said.

Off-key mariachi music blared from shops playing warped LPs as I drove the Chevy down littered streets. I tried to remember the way back to our hotel. The girl turned to Chuck.

"Where is heees date?"

"You're his date too," said Chuck. She rolled her eyes, and I wondered if she was going to get out, but she didn't. Back at the hotel Chuck finished with her, and it was my turn. We took turns all night. The first few times while one of us was with her, the other waited in the dimly lit hallway with a yellow cactus painting made of tiles. But after a while, we didn't bother to leave the room and just waited half asleep, half drunk on the adjacent bed. In the morning, we were ready to start again but the girl pretended to be asleep. The two extra twenties Chuck waved, brought her back to life. After she left, we lay around the room hung over.

The girl wasn't bad looking, and I wondered what it would be like to be married to her. Would she be grateful and always love me because I was the rich American who saved her from being a whore?

I lay around in my beer stained T-shirt feeling dizzy and starting to worry.

What if the girl had syphilis? I just felt tingling. Was it an amoeba?

The sun came through our window and quickly heated up the room. Chuck and I left for breakfast.

"It doesn't show up that fast," Chuck assured me over breakfast.

I wasn't so sure.

"We have to find a doctor." I insisted.

Chuck shrugged.

The doctor spoke perfect English and assured me that Chuck was right. Syphilis signs, he said, appear in months, sometimes years, but not minutes. I made him list the symptoms. Syphilis starts, he explained, with the single chancre—round, small, and painless. The sore lasts six weeks and mysteriously heals on its own. The secondary stage has a skin rash and lesions. You get rough, reddish brown spots on the palms of your hands and the bottoms of your feet.

As he spoke, I turned my hands over quickly in search of reddish spots.

Sometimes, the doctor continued, they are so faint you don't even know you have them. I brought my hands closer. In the late stage, syphilis eats your internal organs, your nerves, eyes, heart, blood vessels, liver, bones, joints, and when it reaches the brain, you die.

I told the doctor he had to give us something. He wrote prescriptions for two manila packets of white penicillin tablets. Chuck and I popped them as we headed back north toward home.

The long drive gave me way too much time to think. I was disgusted with myself, and I didn't know whether my moral depravity or my syphilis would do me in first. As in Montreal, I'd gone along, acted without forethought, followed a friend's lead without considering if a chance to get laid was worth the weeks of guilt that inevitably followed. What kind of man was I? And why, speaking of self esteem, couldn't I get it from a girl other than a whore? How come I had to pay for what my buddies got for free? Was I that undesirable? Why was I so timid? Why on a date couldn't I risk going for more than a tepid kiss? Standing on the steps with my date, under the interrogating gleam of the porch light, I froze at the thought that if I tried something, my date might turn her head away or remove my hand. It would confirm how undesirable I was.

I knew right from wrong. Dad told me the rules governing sex without equivocation and with the same certainty with which Moses might have delivered us the eleventh and twelfth commandments—including the two he would have inscribed if he had a bit more tablet space.

Eleventh Commandment: Thou shalt not crave sex. If you must crave something, crave a good book. Or, crave The Good Book.

Twelfth Commandment: Thou shalt not do the "dirty deed." But if thou doeth do it, do it only to procreate. The sin of liking sex is worse than the sin of having it.

As the weeks passed after Chuck and I returned from Piedras Negras, I began to think perhaps I didn't have syphilis. But I was more sure than ever that I was out of control. As I packed for my new college, it occurred to me that my life heretofore was a chain of spontaneous impulses. I lived unconsciously. I wasn't directing my life, I'd fallen into it. Either I made up the game plan on the spot or I followed peers like a sheep. I gave no thought to emotional consequences, to what the cost would be when my action presented the bill to my self-esteem.

At the same time I felt hopeful this might be changing. My decision to transfer schools was the first time I had assessed my surroundings and, like an adult, decided what to do to make things better. Changing colleges, while the tiniest step in the grand scheme, was a giant leap for me.

Changes would come faster now, because a capacity to look at myself thoughtfully was taking root. It would soon lead me to go for "help" again. But this time the decision to get therapy would be my own.

SIXTEEN

Meter's Running

I STARTED MY JUNIOR YEAR AT MICHIGAN STATE IN THE FALL OF 1963. It was everything I hoped for. My instinct to change schools had been a good one, and my new university was a better fit. Fraternities were inconsequential on the East Lansing campus. The students were more activist and instead of rewarding students who spit back what a teacher shoveled in, professors at MSU stressed conceptual thinking.

But despite my happier campus life, my vise attacks came again. They were growing more potent. Unexpectedly and without warning, I'd race, feeling a piston-pounding excess of energy, only to drop as soon as it passed into a flypaper-sticky lethargy. I fought it every way I could. I tried to exercise my way out of it. I jogged and worked out with weights in the gym until I could bench-press my own weight. But the days still came without warning when my thoughts downshifted, moving against a resistance like a spoon in molasses. It seemed to take me forever to absorb what someone said to me. I didn't respond in the moment, and hours later would think of what I could have said. When I looked in the mirror, I recognized the blank expression as the look I'd seen in the mezzotint pictures of my stunned aunts, the daughters of Grandfather Isaac.

I needed "help," and I wanted it.

The few available psychiatrists were classic Freudians; the more eclectic therapies had not yet appeared, at least not in the Midwest. East Lansing, Michigan, the home of MSU, had few mental health resources, so in the end I had to commute to Detroit for therapy.

I don't recall who recommended Dr. Maynard Razard, but his office was in a glass solarium off his home in a wealthy Detroit suburb. At exactly the appointed time I anxiously knocked on his door. Dr. Razard greeted me in a blue silk suit with excessive sheen for a psychotherapist—an issue he addressed by wearing a muted ivory shirt and a pale blue tie. He allowed an inch and a half of stiffly starched cuff to extend from his sleeve, just enough to admire his pearl cufflinks in their thick gold setting. Gray, swept-back hair completed his disciplined appearance. Every strand of hair lay in its well greased track as if a coach had blown a whistle and the stands hustled into place.

Naturally, I was nervous at my first session. I found it of little comfort that Dr. Razard turned to study me through his narrow silver bifocals. It brought an unpleasant recollection of the way Dr. Cronick had similarly dissected me with her piercing stare. Dr. Razard motioned me to a black leather couch, placing his chair behind my head where it was impossible for me to see him. He told me that after medical school he'd trained as a classic Freudian analyst. After that brief introduction, he rarely ever spoke again. Sessions started with a command to "Begin" and ended when he closed his leather notebook to said, "That's it for today."

My job was to talk for precisely fifty minutes.

He told me to say whatever came to mind, so I talked about Mom and Dad, about how sad I was living in St. Louis, and of my persistent vise attacks. From behind I could hear Dr. Razard scratching mysterious notes with his black-and-gold Mont Blanc pen. He rarely commented on anything I said, so the only drama in our sessions occurred when his pen stopped scratching and he asked me to repeat something. I never knew if it was because I'd said something really important, or if Dr. Razard doubted me or was simply hard of hearing.

You wouldn't typically think of therapy as a lonely hour, but I never felt more alone than in my sessions with Dr. Razard. Years later, when I gained perspective on him, I decided he wasn't the first therapist to be drawn to the profession by his own needs. I think what attracted him was his lack of the very thing psychiatry purported to develop—a capacity for intimacy. Had Dr. Razard chosen the corporate world, he'd have been one of those executives who position themselves behind an ornate, mahogany desk, commanding from a high-back leather seat while a secretary guides visitors to strategically smaller chairs. Had he chosen academia, he'd have been a professor who lectures to a class of four from behind an elevated podium. His choice to be a classical Freudian analyst was no accident. He'd found a modality that feigned intimacy but shielded him from involvement.

Still I was desperate for help—any help at all. So twice a week I made the four-hour round-trip drive between East Lansing and Detroit. I drove rain or shine. I drove the day Michigan had a historic blizzard, somehow managing to keep my green Ford pointed forward on the windblown expressway. I couldn't see much through the heavy snow, and the road was sheer ice. But every time the Ford started to rotate sideways, I was able to gently nudge the hood back into center lane. Halfway to Detroit, the state police closed the expressway. I took an exit and found a phone booth.

"They closed the roads," I explained to Dr. Razard. "The entire expressway."

"Don't worry Michael," he said, "I can mail your bill."

SEVENTEEN

Odd Jobs

I MADE SPENDING MONEY FOR COLLEGE, $1.25 an hour, by washing pots and pans in the dorm cafeteria. I stood enveloped in steam at a deep, commercial sink and scrubbed while I sang in spoof grand operatic style.

But when the cafeteria closed for the summer, I needed work. One of my friends, a football player for Michigan State, got a job through the athletic department working for REO, the Lansing-based truck manufacturer. He said the word at the plant was that REO was hiring laborers. So I drove downtown to the factory, only to find a block-long line of applicants. I got in line at the end. A good hour later I found myself at the front, smiling at a plump personnel lady who apparently put her lipstick on in the dark.

"No more jobs sweetheart," she smiled. "Got all the help we need."

"You don't need anyone?" I asked her.

"Nope," she said waving me off, "'cept truck mechanics,"

"But that's why I'm here," I said.

"You a truck mechanic?" She looked doubtfully at my smooth hands.

"Yep," I said.

"Where you worked at?" She asked.

"Crain's Gulf" I said. "They specialize in trucks."

My actual experience had been pumping gas on two weekends at that local Gulf station.

"Humph," said the lady, her brow wrinkled with doubt. "Got tools?"

"Of course," I said.

"Humph," she said again. "Well, come on back Tuesday for a physical and if that's okay, I guess we can use you."

I went home that weekend to ask Dad if we had any tools. He wasn't sure but told me there might be some in the garage. I found a hammer, two wrenches, three rusty screwdrivers and an old tackle box.

The following Tuesday I arrived at the plant, passed the cursory physical and was led to a production line where seven army troop trucks stood in progressive stages of assembly. The trucks were army green with a white American star on each cab door. Each had a team of mechanics on them like ants, assembling the trucks for shipment to Pakistan.

I stood before the line foreman, a guy named Lindsay.

"The manifold seal's leaking," he said, pointing to the third truck in the line.

I hadn't a clue how to fix it, but I went to the truck and looked around under the hood.

Lindsay came over. "Let's go, fella," he clapped his hands, "get your hammer and some gasket seal and have at it."

Hammer. I reached in my tackle box. A moment later the production line came to a halt. The guys had been eying me curiously, and now they were laughing and pointing at me. How was I to know a mechanic's hammer is noticeably different from the carpenter's hammer I held my hand. The mechanics knew immediately they had a real ringer on their hands, so Foreman Lindsay set out to have some fun.

"Grossman," Lindsay said, "go to Parts on the second floor and get me a left-handed monkey wrench." To a chorus of snorts I dutifully headed off to the second floor, and from there I was directed from department to department up and down the plant until the Parts Manager explained, "No such thing as a left-handed monkey wrench."

Lindsay sent me on one fools' errand after another, and that was fine since I knew I was making $3.75 an hour as long as I could draw it out—three times what I made washing pots. I became Mr. Master of Ceremonies and wise-cracked with the guys, smiling when Lindsay and the mechanics called me "college boy" in a good-natured way.

They tired of playing with me after a couple of hours. Lindsay called me over, I assumed to give me the ax. To my surprise, he said I was such a good sport that I could stay on if I wanted. He gave me the job of pasting American flag decals on the tailgates of finished trucks, sweeping up the bays and driving completed trucks to the parking lot.

Often I went to work with my friend from the football team and his teammates. They sanded trucks in an adjacent area of the plant, muscling vibrating sanders back and forth over fenders and hoods while their hair, clothes and mouth masks got caked in army green paint dust. Pasting decals, I made the same money they did. We all worked the night shift, and some nights around 2 a.m. Foreman Lindsay would tell me to take a break with him. We'd sit outside the plant on the fender of a big military truck, under a bright moon, talking, drinking a beer, and looking up at the starry sky.

Sometimes you just luck out.

My days as a truck mechanic ended when my senior year began that fall. Since I still needed spending money, I responded to an ad for a part time reporter with the *Ingham County News*, a small, family-run paper in nearby Mason, Michigan. Although I had no journalism training, the paper's editor agreed to see me. He was a seventy-six-year-old guy named Hayden Pallard, a former editor now retired from the *Detroit News*.

"Any experience?" Hayden asked.

"I had a weekly opinion column in college. I had to meet deadlines," I added eagerly.

"Umm," he said.

Hayden wore a stained bow tie, a gray sweater and a gold watch fob that ran from his musty blue suit jacket to the pocket of mismatched, wrinkled, green slacks. He parted his thick, white hair down the middle, but it lifted in back in a half circle that looked like turkey feathers. He had the habit of wetting his lips and running his tongue over pipe stains at the corners of his mouth. The yellow ends of his fingers trembled. During the interview he used expressions like "madder than a wet hen," or "shoot the nearest snake first." I liked him immediately.

He sat me at an old Royal typewriter with a threadbare ribbon.

"See if you can give me a story on this," he tested.

I noticed that his hands shook as he handed me a list of facts about a recent meeting with the local mayor. I didn't even know how to format a news story, but I had a newspaper with me, and I copied the way a story looked:

> MASON, Michigan, December 12, 1966 – In a surprise move , Mayor McDonagan said today . . .

Hayden marked up my article with lots of red ink slashes, so I figured I didn't get the job. But when he finished he said, "We can use you."

I loved being around Hayden. He had me cover town meetings, and I did my best to dramatize funding budgets for a sidewalk repair or to embellish a local wedding with adjective-swollen descriptions of chiffon dresses and carnation arrangements.

In the summer of 1967 I had some real news to cover. Detroit's racial powder keg lit off with five days of violent street fighting that left forty-three people dead and eleven hundred injured. The black community let loose all its anger at the Detroit police. Snipers atop tall buildings shot at the police, and fighting was so widespread that Governor George Romney called out ten thousand national guardsmen.

When I learned of the rioting, I grabbed the only camera I owned, an old Polaroid, and drove as fast as I could from Mason to Detroit. About five miles outside the Detroit city limits, the national guard had set up roadblocks and were turning back cars. I rolled down my window.

A soldier leaned in. "Can't pass here."

I acted bored, like this was the third darn riot they'd made me cover this week.

"Press," I said flashing my credentials. "The *News*." I held my thumb over the words *Ingham County* so he'd figure I was with the *Detroit News*.

"Okay," he said, waving me on with his automatic rifle.

It was hard to believe I was in an American city. Soldiers with rifles stood on street corners and Army tanks rolled by, grinding tracks in the Livernois Avenue pavement. I parked and started taking pictures, but I had to wait between each shot for the self-developing Polaroid to finish.

A soldier grabbed my arm and pulled me into a drug store.

"Sniper," he said pointing to the rooftop across the street.

There were pops of gunfire coming from the roof, then a barrage of gunfire toward the roof. Then silence. The building was smoking and flames were coming from the windows when the fire trucks arrived. I thanked the soldier and left. As I turned the next corner, I came face to face with a man who shoved a shotgun into my belly. He was guarding his store.

"Whoa," I said, "I'm with the *News*. Mind if I take your picture?"

He saw my camera and lowered the shotgun.

When I'd used up all my film, I drove home to write my story. I remember being thrilled with the lead that seems so melodramatic now:

> DETROIT, Michigan, July 23, 1967 – The nation's fifth largest city lay burning, smoldering in ruins, with tanks and soldiers at every corner. As I entered the city, sniper fire cracked overhead. This wasn't a third world country. It was Detroit, Michigan. The United States of America.

Hayden didn't mind the melodrama and ran my story unchanged in the *Ingham County News*. The paper's owners ran it in their whole chain of newspapers, giving me a full page with a byline, and they used my pictures of the tanks, the burning buildings and the man pointing his shotgun at me.

EIGHTEEN

Norman Rockwell's Finest

IN THE LATE SIXTIES, progressive colleges like Michigan State University expanded student medical benefits to include mental health services. When I read in the school newspaper that MSU students could get therapy at the Student Services Center, I decided to take them up on the offer. I had been seeing Dr. Razard for two years, but at my next session I told him that the commute to Detroit was too tiring and I planned to terminate treatment with him.

"Don't forget, there is a mandatory final session," he responded. "You might as well come one more time, because the twenty-five dollar fee is billable whether you show or not."

I called Student Services for an appointment and got one with Dr. John Hinkly. I found him listed in Michigan State's staff directory as a Rogerian therapist, so I headed for the library to learn about Rogerians. Dr. Carl Rogers developed the treatment to address shortcomings in classical Freudian analysis.

He's not the only one who thinks Freudians have shortcomings, I smiled, recalling the lonely hours I'd sent with Drs. Cronick and Razard.

The encyclopedia went on to say that unlike the cerebral Freudians, Rogerians encouraged therapists to react emotionally to their patients. As a result Rogerian therapists were characteristically warm and empathetic. They called themselves "client-centered," a term suggesting their respect for a patient's life experiences. Rather than judge a patient's actions, they believed they would be more self-revealing if the therapist simply amplified their emotional reactions to the experience they described. A characteristic Rogerian technique was to repeat the patient's description for emphasis.

> PATIENT: "I wanted to kill my mother, she's such a witch."
> THERAPIST: "So you wanted to kill your mother."
> PATIENT: "What else could I do? Nothing else would stop her. Nothing."
> THERAPIST: "There was nothing you could do to stop her. You felt helpless."

This new therapy intrigued me, and I eagerly awaited my hour with Dr. Hinkly.

At the appointed time, I entered the weathered brick Student Services Building and gave my name as the secretary handed me a clipboard with a sign-in sheet.

She requested the fee up front. "Twenty-five cents for today please."

This is like therapy in a Peanuts cartoon, I thought smiling as I dug in my jeans for the change.

She led me down the hall to Dr. John Hinkly's small office, where it was immediately obvious that Rogerians set a different tone from their clinically detached Freudian counterparts. Dr. Hinkly came out from behind his desk to greet me and offered me a chair with a welcoming gesture of his hand. I guessed Dr. Hinkly's height to be six-feet-two, and he was bald except for a thin, monkish ring of hair at ear height. His lab coat was several sizes too small, so when buttoned at the waist, he looked like a great white pear. He was a gentle man who spoke softly. Unlike the deadpan Dr. Razard, Dr. Hinkly had mastered the art of facial expression. During our sessions, if I talked about some progress we'd made, Dr. Hinkly looked pleased. When I described my vise attacks, he looked protective, his face reflecting my own concern.

Dr. Hinkly remained my ally even after I told him about Freshman Orientation Week and how I'd let so many people down. He wasn't sanctimonious when I confided about Montreal and Piedras Negras. But he wasn't passive. He didn't hesitate to correct me, as he did when I finished my brief family history. He told me I saw Mom and Dad one-dimensionally—a "Norman Rockwell portrait," he called it.

Of course I viewed them one-dimensionally. Bible Belt kids were brainwashed when it came to parents. Boys idealized parents as automatically as we said the Pledge of Allegiance. If a classmate spoke ill of your mom, you didn't tolerate the insult. You were expected to fight him, no questions asked.

But Dr. Hinkly said it was time to go deeper. He said my portrait of Mom and Dad was the thinnest of pencil-sketches, and he urged me to fill it in with dimension and colors. He constantly probed, as he did when I mentioned that Dad was down on me this week.

"What did you do to make him angry?" Dr. Hinkly asked.

"He told me to cut the lawn, but I forgot," I said.

"What exactly did he say when you forgot?" Asked Dr Hinkly.

"He said I was an idiot and he took me to the garage." I said.

"He called you an idiot and took you to the garage," repeated Dr. Hinkly. "Then what? Did he hit you?"

"He might have," I said.

"Might have?" Hinkly asked with his eyebrows raised.

"He whacked my head a little," I said.

"He whacked your head a little," said Dr. Hinkly, looking at me curiously.

He paused a moment and then asked, "How would you handle it if you were the dad?"

"I don't know," I shrugged.

"You must have some idea," said Dr. Hinkly.

"I guess I'd remind my kid that he was supposed to cut the lawn and then I'd make him do it that very moment, even if it was dark out and even if he missed his favorite TV show. Maybe next time he would take me seriously."

"How hard would you hit him?" Asked Dr. Hinkly.

I thought a moment.

"I don't think I would," I said.

"You wouldn't hit him," said Dr. Hinkly with a hint of approval.

"Nope," I said.

"Was your Dad physical with your brother and sister too?" Asked Dr. Hinkly.

"Not really physical," I said defending Dad. "No more than other dads. My uncles were hard on all my cousins. I saw cousin Ira's bruises when he changed his gym shirt. My buddy Dennis's dad was tough on him. I remember going over to see Dennis once, but when I got there, his dad had him out in the garage—for discipline. Dennis looked pretty bad when the two of them came into the kitchen. Dennis's mom questioned her husband about the bruises on her son and he reminded her that, 'The kid needs some sense whacked into his thick skull. Spare the rod and you spoil the child.'"

"How do you feel about that philosophy?" Dr. Hinkly asked.

"I don't know," I said. "Dennis turned out okay. Dad told me he got the strap a lot when he was a kid. Grandfather Isaac was like a Nazi. Dad had to call him 'sir' and stand when he entered the room. Some parents are buddy-buddy with their kids, but no one is palsy in our family."

Dr. Hinkly was silent. As he studied me, his pen dropped accidently from his hand and landed on the desk with a distracting clatter. I let my thoughts follow the sound and they took me to an afternoon many years ago.

"Michael, are you with me?" said Dr. Hinkly interrupting my thoughts,

"Sorry Dr. Hinkly," I said, "but I remembered something about Dad."

"Yes," he prompted.

"When I was about 13, Dad had to go to this office for a few hours on a Sunday afternoon. He was supposed to spend the day with me and my brother Randy, so he took us along. Dad's office was on the fourth floor of Grossman's Department Store, behind walls that separated that floor's retail aisles from the executive offices. The fourth floor contained both the appliances department and the toy department—so there were aisles of white mixers, juicers and chrome toasters that mirrored our faces when we looked at them. There were also aisles of toys—Barbie dolls in colorful see-through packaging, plus slinky toys that walked down steps, cap guns, and monopoly games.

"Dad worked at this massive oak desk with papers and ledgers at each side, but there was little for Randy and me to do except to roam the aisles and play with the toys. We were allowed to play with the open display toys as long as we were careful and as long as the toy wasn't noisy like a ray gun. But there were only a few display toys out, and we were bored with little to do.

"Two hours had passed, and Dad's only appearance outside his office door was to shush Randy when the energetic seven-year-old became too boisterous. The electric wall clock moved in slow motion, and Randy's energy level hit the point where he couldn't sit for one more second. He just had to let loose, so he began to run up and down the aisles of goods making motor sounds, giggling and laughing, arms outstretched like an airplane.

"Dad stuck his head out from his office, and he didn't look happy. I knew the warning signs, but Randy, only seven, didn't get it.

"'Randy, I told you to be quiet and I mean it,' Dad warned.

"Randy sat back down, but in a few minutes he was buzzing the aisles like a fighter jet.

"Dad appeared again.

"'Randy. Sit down, you little shit, and be quiet. I'm not going to tell you again.'

"Again Randy quieted for a time. But it wasn't long before he was racing past the glass display shelves, thundering past toys, giggling and whirling like a tornado.

"Dad came out of his office, eyes molten, raging like a bear from its den. His face was contorted as he headed for Randy like he couldn't see anything else. He spun Randy around by the shirt and, as if he was his punching bag in our garage, Dad slugged him in the gut with the full force of his six-foot frame.

"Randy dropped to the floor with the wind knocked out of him. He was unable to talk but could only suck repeatedly for air, making a gasping 'ahoooop' sound.

"Dad's temper brought him to the edge of a killer's trance, but slugging Randy broke the spell. Like a dog hosed with water during a fight, he shook his head trying to return from wherever he had gone. His face was like stone when he returned to his office.

"I stood frozen, not daring to move. When Dad's door slammed, I went to Randy, who couldn't talk.

"Randy, can you get up?" I asked.

"Randy rolled over, face down on the floor, and just moaned.

"That's all I remember," I said to Dr. Hinkly, shrugging.

Dr. Hinkly shook his head.

"Was Randy bleeding?" he asked.

"I don't recall. I don't think so. But he was really shook up."

Dr. Hinkly paused, I looked at him, hoping he would carry the conversation.

"Well?" said Dr. Hinkly, awaiting my reaction.

"Yeah, I know. There goes Norman Rockwell," I said flippantly, hoping sarcasm could suppress the anguish that tugged at my consciousness.

Dr. Hinkly saw that I wasn't ready to go any deeper. Our time was up, and he stood, ending our visit.

As children, Jill and I could turn to each other for support. We confided in each other and verified each other's perceptions on days when Mom's or Dad's actions didn't make sense. But Randy had no one. He could not turn to his parents, not to the few friends he had, and not to Jill or me. We used to prey on Randy the way bigger fish eat smaller ones.

What's more, Randy's sense of when to stay out of Dad's way

was never honed. He was too impetuous to watch out for Dad's moods. I learned later that Randy's timing that afternoon years ago couldn't have been worse. Dad took us to the office that afternoon choking with unspent anger about a board meeting that had occurred that week. He swallowed bile when his brothers and sisters, equal stockholders but with lesser vision, vetoed his expansion plans for the store.

When Randy got on his nerves that day, Dad's last thread of control snapped. It was more than accumulated frustrations. I believe something in his youngest son mirrored what Dad most disliked in himself. Randy, spontaneous and frequently impudent, rarely lived up to Dad's expectations—however unrealistic they were. But as a constant disappointment to Dad, Randy echoed Dad's own childhood. Dad could never satisfy Grandfather Isaac despite a lifetime of trying.

After my session with Dr. Hinkly, I went home for the weekend. Dad wasn't home when I arrived, and he didn't pull into the driveway until late that night. He stormed through the front door, angrily muttering that his dry goods buyer had resigned. He was in what Jill and I called his "black cloud mood," and it was frightening. But like Randy, I also wasn't smart enough to wait until they passed. Waiting them out made me feel like I was acknowledging that Dad had all the power, that I was helpless, trapped in a situation completely out of my control. So inevitably, I did the wrong thing, the worst thing I could do. I baited Dad, taunting him each time he frightened me. I knew I was poking a sleeping dog, but I couldn't stop myself.

"So Dad, how do you spell workaholic?" I teased as he tossed his hat on the closet shelf.

Dad scowled.

"The reason you have clothes on your back is because I do work 'til eleven," he reminded.

"Bullshit," I said, "you work because you want to. It's who you are. You do it for you, not for me."

Dad's face darkened as he pounded the table and rose.

"You son-of-a-bitch," he growled, heading for me.

Normally when Dad charged I held up my arms to protect my face, but I didn't this time. I hadn't planned to react differently, I just did. I held my position, but before Dad reached me, I ducked under his clenched fist, grabbed his shoulders, spun him around and slipped a headlock on him.

Dad's jaw dropped in surprise.

I tripped him, slid him to the floor and pinned his arms behind his back.

He looked dazed.

Mom heard the ruckus and came into the kitchen running, circling the room hysterically with her hands to her temples.

"Oh my god, don't hurt him," she pleaded.

I never hit Dad, but I did keep him pinned.

"Say 'I give,'" I insisted.

He wouldn't, so I tightened my hold and waited with the full weight of my body over his. He struggled futilely and finally stopped.

"I give," he said.

His voice sounded beaten, a tone I'd never heard from before from the great Mr. Bluster.

At our next session Dr. Hinkly listened intently when I described what had happened.

"Do you know," I said, "I feel sure Dad will never lay a hand on me again. I know it in my gut. A real man would try to muscle me again, but Dad is nothing more than a bully."

"Nothing but a bully," Dr. Hinkly repeated.

Dr. Hinkly looked thoughtful for a moment before asking another of his pointed questions.

"And Michael, what was your mother doing all those years while your Dad hit you kids?"

NINETEEN

Drive-In Movie

EVEN IN COLLEGE, talking to women was nerve-wracking. Just to make small talk I had to pump up my Mr. Master of Ceremonies balloon. As I spoke, I carefully watched for any hint of boredom—so I could end the conversation before the girl did.

During one session Dr. Hinkly asked if I dated much.

"Rarely," I said exaggerating.

"Rarely," Dr. Hinkly repeated. "Do you think you should go out more often?"

"Well, there is a girl in my Victorian Literature class . . . Madeline."

"Might you ask her out?" Hinkly said.

"What if she turns me down?" I asked.

"What if she doesn't?" said Dr. Hinkly.

Madeline had short black hair, a warm laugh and a well-proportioned body. I steeled myself for a "no" as I asked her out.

"Sure," she said, "I'd love to go out with you, but you need to know that I have a boyfriend at the University of Michigan."

To my surprise, I was comfortable around Madeline. After a

third date, I began to wonder what it would take to knock her boyfriend out of the picture—or at least to sleep with her.

With that goal in my mind, we headed for the drive-in movies. The back seat of my Buick was loaded with anything Madeline might want to drink. I had beer, whiskey, scotch, vodka, mixers, ice and even a Styrofoam cooler chilling a bottle of champagne. We pulled in to the East Lansing drive-in, and I pulled into an open space, reaching for the heavy metal speaker as James Bond in *Goldfinger* came on the screen.

"Refill?" I repeatedly asked Madeline, offering more vodka and filling my own glass as well.

About mid-show Madeline left for the bathroom, noticeably weaving en route to the old cinder block building.

Excellent, I thought. *I'll make my move when she gets back.*

But out my front window I saw multiple Madelines returning, and when she slammed the Buick's heavy door closed, I had to sink both hands into the seat to stay upright. When that became questionable, I shoved open my door, leaned out and puked.

I was drunk. Madeline was merely bewildered.

"Home," I moaned starting up the Buick.

I remembered to return the drive-in speaker to its metal stand before I drove away, spinning the wheels in search of an exit. The "closed" sign at the first gate seemed an unnecessary delay, so I plowed through the barrier, dragging the fence with me until it fell away when the dirt road became the highway. Madeline's eyes were wide open, while mine were half shut. I clung to the steering wheel until we reached her dorm.

I was the talk of the campus next morning. The police were looking for the fool who drove a car through the drive-in wall. They never found him.

And I never made love to Madeline. After our next class she confided that she'd called her old boyfriend and they were back together. She could overlook his gambling problem after all, she said.

I didn't tell Dr. Hinkly about the drive-in for fear he'd have to report me, but I mentioned that I'd struck out with Madeline.

"You struck out with Madeline," he repeated. "But you met a lovely girl and had a few nice dates. Isn't that better than weekends at the dorm?"

I had to acknowledge that it was.

"So maybe you'll try again?" urged Dr. Hinkly.

TWENTY

Introduction

I DISAGREED WITH EVERYTHING SUSAN DAVID SAID. But it wasn't her point of view that struck me when the well endowed brunette raised her hand in English Lit class. She rose to say *Paradise Lost* was bent on "justifying the ways of God to men." I argued it was more about free will and the battle of good and evil. After class I caught up with her, hoping we might continue the discussion over coffee. She accepted.

Like Madeline, I could talk to Susan David without feeling on constant, anxious guard. But, stirring neatly poured cream, she made sure that I understood that she was Jeff Terry's girl. Who on campus didn't know of Jeff Terry, the University's All-American swimming star? We met for coffee after the next several classes, but always her conversation turned from great works to the great accomplishments of Michigan State's swim star.

I figured if I had any chance at all with Susan, I had to plant the seed that athleticism wasn't such a big deal. With a minimum of subtlety, I suggested that high school girls swooned over athletic prowess but as girls matured in college, they looked for intellect, and sensitivity. We talked late into the night about the Plight of Humanity, World Injustice and God. I read her passages from *Catcher in the Rye* and *Siddhartha* and *Walden Pond,* all to remind her that the Buddha and Thoreau weren't talking about athletic achievement.

One night we met for dinner, and Susan mentioned she was traveling that weekend to see Michigan State swim against Ohio State.

"Jeff has tough competition in this meet, but I know he can do it," said Susan, showing more admiration than I'd have liked.

"We should live together," I blurted out, desperately upping the ante.

I hadn't planned to ask her. It should have been an important decision, but I had given it no forethought at all. It was all I could think of to head off Jeff Terry. It's what came out.

What surprised me most was Susan's reply.

"Give me some time to think about it," she said.

I was sure Susan would say "no," I thought. *I just said it so she would take me more seriously, think of me also as a boyfriend. Was she really considering if we should live together?* I was stunned. *Was I ready for this? Could I handle it? It all happened so fast.*

A week later Susan accepted my offer, and the following week she moved into my apartment, an off-campus second-floor walk-up.

Our apartment—suddenly it was *ours*—had three small rooms. The bedroom had three bookshelves crammed alongside a mattress that lay on the floor with no frame. The living room window looked out on a neighbor's hanging laundry and included a Pullman kitchen with a two-burner stove and a refrigerator. You could shower in the bathroom tub if you pulled the curtain around in an oval. All three rooms had the same floor—chipped linoleum with a checkerboard pattern that alternated between a red flower in a pale yellow square and a yellow flower in a faded red square.

In my mind, Susan's arrival meant that I'd won. Jeff Terry was out, she was my girl now, and there was only room for one in the winner's circle. I assumed all cameras would focus on me. It was in fact, my idea of a relationship—what I thought it meant to be a couple—that two people were devoted—chiefly to me. If the spotlight shifted from me even for a moment, I took it as an affront. I felt insulted, defensive and diminished. I didn't see compromise as the way to meet another's needs, and Susan's slightest disapproval, her smallest criticism, called me to marshal every defense, when all I had to do was listen.

"Let's see *Thunderball* tonight," I said.

"How about Bergman?" she said. "*The Virgin Spring* got great reviews."

"I don't want *The Virgin Spring*. I want action. You see Bergman, I'll see *Thunderball.*

"What about *Zorba the Greek*? They say it's very well done."

"*Thunderball* starts at 7:00," I said. "You want Kazantzakis, go to Kazantzakis."

"Can we go to Spartan Village for Italian after the show?" she asked.

"I'm not in the mood for Italian. I want Crawdaddy's for fish," I said.

"But we had fish last night."

"Crawdaddy's is closer to the theater,"

"Why does it always have to be what you want?"

"You got Spartan Village last time,"

"Michael, we ate at Spartan Village two months ago," Susan said. "Some convenient memory you have."

"Well, if you dislike my memory so much, how come you moved in?"

"That fact that I'm here doesn't give you the right to ignore what I want."

"Who's ignoring you? You get what you want a lot."

"As long as what I want is your choice."

"You're no captive. You can go if you don't like it here."

"I'm moved in now."

"If that's all that's keeping you with me, that can be remedied"

"I didn't say that. I said you always want what *you* want."

"Well, if that's so painful, maybe you'd prefer I wasn't here," I said defensively.

"Yes, maybe I would," Susan flashed angrily.

I felt the air sucked out of my lungs, but I kept in battle posture to pretend her words didn't sting.

"Fine then. I'll get the hell out. You shouldn't have to be with someone you hate," I said.

Our apartment had books piled everywhere. Morosely, I gathered my half, silently stuffing them into boxes and carrying them down a long flight of stairs to the car. When it couldn't hold another book, I peeled out the driveway. I got about a mile before my panic got the better my wounded ego.

Am I crazy? She'll go straight to Jeff Terry. I'll be all alone.

I did a tire-screeching U-turn and rushed home to beg for forgiveness. Susan accepted my apology, and as my petulance dissipated, I carried my books, carton by carton, back up the stairs.

That night we saw *The Virgin Spring* and had dinner at Spartan Village.

It was a regular scene, a weekly performance of the only script I knew. As a boy I'd seen it choreographed a hundred times, acted by Mom and Dad, though it resembled two children playing seesaw. Generally Dad took the bottom sea-saw position, more than content to swing Mom high. And she, from that lofty perch, could imperiously command while he would obsequiously obey. There were moments when they briefly changed position. When Dad lost his temper, he swung up, and she allowed him a few minutes aloft before she pushed off and sent him to the bottom, regaining her natural perch. Position was everything, and neither questioned that it was Mom who belonged on top. I had reversed the roles, to keep Susan on the bottom, but I knew the scene by heart.

I hadn't known intimacy. I didn't know its texture or how to spot it or what it felt like. More than anything, I wanted to love a woman. I ached to have a woman look at me and to see in her eyes that she thought I was special. But I didn't have a clue how two people ever reached that point, how one cared for another's needs. My well of having-been-given-to, that reserve we draw from to love another had as yet nothing to spare. I knew only that if there were two of us, there was a potential for an alliance, an arrangement of terms, something negotiated like the division of spoils after a battle for territory or a meeting to determine the hierarchy of command. To protect myself in a partnership, it had to be my way no less than 50 percent of the time, not so much because I was uncaring but because I saw safety in measured percentages.

One afternoon Susan entered the apartment, and it was clear she had something to say, something well rehearsed.

"I've had enough," she said. "My dad's not that well, and I've decided to move home to D.C."

Initially, I felt relieved. Our bickering was exhausting, and it was fuel for the secret vise attacks I could never tell Susan about. So she could take her disappointments with me and go—even to Jeff Terry for all I cared. Maybe I'd ask the blonde in Psych class out.

I began to have second thoughts.

The girl in Psych class will never go out with me. I'll never get a girl as pretty as Susan again. That she chose me over Jeff Terry was a fluke in the first place. Any woman who gets to know me will run just as Susan's trying to run now. The only decent woman I'll ever have is slipping through my hands.

"Let's get married, Susan," I said.

Susan looked startled.

"The whole point, Michael, is that I'm leaving. I'm going home to D.C. Marriage is the last thing on my mind," she said.

"Listen, just listen." I felt spurred by the rush of panic. "The only thing missing from our relationship is commitment. That will change everything. I'm ready. You are too. We could have the wedding in Washington. Your parents will be thrilled. Your father gets the Jewish boy he wants for a son-in-law. Your mom thinks you should be married by now. We can find a little house around here and finish our graduate degrees. It will be great. What do you say?"

Susan stared out the window.

"Your friends Margie, Jean and Linda are already married," I said.

"This is crazy," Susan said.

* * *

I worked on Susan for three days, using every argument I could muster. I said that it was the right time in our lives. I painted enticing pictures, but that fact that her old college roommates were already married seemed most persuasive.

Finally she agreed and to seal the deal, I had her call her parents to announce the news.

"Could we keep the wedding small and simple?" she requested.

"Small and simple, yes. We feel that way too," they concurred.

That afternoon, Susan's parents reserved the ballroom at Washington's posh Madison Hotel and hired the White House calligrapher (who moonlighted) to handwrite several hundred invitations. In June of 1965 Susan and I drove to Washington to get married.

At the routine pre-wedding physical, Susan's doctors discovered that one of her ovaries was the size of a melon. It wasn't malignant they assured, but it had to come out.

"Not to worry. The two of you can get into plenty of mischief vit her one ovary," her Yiddish doctor said, horse-snorting.

At the reception, friends of Susan's parents approached me.

"How good of you," they said to me, "to go through with the wedding even though Susan will have only one ovary."

They said it like I should have requested my deposit back on a lame mare.

After a wedding ceremony at the temple, we headed for the Madison Hotel ballroom, which was filled with well wishers in black tie. Waiters in stiff white shirts carried trays of Dom Perignon. Hors d'oeuvres spilled from artfully arranged silver cornucopias—caviar, shrimp, mushrooms, iced steak tartare, canapés and cheeses. When guests could eat no more, the hotel staff ushered the crowd into the flower-filled dining room, where a choice of pheasant, filet minion or beef Wellington sat artfully arranged on fine Limoge china.

* * *

Because of Susan's scheduled surgery, we changed our honeymoon plans. Instead of Barcelona we went to nearby Ocean City, Maryland, and sat on deck chairs by the ocean, our noses covered with white sun lotion. Susan tanned while I complained about resort prices.

Being married did nothing to abate our bickering. Out for a drive on a Sunday, we fell into our well-worn groove.

"You want only what you want," Susan said.

"Because you never want what I want," I said.

"How about thinking of *me*? Just once. I've never met anyone so selfish."

"Me selfish? You get to be the judge of me, right? You sit like the Queen of Hearts and render verdicts."

"Selfish—it's who you are."

Lacking a comeback, I escalated. "If you hate me so much, how come you married me? How come you wear my ring? Maybe you don't want to be married to me?"

"Well, maybe I don't," Susan pouted.

"So why wear my ring?" I taunted.

"Okay, I won't wear your damn ring." She wrenched it off her finger and thrust it in my palm.

Susan's engagement ring was a triangle-cut diamond held by gold prongs at three corners. I'd designed it myself, and we both loved it. But the fight ran on its own steam now.

"Fine with me," I said taking the ring.

Impulsively, I rolled down the car window and threw it out.

Black silence.

A quarter mile later I turned the car around. We searched the field for hours, but we never found the ring. Maybe it was a sign.

TWENTY-ONE

Susan's Story

SUSAN WAS ELEVEN when her older sister Miriam went to the hospital with a high fever. Nurses worked around the clock to bring the fever down, placing Miriam in a bath of cold water and sponging her forehead with a cold washcloth. Gertrude and Arthur, Miriam's parents, were told that it was polio and all that they could do was watch as over time the left leg grew thinner.

Afternoons after school, Susan listened for the thump of Miriam's steel brace as she doggedly climbed the stairs to the bedroom the sisters shared. Miriam's sweet disposition grew caustic and her sense of humor turned to sarcasm. She formed a club, The Avengers, declaring herself chief and making lieutenants of Susan and their brother Phillip. Chief Avenger Miriam barked orders, routinely berating Susan and Phillip for failing to do her bidding properly. Although Susan and Phillip tried their best to dance to Miriam's tune, demotions in rank brought the siblings to tears. Miriam wasn't dancing at all.

Life was not the same at the family's pleasant Tudor home just up from Washington's wooded Rock Creek Park. Gertrude, an immigrant from Hobblestad, Germany, spent much of her day tending to her daughter, driving her to schools and appointments and secretly hoping that bowls of chicken soup and plates of sugar cookies would mend what modern medicine could not.

Arthur had his own way of responding when daughter Miriam's illness unsettled his well-ordered world. A brilliant businessman, Arthur was not used to encountering obstacles he couldn't overcome. So he distanced himself from the problem by working longer hours at his Georgetown liquor store and by devoting more time to his growing real estate portfolio.

The value of one of his properties was the subject of some debate. Friends scoffed and said Arthur was foolhardy when, in the 1950s, he purchased worthless Virginia farmland 22 miles out from Washington D. C.

"Don't you know," a business associated warned Arthur, "that no District resident goes out as far as Centerville, Virginia? Hell, even Virginians don't go there."

Arthur ignored them, bought the land and on the weekends enjoyed driving to the country to walk his acreage.

When Arthur bought his land, Washington D.C. still had the feel of a small Southern town. The local businessmen still knew each other and they could count the major players on their hands. But as government centralized and the capital city grew, the burgeoning bureaucracy required new homes for more staff. They built an eight-lane beltway that circled the capital to accommodate the added traffic. Then came Washington's subway system. Real estate prices climbed. Soon the eight-lane beltway was jammed with traffic, and the scent of exhaust fumes hung in the air. Downtown, people fought over parking spots that used to be plentiful.

When there was no more land for construction in Washington proper, the mega-developers moved across Key Bridge and built the city of Roslyn. And when Rosyln's marble high-rises could no longer accommodate the demand for homes and commercial space, they built north, pushing the Virginia suburbs further out. Since home prices depended on a property's proximity to Washington proper, the middle class looked farther out for affordable homes. The subway system followed them, and soon even

Centerville, Virginia—once farmland—had subway service to the capital and the Pentagon. Arthur's "worthless" acreage was suddenly the prize of a developers' bidding war, and the winner paid millions for the land.

Yet Arthur's money couldn't restore his oldest daughter, and he did his best to hide his shudder when the slit in Miriam's skirt exposed the metal and leather grid of her leg brace.

Then the rumors about Arthur began. Gertrude overheard her friends whispering at the hairdresser and the doctor's office.

"Arthur was with her again last night. At the Rive Gauche."

"The blond?"

"Yup, arm in arm."

"That woman is a foot taller than Arthur. He looks like a dwarf beside her."

Gertrude ignored the gossip and focused on keeping Arthur's home immaculate and on getting Miriam to her physical therapists.

Susan was keenly aware of the gossip. She watched her mother's cheeks grow gaunt and saw her lightheartedness fade as night after night Arthur either came home late or failed to show at all. More than once Susan was awakened by muffled sobs from Gertrude's bedroom. Susan hated her father for it—and for other reasons. He'd begun to ignore Miriam and he didn't keep his promise to teach Phillip how to drive. Susan was furious at him too because she'd always been Arthur's pet, and now didn't see much of her father either.

Susan's fury erupted the night that Gertrude and Arthur gathered the children in the living room. Arthur sat uncomfortably and coughed as Gertrude told them that their father was divorcing her. Gertrude buried her face in a napkin and sobbed. Susan cursed her father and rose and flung a china candy dish at him as she stormed out of the room.

About a year after Arthur's intent to divorce Gertrude was announced, Susan and I were in Washington visiting her family. I'd been briefed on the pending divorce. Gertrude had planned a family dinner for the second night of our visit, and Arthur promised Gertrude that he would be on time. But at dinnertime, he called to say something had come up and he wouldn't be home until late.

"He's a bastard," said Susan seeing her mother in tears.

Susan threw the dish she'd been drying and it shattered against the wall as she ran from the house, slamming the heavy front door. I caught up with her on the lawn where she was on her knees, raging and pounding the ground.

"I hate him. That son-of-a-bitch. I hate him."

I tried to comfort her, to help her rise and bring her to me, but she pummeled my chest with her fists. Her eyes were wild.

"Bastard," she screamed. "He can't do this to Mom. I hate all men. You're all bastards."

It was a fragile moment, and I tried to put my arms around her, but she shoved me away, raging even as I tried.

"I am not the enemy. Let me help you," I urged.

But Susan had seen the hurt in Gertrude's eyes, and it made a lasting impression.

In fact, Gertrude and Arthur did not divorce. A year after Arthur had announced his plan to leave his wife, the doctors said that his frequent coughing was the first stage of terminal lung cancer. In mere weeks, Arthur became very thin. We transferred him to the Washington Hospital Center where, in a mere three months, he weighed ninety pounds. I had to carry his tiny frame to the bathroom. As if nothing had happened between them, Gertrude stayed with him always, fluffing up his pillow, offering him ice water from a straw and bringing bowls of chicken soup that went uneaten. She loved him none the less on the sunny day two months later when she buried him.

TWENTY-TWO

Street Savvy

AFTER THE FUNERAL IN THE FALL OF 1967, Susan and I returned to Michigan State University to finish our degrees. I still found it hard to retain material and had to prepare for weeks in advance of my exams. Susan crammed the night before and did as well as I did.

After we got our masters degrees, I took a teaching position at Oakland Community College and we moved to Farmington, Michigan outside Detroit. I taught English, Journalism and, ironically, a Freshman Orientation class. I proposed such a class to the administration and received permission to develop and teach it. It ran like a support group. We sat in a circle, and the freshman had an opportunity to talk about what living away from home for the first time was like, an issue I strongly identified with, vividly recalling how lonely I felt in St. Louis. Many first semester freshmen felt isolated, and it helped them to see they weren't alone in finding the transition difficult.

I liked teaching and was determined to make my classes relevant and fun. I dropped the formalities between myself and my students, but not everyone at the community college wanted me to. The English department secretary, Jody, liked my prestige as a member of the faculty and said I should be proud to be an instructor, and that, yes, it was a big deal. Jody had waist-length hair and long, beautiful legs that contributed to her stately if somewhat Barbie-doll appearance. Jody spoke deliberately, measuring every word, her way of insuring that though she had no formal education, she would never embarrass herself with an uneducated choice of phrase. Jody was bright, and it was irrelevant as far as I was concerned that she hadn't gone to college. But it humiliated her as did her modest lifestyle. Her father had left when she was three, and her mother was often too ill to work, so the two of them lived on Jody's salary as a secretary in a one bedroom cottage near campus.

Jody and I began spending time together. We often met on freezing winter nights in my car in the parking lot, and soon we were fogging up the back-seat windows. When Jody didn't know I was watching, I caught her admiring me, looking at me like I was the most important man in the world.

It wasn't long before I was calling Susan from short-stay motel rooms, lying about late night meetings that never occurred. Once again I was ashamed—but not enough to stop seeing Jody or to halt the endless comparisons I made between her and Susan. Jody was so sweet to me; Susan was always so angry. Jody admired me; Susan said I was selfish. It was fun to be with Jody; Susan and I bickered constantly. And then there was the sex . . .

I ought to be with Jody, I decided.

So the following Saturday, in the heat of another who-is-the-more-selfish debate, I told Susan I had had it. I never told her about Jody, but I announced that I was leaving and, following old habits, I filled the car with books and drove away. I got about five miles this time before fear seized me completely and I could barely catch my breath.

I can't do this. I just don't have the balls.

I made a hurried retreat.

When I got back, Susan had locked the doors. I pounded frantically on them, but she refused to let me in. I ran around the house and found an unlocked window in the rear and jumped through it.

I hurried to the kitchen and threw myself at her feet, pleading and hugging her shoes while she angrily kicked me.

"We can make it this time," I begged.

Before long she acquiesced, and later that day I quietly left the house to call Jody.

"I just can't see you anymore," I said.

"I understand Michael," she said sadly.

That night the vise clamped powerfully again. Susan was asleep, so I didn't have to hide it. Leaden arms took me, and I had no choice but to let the force drag me by the feet me across a waterless desert, leaving parallel heel tracks in parched sands. I had to wait it out, observing my ennui like a detached journalist.

When it finished, I reentered a joyless world. My marriage was sour, I'd been unfaithful, and I was becoming disillusioned with teaching. The administrators at the college thrived on paper flow, but where was their passion for their students?

As if an echo of my own disillusionment, the nation had become disenchanted with its own administration and was tearing itself apart with political strife. We lost President Kennedy and then Martin Luther King and then Robert Kennedy. The guys I knew got drafted and were sent off to Asian rice paddies. Weekly I learned someone else wasn't coming back from Vietnam. Lyndon Johnson was president, and though Kennedy may have started it, Vietnam was Johnson's war now.

Nightly I watched CBS and Walter Cronkite report on Vietnam. Cronkite toured the battle zone, returning after the Tet offensive to warn Americans:

"It seems now more certain than ever that the bloody experience of Vietnam is a stalemate."

Cronkite tallied the growing losses—the deaths of young American boys, children really, who should have had their whole lives ahead of them. They became "body count." Five thousand dead. Ten thousand. Twenty, thirty thousand. It was impossible to grasp the collective damage—wives who could never feel secure with their men again, children raised without fathers. And it was happening to innocent Vietnamese as well as American families.

The war seemed to drag on endlessly. Americans torched Vietnamese villages, supposedly to save them, and our own boys were fired on by children who could barely lift the rifles they carried. At home, the military carried rows of flag-draped caskets off transport planes.

I had a teaching deferment. Susan and I found common ground in our opposition to the war, and we joined Senator Eugene McCarthy's presidential campaign. We distributed leaflets and talked to growing numbers of people who were also disillusioned with Vietnam. In my spare time, I worked in the senator's Detroit campaign office, drafting press releases and speeches. Within six months they made me the senator's Michigan press secretary. I wrote William Clay Ford's speech when he endorsed McCarthy at what was then the largest political rally in Michigan history.

I ran for election and became a precinct delegate in Muskegon's ninth congressional district (since redistricted). That put me in line to go to the successive party conventions—first the county, then the state and finally the national Democratic Party Convention if I was chosen. Naively, I imagined I would go to Chicago to cast a vote for Senator McCarthy. I would soon find out that elections aren't exactly run by the book.

In Muskegon, labor controlled the Democratic Party, as it had for fifty years. When I arrived for the county meeting, the chairman, a union boss, was seated at a desk on the auditorium's front stage. He gaveled the meeting open.

"Would delegates who want to go to the state convention line up at the desk," he announced.

The Eugene McCarthy and Robert Kennedy delegates scrambled to line up at his desk. Curiously, none of the union-backed Hubert Humphrey delegates were in line. When the noise quieted, the union boss nodded to one of his men who opened the stage curtain, revealing a second desk and a line stacked with Humphrey delegates.

"*That* desk," the union boss gestured with his thumb. "First come, first served."

That crude ruse eliminated all the McCarthy and Kennedy delegates from the ninth congressional district.

It didn't take long to learn how democracy is played in the streets. Chicanery was the norm, district after district. In Lansing, Michigan's sixth congressional district at the time, they didn't even bother to have the county convention. Precinct delegates were told to drop a postcard to the county chairman, who would pick state delegates from the cards. If that wasn't ludicrous enough, the county Democratic office wouldn't give out the chairman's mailing address.

State by state across the country, Democratic Party machinery filtered out Eugene McCarthy and Bobby Kennedy delegates. Despite his wins in New Hampshire and Minnesota and his high national poll numbers, Senator McCarthy had only a handful of delegates when the vote was called at the infamous Chicago convention of 1968. The anti-war groups came to Chicago too, to express their frustration and anger at an illicit process that had betrayed them. Chicago's Mayor Daley greeted them with his ruthless police force.

At Oakland Community College I pleaded with my fellow faculty to take a stand, any stand, for or against the war in Vietnam.

"Other colleges have formalized a faculty position on Vietnam," I pleaded.

We circulated a petition, and finally the administration posted notice that at the next faculty meeting, Vietnam would lead the agenda. On the appointed day I filed into the auditorium with my fellow teachers, waiting anxiously for the chairman to finish reading the minutes of the last meeting. At last he opened the floor for comments about Vietnam and recognized a teacher waving her hand furiously in the first row.

"Now I ask you, "she asked indignantly, "you tell me why the faculty is not allowed to carry coffee cups through the restricted hallways?"

Her indignation sparked others and an impassioned exchange

erupted about coffee spills and the need to respect teaching professionals by allowing them to carry coffee cups anywhere. The Great Coffee Cup Debate echoed through the auditorium with excited opinions offered from every side. After an hour had passed, the chairman gaveled the meeting to a close. There was no discussion of Vietnam.

I left, disgusted.

The faculty never took a position on Vietnam. We pleaded with the administration to put Vietnam on the agenda again, but they never did.

Fed up, I resigned at the end of the school year.

We'd campaigned to end the war. This was an unpopular position in the beginning, and once more I felt like the boy back in temple, angering the people around me by challenging authority. Again the elders rose, this time to tell me I was un-American. Yet the war made no sense to me. It was another Red Sea—this one of blood.

The public lethargy about the war, the political thievery I'd witnessed, and the Mayor Daley types I encountered fed my sense of impotence. Why didn't the good guys ever win? What about authority attracted men who, like my father, ruled by intimidation if they could. Why did positions of authority collect men with such an amazing ability to prioritize backward?

TWENTY-THREE

The Real World

On one issue, my fellow instructors at Oakland Community College agreed.

"Academia isn't the real world," they said. "College life is an ivory tower. The business world is where it gets real."

If they are right, if success in academia doesn't test your mettle, am I wasting my time? I wondered. *Can I even make it in the business world—in the world of my father and Grandfather Isaac?*

That question and the lethargy over the war led me to resign my position at the end of my second year of teaching. Rather than teach somewhere else, I decided to see if I could make it in the business world. But what kind of work could I do?

Out driving with Susan one Sunday, I pointed to a billboard promoting a local bank. The graphic was of a man planting pennies in the soil with a shovel. The billboard read:

Your Money Grows at Federal National Bank

"Can you believe Federal National paid money for that billboard? I could do better ad copy in my sleep."

"So do it," Susan challenged.

"I will," I said. "I'm going to work in advertising."

McManus, John & Adams, one of Detroit's largest advertising agencies, let me interview for a job. Without advertising experience, the creative department wasn't interested in me, but my credentials as the state press secretary for Senator McCarthy interested the vice president of public relations, who had an opening. He hired me to edit the *Pontiac Chieftain,* a monthly car dealership trade magazine. I wrote stories about enterprising Pontiac dealers who moved a lot of "units." What I really wanted was to write advertising copy. When I saw a copywriter position advertised in the help wanted section of *Advertising Age,* I sent my resume. I got the job, and in 1969 Susan and I moved again—this time to Cleveland, Ohio.

Cleveland was industrial and grim, especially in wintertime. I drove to work in the morning past the Cuyahoga River on my left—burning, its surface polluted by oil. Fire trucks routinely doused the river's flames and the heavy smoke that tunneled up to the Cleveland sky smelled like burning tires. On my right was Lake Erie, rotting with sewage. The scene inspired the headline of an ad I wrote for a local environmental group. The graphic was a huge human nose, and rising into one of the nostrils was a factory smokestack—spewing black clouds of smoke. The ad headline read:

ISN'T IT TIME WE STOPPED PUTTING OUR BUSINESS INTO OTHER PEOPLE'S NOSES?

One February night Susan tugged at my bed covers. She had recently announced that she was pregnant.

"Michael, I'm spotting," she said, tearfully shaking me awake.

I quickly wrapped her in a blanket, bundled her into the car and drove to a hospital through the snowy night.

In the emergency room, a fat nurse stood chatting with the receptionist. She looked annoyed by our interruption.

"You should have handled this with your family doctor," she barked at me. Susan was in tears.

"It's not like we planned the bleeding," I fired back. "Bleeding. You know. Lots of red blood. I think that's what you call an emergency?"

"Do you at least have insurance?" Big Nurse demanded.

"I have Blue Cross *'at least,'*" I handed her my card.

She scowled, "Come this way."

Susan had a miscarriage. I sat with her on the hospital bed and held her hand until she fell asleep. Then I went home for a few hours of sleep. When I returned, Susan was distraught.

"I just wanted to have a baby," she said crying.

I gently stroked her forehead.

Big Nurse returned and shoved papers at me with X marks where she wanted me to sign.

Susan and I talked later that afternoon about future plans for a family.

"We can try again," I said. "Soon, if you want."

Susan said she wasn't very happy in Cleveland, and I admitted that I wasn't either.

"Could we possibly move to D.C.?" she asked. "I could be near my family."

"I don't see why not," I agreed. "As long as I can find a job."

I sent my resume to several Washington ad agencies and accepted a job with one in Georgetown. We moved to the nation's capital.

Relocating to a new city distracted Susan and me from our bickering, but when things settled, it began again. I chose to escape to my work. My boss teased that I was a workaholic—high praise in advertising circles. I liked writing ad copy, but the agency president thought I was stronger at handling clients and asked me to move to account management. That meant leaving the quiet, reclusive safety of my copywriting cubicle to spend my day at client meetings. Now my job was to call on accounts, sit in cherry boardrooms, show storyboards, propose media schedules and force a hearty laugh when a client told a crude joke after his third lunchtime martini. I hated the social aspect, but the reward for switching departments was a salary increase and a better title. Dealing with agency clients meant that I had to constantly become Mr. Master of Ceremonies, and each time I did, I felt ever more isolated from myself—and from Susan, who was unaware of my internal conflict.

I stayed home from work on Sundays, which meant there was no escape. Without the distraction of frenzied deadlines, I couldn't avoid the terrible isolation that came over me—a feeling like sitting alone for an eternity in a white, empty room, void of stimuli, where nothing ever moved, nothing ever happened and no human contact could occur. On Sundays the sadness so enveloped me that this vise attack washed away all color, turning the landscape to grayscale.

Though my despondency fit the oppressive humidity of summertime in Washington, it wasn't just the weather, and it was more than the constant friction between Susan and me. Something I couldn't yet identify caused me to clench my jaw so tightly that I was in constant pain—even while, incongruously, I grinned all the time.

I didn't know what it was yet, but I knew they were warning signs.

TWENTY-FOUR

Walls

THE STABBING PAIN IN MY CLENCHED JAW told me I needed therapy. But I didn't know any Washington therapists, and I surely couldn't ask at work. So I turned to the Yellow Pages. There were no psychiatrists whose last name began with "A," but I found three under "B'" and scheduled an-hour long session with each. In the end I settled on Dr. Robert Bowman because he seemed kindly like Dr. VanDervort, yet capable of asking penetrating questions like Dr. Hinkly. It was a lucky choice. Years later Dr. Bowman would win world acclaim and a Pulitzer Prize.

Therapy had come a long way from its Freudian roots. Now it was the norm rather than the exception to combine Freudian methodologies with the newer approaches that had emerged in the 1960s. Dr. Bowman was Rogerian by nature—kindly and client-focused. But he used an eclectic mix of techniques including some from Murray Bowen's family-centered therapy, some of Reich's work on character armoring and some gestalt therapy practice, especially dream interpretation the way Fritz and Laura Perls did it.

Though I chose Dr. Bowman because he seemed the most insightful of the three therapists I interviewed, from the first session on I resisted his efforts. I dodged his keen probing and felt anxious each time he suggested that I saw my parents through rose-colored glasses—although Dr. Hinkly had said the same thing years before. I felt compelled to defend Mom and Dad—mindlessly, blindly, in a kind patriotic reflex. I argued with Dr. Bowman any time he offered his insight.

"It wasn't Dad's fault that he was always at work. He had a store to run and a family to feed," I insisted.

Or, "Mom wasn't being seductive with me. She simply thought I could do better than Connie Riley," I insisted.

At one point Dr. Bowman asked if I thought my parents were relieved to send me away to St. Louis.

"If they didn't care about me, why would they pay so much to send me away," I argued.

"So they sent you to away because the three of you were getting on so well? Dr. Bowman persisted.

"That's not the point. They did what was best for me," I said.

"Really," said Dr. Bowman.

I was late for my next session. Dr. Bowman asked me why.

"My sister Jill called. My aunt died," I said.

"I'm so sorry, Michael. Were you close to your aunt?"

"Sort of," I shrugged.

Something about my vagueness sparked his interest. "You've never talked about anyone dying before. Do you think much about death? Does it scare you a lot?"

"That assumes I will die," I said. "Suppose I'm immortal?"

Dr. Bowman shot me a curious look and asked, "Do you think you won't die?"

"I'm simply saying that you can't prove I will die. Take the sunrise. Actuarially, we expect the sun to rise tomorrow because it always has. But until it does, it's not a proven fact. That's true of death too," I chuckled.

"That is a really sophomoric argument Michael. Why even bother to make it?" He asked.

I thought about his question for a while. Finally I responded, "I guess that's how I deal with death . . . because it's so overwhelmingly frightening. And maybe it's how I handle a lot of scary things—flippantly. Joking about death lets me distance myself from it. Being sarcastic, rebelling against the inevitable, is my way of refusing to go softly into that good night. Joking in death's face makes me feel a tiny bit of power against a force overwhelmingly stronger than I am."

"Sound like anyone in your family?" Dr. Bowman raised his eyebrows. "Someone who scared you?"

I owned that Dr. Bowman had a point. "I guess I deal with lots of my issues that way, don't I? Especially if I feel really scared, or really sad or if I fear some memory is really going to hurt. It's easier to joke the whole thing off."

Dr. Bowman looked pleased. "Isn't that how you handled your Dad? You couldn't control him, but you could mock him?"

"Something like that," I acknowledged. "Dad can be scary and threatening like Death. You can't argue with either one. You can't trick either one. All you can do is dodge until the force gets you."

"So which frightens you more, Dad or Death?" he asked.

I changed the subject. "Come to think of it, Mom and Dad hardly ever spoke about death," I said in a second moment of insight. "When a family member died, we kids were never told."

"Seriously?" asked Dr. Bowman. "What did they say when a relative died?"

"That's just it. Nothing. Jill, Randy and I had to find out from someone else, often months later."

The doctor looked astonished.

"I learned of my Uncle Eddy's death that way—during a casual phone conversation with my Cousin Ira. 'Say, how is Uncle Eddy?' I asked him. After a pause at the other end, Cousin Ira replied, 'Are you serious? Uncle Eddy died three months ago. Didn't you know? No wonder you guys weren't at the funeral.' 'Uncle Eddy is dead!' I said, shocked. I called Mom, and she said, 'Did I forget to tell you? Yes, Eddy had a heart attack.' So then I called Jill and Randy. They didn't know of Uncle Eddy's death either."

"Why do you think your parents never told you?" Dr. Bowman asked.

"I could suppose it was their misguided attempt to protect us. But I know it goes deeper. I think Mom and Dad were runners. Lots of people are. It was easier for them to ignore painful things than to face them."

"Accepting death is one thing," said Dr. Bowman, "but not telling family members is quite another."

"Mom's a skilled avoider," I explained. "She rarely faces any difficult issue directly. If the subject makes her uncomfortable, flash, she's outta there. Maybe to Cuba."

"But weren't you put in an awkward position by not knowing?" Dr. Bowman asked.

"Relatives assumed we couldn't be bothered to go to family funerals or even to send our condolences."

"How did you feel about that?"

I shrugged.

"Did it make you angry? They left you in the dark," Dr. Bowman prompted.

"Actually," I said, ignoring his question, "once Mom did tell me when someone died."

"When was that?" asked Dr. Bowman.

"I was in my office when my secretary poked her head in. 'Your Mom's on the line,' she said. I picked up the phone. 'Hi Mom. "Dad's *dead*,' she said. 'My god, Mom,' I gasped. 'What happened? Mom? Mom? Mom!' The line was dead. In her confused state, she'd put me on hold. I redialed for an hour before I finally got past her busy signal."

Dr. Bowman shook his head. "How did your father die, Michael?"

"He had a heart attack in a Houston motel room. He moved to Houston to start a new business when the department store failed. You remember—the labor strike?"

The doctor nodded.

"Mom was supposed to move from Muskegon to Houston the very morning they found Dad's body."

"My god, how hard that must have been or her."

"Yes," I agreed.

"Michael, I'm truly sorry, but the hour is almost up, and I'd like you to summarize what you're taking away from today's session. What have you learned about how you handle things and how you deal with fear?"

"Well, I do see how much I dodge what scares me," I said, "and lots of things scare me. To be honest, I feel a lot of underlying panic—almost a free-floating terror just below here," touching my forehead, "and here," rubbing my hand across my stomach. "I feel like all that fear contributes to my sense of helplessness—and to my depression. Because I'm too afraid to deal with the big fears, I drain them off into lots of tiny fears—small but constant survival worries like, what if I end up hungry and homeless? What if my agency clients don't like me? Will I keep my job? What if I get cancer? I feel scared a lot, and it's hard to feel self-confident with the sense that the ground under my feet may not hold. Some days it's overwhelming. That's when I'm vulnerable to an attack."

"You think your depression is closely tied to your fears?" Dr. Bowman asked.

"Sometimes I wonder if the numbness of my depression comes to provide relief from my fears," I said.

"Very good Michael," Dr. Bowman smiled warmly. "That's an excellent starting place for next time."

Despite my resistance, Dr. Bowman and I made progress. Though I clung dearly to my romanticized image of my parents, Dr. Bowman persisted, probing about St. Louis, about the death of our dogs, about Dad's temper, about Mom's seductiveness, until slowly I saw them as real people—as imperfect. I began to look at them with adult eyes instead of those of a needy child who had to idealize, driven to embellish so his fantasy image stays secure. I felt safe owning that I was mad at them. I took Dr. Bowman seriously when he wondered aloud if the pain in my clenched jaw was restrained anger. Did raw fury lie beneath my locked-on smile? Had I had turned it inward because turning it outward was too scary? How much did the rage I'd internalized contribute to my depression?

Had I been able to chart the progress of the work Dr. Bowman and I did, I would have made a graph with two lines. One line would go from left to right and rise progressively across the graph. The second path would be concentric counterclockwise circles showing how often I had to circle back and return, again and again, to re-immerse in old material. Fears and self doubts that took years to layer on were not quickly stripped away.

But our progress was real, if difficult to quantify. You can't grade a therapy patient the way you can a student. The academic model doesn't apply because it isn't about subject mastery. A better model is a journey. Think of walking along a path until you come to a wall. On some days you can't breach the wall at all. But on other days, you find a gate and pass through easily, only to find yourself faced with a second wall, and after that a third. In time it becomes clear that the row of walls is endless and that you'll never breach them all. That's when you get the point. That's when you understand that getting past the walls isn't the goal at all. The goal isn't a destination but the strength you gain by choosing to stay on the path.

That realization matured my conception of therapy. I no longer saw myself as a patient seated before the master, awaiting the big one—the lightening-strike breakthrough that would change everything. Rather, I saw progress in therapy as an accumulation of small moments of clarity, instants when my vision focused, permitting me to wrench free from the seductive, false comfort of an idyllic family portrait. Every breakthrough was a small recognition made in real time that moved me toward an adult's perspective. While the therapy itself might terminate, there was no finish line for the patient because the work of uncovering should never end.

It seemed a good time to pause and look back at my "help." I'd rebounded from a terrible start when, as a child of eight, I encountered the disinterested, judgmental Dr. Cronick. She might have driven me from therapy forever if I'd taken her contempt to heart. In time I met Dr. VanDervort whose intervention landed me in St. Louis, feeling abandoned, sent away by my parents and painfully lonely. Yet perhaps sending me to St. Louis saved me. It pulled me from a toxic environment and may have spared me from the fate that befell my three cousins.

Then I saw Dr. Razard, the disengaged Freudian who hid behind his couch. When I think of his considerable limitations—I recall something Ram Dass said in *Grist for the Mill*. To paraphrase, the therapy can be only as high as the therapist. Yet even my lonely hours with Dr. Razard provided a vent for my anger and released enough pressure so I could function in college despite my depression.

I made significant progress with the kindly Dr. Hinkly, whose natural warmth and Rogerian methods gave me the first experience of therapy as a safe haven and the knowledge that I could trust someone without fear of betrayal. My ability to be vulnerable with Dr. Hinkly laid the foundation for Dr. Bowman and me to build on years later.

Which brings me to the present and Dr. Bowman, who helped me accept that my parent's capacity to nurture was very limited, something that is universally difficult to accept. As a child it was safer for me to believe that the bone-deep emptiness engulfing me arose from my own unworthiness, that surely things at home would improve if I could just get it right. I blamed myself because the alternative—seeing that I was in a dangerous, unforgiving, unwholesome, toxic environment—was unimaginably threatening. My depression, my rebelliousness, the anger in my jaw all had to be signs of my own inadequacy. I had to be flawed, not my mom or dad. I had no choice but to remain befuddled so that I could idealize them as loving parents and cling to them. It provided a badly needed sense of safety, like a child's life vest, a garment so essential that many continue to wear it even after adolescence—some even on their death bed. No matter that it no longer fits.

When my clichés did shatter and I looked realistically at my parents, I had to recognize their indifference. That was frightening and sad, and I experienced a terrible aloneness. But I did begin to see them more clearly, and as I did, I prayed for help getting past the sense of isolation that followed. I was angry. I was cynical. I assumed there was no parental love—that there was no love at all. Every man for himself.

I continued to feel that way until the day I came home from work and Susan greeted me with her announcement. After hearing her news, I felt challenged. How well would I do as my perspective shifted from that of the child to that of the parent?

TWENTY-FIVE

The First "The End"

In the summer of 1975 Susan called to ask me to leave work early.

"Sit down I have something to tell you," she said when I walked in.

"Okay," I said.

"I'm pregnant," she said proudly.

"Wonderful," I said turning pale.

I felt a band twist in my abdomen.

How much does it cost to raise a baby? Can we afford it? What if the baby isn't healthy? Would our fights upset the child? Will his teachers call me some day to suggest our child needs "help"?

Next session I told Dr. Bowman I was going to be a father.

"That's great, Michael" he said.

I said nothing.

"Well, isn't it?" he asked.

"To be honest, it really scares me. How am I supposed to raise a kid? I'm a kid myself."

"Michael you're in your thirties," he said.

"But can I afford a child?" I asked.

"People raise children every day with a lot fewer resources than you have," said Dr. Bowman. "You have a good job."

"But how much does a baby cost to feed and clothe?"

"Are you honestly worried about that?" Dr. Bowman asked, his brow wrinkling with curiosity.

"Worried? No. How about scared to death."

"How come? Why does it feel so overwhelming?"

I shrugged my shoulders. "Overwhelming. You picked the right word."

"Good, so let's look at that. Do you remember what you told me your dad said before he left for work every morning?"

I was impressed that Dr. Bowman remembered something I'd mentioned over a year ago.

"Dad said that if we kids wanted bread on the table that night, he had to leave for work. 'Bread' was his synonym for survival."

"Yes . . . ?" prompted Dr. Bowman.

I wasn't sure what he wanted.

"Do you recall your description of the way your dad said it?" he asked.

"He wasn't joking," I said. "He was deadly serious, and he even looked frightened. As a child I literally thought we wouldn't eat that night if Dad didn't leave for work. I still feel that fear sometimes, as if the day is just around the corner when there won't be food for dinner. I worry about being homeless and imagine I have to ask my neighbors for food. I know it's stupid, but I think about it at least weekly."

"Can you accept that your father's fear wasn't rational? That yours isn't? Your dad was well off and you have a good job," Dr. Bowman reminded.

"Yeah, but people lose jobs. Then how could I feed a helpless infant?" I said.

"What's the likelihood of losing your job? You just got a raise."

"Anything can happen in business. There could be a takeover or a recession, or I could lose a major client. Dad lost his store."

"So he did," said Dr. Bowman pointedly. "But according to you, your father talked about going hungry even at the height of the store's prosperity. So what was going on? Was he dealing objectively with a realistic fear, or was he venting, letting his anxiety spill out without worrying who he scares? Isn't a parent's job to shelter children from such concerns, especially if they aren't real in the first place?"

"But I too feel that nothing is safe. Will I be able to hide that from my child?"

"You won't need to hide it if you understand it," said Dr. Bowman. 'The fear will dissipate on its own. So what can you take from our session to explain your fear?"

I didn't have an answer, and besides, the hour was up.

"This is important, and we're getting to an area where you're avoiding. Let's return to this issue, Michael," said Dr. Bowman, rising from his chair.

I arose too, but he stopped me at the door.

"Meanwhile, congratulations are in order," he said, putting his hand on my shoulder and smiling warmly.

Six months later, we had a daughter. We named her Lauren Esme Grossman, the middle coming from J. D. Salinger's "For Esme with Love and Squalor," a short story about a precocious little girl whose kindness saves an emotionally battle-scarred soldier.

A year and a half passed.

It was a typical Washington summer night, so humid you could almost squeeze the air like a dripping towel. The central air conditioning struggled to keep up. I was comfortably indoors, babysitting Lauren. Susan had gone for a girls' night out with her friend Linda.

It was getting late, and I hadn't heard from Susan, so around midnight I dialed Linda. "Oh," she said, "She just left. She's on her way."

At 1:00 a.m. I called again.

"She should be there very soon," Linda reassured me.

At 2:00 a.m. I called again.

"Linda, she's still not home. Maybe she's hurt or broken down on the parkway. I'm calling the police. Please call if you hear from her," I said.

There was a pause at Linda's end.

"Michael, don't call the police. Susan wasn't here tonight."

I felt stone struck as I slowly cradled the phone. That could only mean one thing. Some stranger was probably thrusting into my wife at that very moment. I wanted to rip my hair out. Or rip his out. Or hers. I paced frantically until 3:00 a.m., when car lights flooded our driveway. Susan came up the front steps.

"Hi," I said, "Did you have a nice time?"

"Yeah," she said brushing past me.

"And how's Linda?" I said.

"Fine," she said without turning.

"That's interesting, since Linda said you were never there," I said.

Susan kept walking.

"What do you have to say about that? Any excuse? Any explanation?" I trailed her down the hallway.

Susan walked past our bedroom, entered the guestroom and slammed the door. I went to our bedroom and I slammed the door. I tossed in bed and stared at the walls. I got up, paced and went back to bed, in an agony of panic until sunrise. I couldn't stand it anymore. I went to the guestroom and climbed in bed with Susan. She turned away. I waited hopefully. Finally she spoke.

"I want a separation. Lauren and I will leave."

My throat contracted. *Could she mean it?*

For a week Susan barely spoke, and when she did, she confirmed she was determined to leave me.

"But I think you should leave the house so Lauren doesn't have to," she said. "It will be better for her."

"Okay," I said.

Am I supposed to beg her to stop treating me so coldly, I wondered, *after what she did?*

The fight had its own momentum, and neither Susan nor I had the maturity to alter its course. Though I felt betrayed, I'd had my own affair with Jody, and besides, it was the 1970s—the "open marriage" era. I assumed this fight, like all our others, would not last. I'd take my books and leave and in a few days Susan would call me, we'd make up, and I'd come home.

I rented a studio apartment and I waited.

Dinnertimes were especially lonely, because that had been my time with Lauren. The dollop of tasteless, gluey stuffing in my frozen turkey dinner matched my mood. The loneliness differed from a vise attack. It wasn't as paralyzing, but it was sadder, and it never let up.

"You said it would get better with time," I reminded a recently separated friend.

The phone in my apartment rarely rang. I thought I heard it ring late one night. I hurried to answer it in case it was Susan calling, but all I got was dial tone.

On another night as I lay in bed, I couldn't take the agitation. I'd been thinking of Susan and her lover. I dressed and drove to my house, and sure enough, his car was in the driveway. I hid in the bushes and watched him in *my* living room, on *my* couch, with *my* wife. I came again the following night, but this time I lost it and pounded on the front door. Susan appeared behind the glass demanding that I leave or else—so I did.

In bed again, I wondered who among our friends would stay loyal to me. I'd lose Linda to Susan, but Bill and Marlene might stick with me.

As the time passed I felt increasingly desperate. Our time apart was lasting much longer than I expected. I called Susan, who agreed to meet me in the morning for coffee.

"Only to discuss arrangements," she clarified.

At breakfast Susan looked out the window while I begged for another chance.

"Before we toss out eight years of marriage, can we at least see a marriage counselor?" I said.

Susan reluctantly agreed to see Dr. Bowman's assistant, a social worker whom Susan knew, liked and believed would be neutral.

A week later we sat facing the social worker like opposing parties in court.

"I don't want to be married to him," Susan began.

"I wasn't the one who had the affair," I said self-righteously. "We could have worked on our issues, but she was too busy cheating with her new boyfriend. That did wonders for our marriage, didn't it?"

I grew self-righteous as the session continued and almost deluded myself that Susan alone had been unfaithful, as if I'd never had an affair with Jody. That secret was safe with Dr. Bowman's assistant. Professional ethics wouldn't permit her to tell Susan.

"And you, Michael?" said the social worker. "Have you ever strayed?"

My mouth dropped. *She's not allowed to suggest that,* I thought.

"Well, Michael?" she waited impatiently.

"Well, yes," I mumbled. "I suppose I have."

Susan turned and stared angrily at me.

"This will be our last session," she announced.

TWENTY-SIX

Long and Short of It

I PRAYED THE PHONE WOULD RING, but as the weeks passed I began to accept that Susan really was finished with me. Our trial separation would prove final. It was like the definition of a chemical reaction that I learned in high school: matter is permanently altered so that the change can never be reversed. That can happen in a marriage, too.

I only left my apartment now to go to work. Friends asked me over, but I preferred not to see anyone. I lay in bed at night feeling abandoned and reviewing my mistakes with Susan: my always insisting on the movie I wanted to see; the engagement ring I threw away; my adolescent departures when we fought, and of course my affair with Jody. I worried too about something Susan told me during our final fight.

"I hated sex with you," she said angrily. "Your penis is so tiny I never felt a thing."

What if it is too small? I worried.

Bill Wayland and Marlene Ruger were my two best friends. We'd known each other for years—and there was little about one another other we didn't know. I met Bill when the agency teamed us up to write advertising copy. He was tall and muscular but quirky, with

Albert Einstein hair exploding from the sides of his otherwise bald scalp. He was a chocoholic, addicted to the nonpareils he always carried in a wrinkled, white paper confectionary bag he'd pull from his jeans. Bill had a habit of repeating the first words of his sentences, a verbal style that gave him a certain thoughtfulness.

"You know . . ." he'd say, waving a finger for emphasis, "You know, I think we can do better on this headline."

Bill tired of copywriting, quit advertising and went to the University of Rhode Island, where he earned a Doctorate in Psychology, completing both his degree and his internship in record time. Marlene Ruger, already a psychologist, was Bill's lover. Bill called her Sweet Lips for no particular reason and the name stuck. Sweet Lips was almost stereotypically a New Yorker—brassy and assertive, but warm and funny beneath her brazen surface. And she was devoted to Bill.

When Susan and I separated, I called them frequently.

"Will I ever find a woman again?" I asked one night.

"Not in your apartment," said Marlene. "Try going out."

"Even if I find one, I might not be up to the task," I said

"Meaning what?" said Bill.

I told them what Susan had said.

"I may be anatomically challenged," I added.

"Grossman, you jerk, get on a plane to Rhode Island and spend some time with us," said Marlene.

I flew to their home, a converted barn with massive beams and beds in the loft. We sipped wine and talked into the night. It was like old times, except that Susan wasn't there.

I brought up my anatomical concern. Bill rose and told me to follow him to the bathroom. He took a ruler, measured and we were exactly the same length. When we returned to report the results, Marlene made a point of remarking that Bill was plenty adequate for her.

In our next session, I told Dr. Bowman about the visit.

"Bill and Marlene were wonderful. But what if Bill's penis is too small?"

"Marlene has no complaints," said Dr. Bowman.

"True," I said, unconvinced.

"Have any other women ever complained about it?" asked Dr. Bowman.

"No." I said.

"Did Susan ever complain before your last fight?" Dr. Bowman asked.

"No, but I've always wondered if I was big enough."

"Why would you?" Dr. Bowman asked.

"I remember when I was a kid, I saw Dad's in the shower. His hung like a tree trunk, while mine was only a twig. I figured mine would never be as big as Dad's."

Dr. Bowman was about to say something when I interrupted him.

"You know, I recall another time that I worried about it," I said.

"Go ahead," prompted Dr. Bowman.

"I was nine. Our family doctor was my Uncle Ralph. You know, Cousin Irwin's father. Well, he asked Dad to bring me to his office. He'd given me a physical exam the week before, and he told Dad he wanted to go over the results with him.

"Herman, *you* bring him, not Rosalind, please," I heard Uncle Ralph tell Dad emphatically.

But Dad got tied up in a meeting, so Mom brought me after all.

The nurse led me down the hall to the exam room and told me to undress. I waited alone, bored, and looking around the room at the hanging stethoscope and the glass jar filled with wooden tongue depressors. It was cold on the stainless-steel exam table, and I got goose bumps and wished I had a blanket. Soon Mom and Uncle Ralph came in. Uncle Ralph took a tongue depressor from the jar and started poking my penis.

"See here Rosalind. Way too small," Ralph said, tapping my scrotum like a drum. Each time he tapped, Mom would nod in agreement. He kept lifting my scrotum and letting them flop like a bean bag. The head of my penis withdrew like a turtle.

"See how drawn up into his fat he is," said Ralph jamming the tongue depressor in again.

"Um huh," said Mom clinically.

"Thyroid injections could help," Uncle Ralph said.

"You think so?" asked Mom hopefully.

"Bring him in once a week. Or maybe Herman could bring him. See my nurse—tell her to find a time."

The trail of cigar smoke marked his departure from the room.

Each week Mom brought me for shots, and each week the two of them poked at my scrotum until Uncle Ralph said I didn't have to come anymore.

TWENTY-SEVEN

Weekend Parenting

THOUGH SUSAN WAS CORDIAL EVERY WEEKEND when I arrived to get Lauren, I felt like I was behind enemy lines. Lauren and I would go to a movie, to the National Zoo or to the carousel near the Smithsonian. Once we saw Big Bird at the PBS studio. But all were poor substitutes for daily life with my daughter. I'd become a weekend father, and I felt like an uncle.

I grew increasingly short-tempered at work. They gave me a new account—a major jewelry store client. The president of the jewelry firm was nothing if not set in her ways. She insisted on staying with her old fashioned ads—reminding me that despite my advice—she'd built a thriving business with them. I arrogantly warned this successful businesswoman that she'd better change her ways. To make my point, I asked if she communicated by phone or by smoke signals. She threatened to find a new agency and management sternly warned me to shape up. But at our next meeting I said that if she didn't change her antiquated ads, she should buy stock in her competitor. When she threatened to get a new agency instead, they fired me.

With no job and with child support payments to make, I panicked. I grew more and more frantic worrying that I'd run out of money. To calm myself, after a mere two weeks of joblessness, I took a terrible job with Warren Kristo Public Relations, a small, relatively unknown Washington firm that specialized in real estate publicity. Had I bothered to get the word on Warren Kristo, the president, I'd have learned he was an irrational bully, usually contradictory and always condescending. Cohorts summed up his management style as "If-I-wanted-your-opinion-I'd-ask-for-it." When Warren Kristo didn't get the newspaper coverage he promised a client—and coverage was never a sure thing—he'd scream in our faces with spittle popping off his lips. Warren relished calling Sunday morning meetings where he'd circle the conference table to ask why he ever hired such a group of "fucking idiots." In six months I'd had enough, paycheck or no paycheck.

One of my PR accounts was a sharp group of Washington real estate developers. I especially liked my client, Jim McMullen, the marketing vice president. When I gave Warren notice, I called Jim to say goodbye and, as an afterthought, asked if he knew of any marketing jobs.

"Get your butt right down here and let's talk," Jim said.

When I arrived, Jim's secretary Mariana was not at her desk. I knocked on Jim's door and he yelled to come in.

"Hey Jim," I waved.

"Hey," he smiled back.

Jim was a six-foot-four-inch Irishman with a handlebar mustache and arms like calves. He sat at his desk, to my amazement toking on a "left-handed cigarette." A pair of high heel shoes retracted from under his desk as I entered, and Jim's assistant, Mariana, climbed out, her blond ponytail shifting shoulders as she arose.

"Hi ya Mike," she grinned brightly as she left.

Jim winked and motioned me to a chair.

"So, Jim, I left Warren Kristo," I said.

Jim and I shared a knowing look. He took a deep toke, holding the smoke in his lungs until he opened his mouth and artfully let the white rings float up his cheeks.

"Just what this company needs," he said thoughtfully, "a smart Jew. Wanna start in the morning?"

"God that's great, Jim," I said. "As a courtesy I suppose I ought to tell Warren. I'll do so this afternoon."

Later that afternoon, Warren Kristo smirked when I was ushered into his office.

"Your job is filled, Grossman. Don't bother to beg," he said, shooing me off like a horse fly. Sadistic by nature, Warren was thoroughly enjoying my visit.

"I'm here as a courtesy Warren," I said, "not to ask for my job back. I've taken a job with Jim McMullen."

Warren's eyes narrowed.

"You can forget about working for McMullen, you little prick," he snarled. "You're not working for him or anyone else in Washington."

He grabbed the phone and speed-dialed Jim McMullen, screaming through the speakerphone when Jim answered.

"You can forget it, McMullen. Our contract specifically prohibits you from taking my staff for a year after they leave."

What a blunder, I thought. *Nobody yells at big Jim McMullen. Warren you are even stupider than I imagined.*

The speaker box stayed silent a moment, and then McMullen's powerful voice made it jump.

"Warren, here's the deal," McMullen said. "Michael works for me or I'm coming up there with this bat."

We could hear McMullen tapping something wooden on his desk.

"Your choice," McMullen said loudly, tapping the bat again. "Oh, and when I'm done with you Warren, I'll fire your ass and you'll lose my PR account too."

Warren paled.

"Warren . . . ?" Jim said with mock patience.

Warren muttered his approval and the phone clicked off at McMullen's end.

Jim McMullen practiced what my old rabbi only preached. He questioned everything until he found a better way—which he always did. The company designed, built and sold medium priced single-family homes, townhouses and condos in metro Washington D.C. We had competition, but Jim didn't market like other developers. Even our model homes were different. Most developers created models in four standard décors: Colonial, Victorian, Modern, and Mediterranean, but not Jim, who told me the potential condo buyer visits four developments and sees sixteen models in a day. By the time he's done looking he can't remember one development from another. So Jim decorated outlandishly. Prospects inevitably snickered when they entered the model bedroom painted in bright crimson, and they couldn't help but smile at the mirrors over the chrome four poster bed, but they didn't forgot it. They also remembered the placards placed at key stations on the tour, describing our heating and cooling efficiencies or underscoring our superior construction quality. Jim's homes sold faster, and he got a higher price per square foot.

Hanging around big Jim McMullen boosted my self-confidence. I got the kind of contact high you get at a Clint Eastwood movie—that feeling of invincibility. Women loved Jim, and I mimicked his self-assured style. So when Carol, a secretary in our commercial division, laughed aloud while touring our crimson bedroom model, I edged up to her and whispered, "We ought to try it out."

"Definitely," she winked.

"Tonight?" I asked.

"Pick me up," she said.

I alerted security that I was coming, but the second shift project guard never told the third shift guard. Carol and I were naked in the chrome bed when flashlights started dancing on the walls. Police car strobes pulsed through the window blinds, turning the room from red to white to red while officers beat at the front door. I tripped trying to get my trousers on as I wobbled to the door.

"Ah . . . I'm with the project," I explained to the officer. "I'm the director of marketing."

Our amused project guard confirmed my story as I stood barechested until the officer finished his notes.

In the morning Jim McMullen poked his head into my office.

"Grossman, you asshole," he said laughing.

He continued laughing all the way down the hall.

TWENTY-EIGHT

Bar Maidens

DATING AGAIN AFTER YEARS OF MARRIAGE was like attending a film festival for grade-B movies. Night after night, the conversations were predictable—the search for people we knew in common, then restaurant and movie reviews, filling what would otherwise be the loud sound of silence. I would take a deep breath and pump up Mr. Master of Ceremonies before I rang the buzzer at a date's apartment building.

Some evenings after work I went with Jim McMullen to Beowulf's Bar in Georgetown. Washington's famous three-to-one, women-to-men ratio meant that I'd almost always meet someone. Talking to new girls was an effort, but the awkwardness dissolved after a few beers. After a few more I could confidently approach a girl seated at the bar. If I felt any chemistry, I'd soon propose something crude. Her face would flush, but more often than not, she'd follow me to my car.

Nights that I didn't spend at the bar, I lay in bed, scripting imaginary calls from Susan. I'd created a variety of reconciliation scenarios and played them out using my ceiling for a screen. In most scenes, Susan approached me timidly.

"Michael," she'd say.

"Yes, Susan . . ."

"Michael, I, I . . ."

"Yes," I'd say patiently.

"Well, I was wondering if . . ." she would hesitate.

"Yes . . ." I could be wonderfully patient.

"Well what if, maybe ah . . ."

"Yes," I'd encourage.

"Do you want to come over for your favorite—Hawaiian chicken?" she'd say too quickly.

I was magnanimously taking her back one night when the phone interrupted my fantasy. It was, in fact, Susan.

"Yes, I'll come earlier for Lauren on Friday. So tell me, how you are?" I said, settling in for a nice conversation.

"Oh. Well, sure. I understand. Okay, then. 'Bye."

I don't need her, I assured myself. *I'll find a lover somewhere else—a perfect woman, my soul mate.*

I made quick script revisions on my ceiling screen. Susan's face dissolved, and in its place my imaginary soul mate appeared in a gown of shimmering pearls, her golden hair reaching the emerald belt at her waist. She would be perfect, uniquely oblivious to my imperfections.

Is she divinely sent, I wondered, *this angelic guide who will lead me to her earthly counterpart? Surely my blond angel has come to help me find my ideal woman.*

Driven by my fantasies, my visits to Beowulf's Bar were no longer solely for beer or to get laid. Rather, when I pushed through the bar's swinging doors, I entered as a grail knight on his quest, that higher purpose coloring my perceptions like 3-D glasses.

I came for my soul mate, and with the aid of the potion in my Heinekens, I could superimpose the face of my angel enchantress on the blond at the bar stuffing peanuts in her mouth. More potion would get me past her raccoon eyes and allow me to follow her vacant pupils to a presumed depth. Her slowed, slurred, speech would permit me to thoroughly admire her wisdom.

"Come with me," I'd whisper.

She'd stand, grinding a cigarette into the hardwood floor, and the two of us would negotiate the bar stools en route to my car. As we drove off she might touch my leg, a gesture that would awaken my other mystical force.

Each one of these encounters headed a week of intense dating—a singing-in-the-rain, euphoric week with culinary discoveries, tasty wines and talk of possible life plans. There was lovemaking, too, not unlike clumsy sex.

But trouble would brew when, in the second week of dating, a shadow would be cast over my fairytale. As if my sparkle-power gauge read empty, my soul's twin flame would go out. I'd often sense the very instant my date morphed from an angel back to a blond with a disproportionate nose and nasal voice. Then her hand on my leg would fail to arouse my forces because I couldn't stop staring at the sparkles in her airbrushed nails.

I went through strings of Beowulf maidens, my supposed soul mates. Roberta, for example. I first saw Roberta, a stately, well tanned woman, sitting on a bar stool. One inebriated glance and my intuitive knowledge assured me my lifelong search was over. This was the woman. Minutes later we left the bar.

After love making, as we shared a cigarette, I imagined our life together. *I preferred modern, but our home could be a traditional if Roberta wanted.* I mused.

I whistled through the following work week, eager to begin the romantic Vermont weekend I planned. We drove north on I-95, but twenty miles past New Haven I knew that something was amiss. When Roberta placed her hand on my leg, a cruel reality attached. Roberta smiled. I smiled and then did a double-take. Did she always have a lip ring? And where did that pockmark on her cheek come from? My focus sharpened. This was all wrong. She might as well have been an inflatable doll.

In my loneliness, I used these women, like blank canvases without a clue who they really were. My brief relationships were magical thinking, driven by how badly I wanted to love a woman and to feel loved by one. But I wasn't having real relationships, and if I really wanted something more adult, it was time to abandon my fantasies.

There was something else I needed to do, too. I'd been aware for some time that my therapy with Dr. Bowman had bogged down and was becoming my other rut. I owed Dr. Bowman a tremendous debt, but these days I was too successful resisting him. If I was going to make it through my resistance, I had to make a change.

TWENTY-NINE

Body Block

FROM OUTWARD APPEARANCES, I was doing fine in Washington. I dated attractive women, my job paid well, and my name was known in Washington's small marketing community.

But appearances could be misleading. In the privacy of my office with the door securely locked, I gasped for breath while vise attacks in manic mode twisted my intestines. Or, in their slow motion phase, my consciousness had a liquid quality and my heavy eyes saw as if through a sheet of film that gave everything the flatness of mezzotint. Yet when an attack passed, I would straighten my tie and nonchalantly emerge from my office, shoulders cocky, with no hint of the hell that occurred behind the closed door.

Only my therapist knew of these episodes. My office associates didn't, and I hid them from my clients. In eight years of marriage, I'd never told Susan. Secrecy was a childhood habit. I'd learned to concentrate with all my might to hide a vise attack lest I be sent again for "help," or worse, sent away from home. That habit became an automatic response, so that now the curtain fell involuntarily at the onset of an attack. My smiled locked into place, and my glib jokes provided further camouflage. Collectively they masked the painful hypersensitivity that accompanied the imaginary vise tightening in my head.

It was also no accident that I chose to work sixty- and seventy-hour weeks at the agency. My workaholic routine provided a welcome distraction from the sadness that was falling. Rigid work schedules kept my thoughts on track from point A to B, eliminating the leisure time that let them pinball randomly on a C-to-Z path of unrestricted emotions. But that also meant I was vulnerable when I left work. Leisure time was risky business. It was painful, so I skipped vacations. But I couldn't avoid Sundays. On Sundays the floodgates opened.

I'd found Dr. Bowman in the nick of time when I moved to Washington. With his help I managed my swings from mania to depression well enough to function in the high-pressure world of advertising. His considerable warmth made it safe to continue the unwrapping process I'd started with Dr. Hinkly, and I looked more deeply into the threatening reality of my chaotic, septic family environment. Something as simple as knowing that there were reasons for my mood swings brought relief to my painful jaw.

In one session Dr. Bowman asked me to describe a typical meal with my family when I was a child. It was a clever question, since dinnertime memories have an uncanny ability to show the dynamics between children and parents. Even fully-grown adults see their childhood patterns reemerge when they return home for holiday dinners. Siblings find themselves jockeying for position and embarrassing parental behaviors, almost forgotten, go on display again. Dinnertime is a time capsule preserved for the family—or for a keen analyst.

"My family didn't converse in the normal way at the table," I explained to Dr. Bowman.

The day Richard Nixon made his famous Checkers speech, it went unmentioned at our table. When Dave Garroway and the *Today Show* premiered, and *High Noon* and *Rebel Without a Cause* opened at the local movies, those entertainments would not have been discussed. Instead the five of us, parents and children alike, sat with fists clenched below the table, ready for whatever came at us, and what was coming wasn't polite conversation.

"I don't care how full you are, you eat every last bite, and I'll wait until you do," Mom would say, forcing a loaded spoon through my sister Jill's clenched teeth. Jill would cry hysterically, spurring mother to reload the spoon.

"Poor, poor baby. How you suffer," Mom would say sarcastically.

"Shut up, you idiot," Dad would bark at my brother Randy, raising a threatening hand, but with perfect timing Josefina would place a bread plate between them, giving Dad just enough time to think better of it. Under the table Randy banged his knees like windshield wipers.

"Jerk," Dad would scream at another infraction. The pace of Randy's knee-banging would increase.

"You're not going to the dance because I say you're not," Mom would tell me.

"But why? Just give me a reason," I'd plead.

"I don't have to give you a reason. It's enough that I say no."

"Then I'm going," I'd say defiantly.

That would be Josefina's clue to place the meat platter in front of Mom, interrupting to ask how many pieces she wished. If Josefina succeeded, everyone would quiet down and go back to his or her plate. We'd eat deliberately, picking at our food as if half the morsel were nourishing, the other half toxic and ours was the impossible task of sorting the two out.

Thanks to Dr. Bowman, I saw my parents more realistically, but my understanding was only conceptual. Emotionally, I was still stuck. I could describe Mom and Dad more realistically, but the feelings in my gut remained sequestered. If I wanted more relief, I had to get past the conceptual—past mere labels on behaviors—and reach the feelings. Dr. Bowman urged me to do this continually. Each week we stood together at the edge of that cliff. He was willing to go hand-in-hand, but I refused to jump. Instead, I dodged his questions and responded with platitudes that deflected his probing. I might answer his question with another question, pleased to escape but disappointed that I had.

"So, how did you feel when your Dad called your brother an idiot?" Dr. Bowman would ask.

"What kind of father calls his son an idiot?" I would say.

"And it made you feel what?"

"How could he use words like *idiot* and *dummy*?"

"But I ask you again, Michael, when he used those words, how did it make you feel?"

"It can't be very good parenting, can it be?"

I knew perfectly well where Dr. Bowman wanted me to go, but I wasn't going there. This went on for months until I felt like I was on a hamster's exercise wheel. At that point I knew I had to move on. It wasn't Dr. Bowman's fault, but I sensed it would take someone else to jump-start the process. What kind of therapist should I look for, and what modality could get me moving again?

I turned to Peggy Martin for help answering those questions. I'd had a few dates with Peggy shortly after my divorce, but she quickly demoted me to "just friends" status. I wasn't surprised. It was obvious even to me that Peggy was light years ahead on the holistic path I'd recently began to explore. Peggy earned her living as a reflexologist, providing an alternative system of healing through foot massage. She was a true believer in alternative medicines, while I was "just looking."

Peggy had a broad knowledge of psychological therapies, and I sought her advice, confessing how I sabotaged my sessions with Dr. Bowman despite my best intentions. Peggy told me to see a Bioenergetic analyst.

"Bioenergetics is perfect for a high-verbal guy like you," she said. "The process circumvents words and uses bodywork—physical positions—to reach your feelings."

"But analyzing words is how I process," I said. "I don't see how some kind of body workout can replace that."

"Well, it can," she said confidently, "and frankly Michael, from what you tell me, you're intellect isn't getting you very far."

"But bodywork?" I said.

"Where do you think we hold feelings, Michael?" Asked Peggy.

"You think feelings reside in your head. But the body holds them even more powerfully. The very language we use tells us to listen to our bodies. People don't die of a broken intellect. They die of a broken heart. People don't tell you to get off their thoughts. They tell you to get off their back!"

"What about trauma?" I asked. "Isn't trauma exclusively psychological? It's a mental reaction. How could an exercise deal with trauma?"

"Your body's muscles retain trauma too," Peggy explained, "They hold onto shock. They tighten around it, just as your mind represses trauma. When memories get locked in the musculature, they block the flow of energy through the body, and when energy doesn't flow freely it plays havoc with your state of mind. That's when you feel ungrounded, out of it, sluggish or speedy—like the 'vise attacks' you describe. People flip from depression to mania when their energy is too blocked to maintain a proper balance."

"But all the therapy I've had has been talk therapy."

"And yet here you are, stuck, because all you do is talk. You can't bullshit the body, Michael," she said. "Get into your body and get some feelings out. Afterward you're free to analyze 'til the cows come home."

Peggy's suggestion seemed too radical, and the process was too new to have been scientifically documented. I might have tossed it off as New Age hocus-pocus, but what stopped me was an incident I recalled. As part of my growing interest in holistic healing, I'd tried a series of deep massages based on a technique called Rolfing. The masseur pressed his elbows into my back, throwing his body weight over his elbows so they really dug in. It hurt, but with the pain came a memory.

I was around twelve. As Dad was leaving for work, he rolled down his car window.

"Sweep the garage today, Michael" he said.

I forgot to do it, and when Dad got home and found the garage upswept, he was angry. I mouthed off to him as I always did when I was really scared, so he pulled me up the stairs to my bedroom. I knew the routine. I had to drop my trousers and lay over the bed while Dad went to work with the hairbrush. But the wood hairbrush snapped in half over my rear, and he had to go for another one. I mocked him and said the broken hairbrush meant that I'd won.

That memory floated into consciousness the very moment the masseur dug his elbows into my back. Was Peggy on to something? Maybe it was worth a try.

Peggy told me to go to the Bioenergetic Institute of Washington D.C. I choose to visit on a group night that was open to the public. The institute was hardly an "institute" at all but rather a small loft, a carpeted, otherwise empty room. Several therapists moved from person to person to help people get into the various Bioenergetic stress positions much the way a yoga instructor helps position students. After a few positions, they paired us up and handed each of us a foam-covered battle bat they called a bataka.

"Tonight let's explore our anger," said the leader.

My partner had some experience with Bioenergetics, so he was instructed to work with me, to goad me by playing the role of a sarcastic parent. He mocked me and aggressively hit my legs with the cushioned bataka. I would not give him the satisfaction of reacting, and I stood rigidly with my arms folded, ignoring his abuse. Finally my more experienced partner, frustrated with my passivity, dropped his bataka and sprang in my face.

"You are an asshole," he screamed.

When even that didn't faze me, he shoved me forcefully in the chest. He threw me off balance and kept pushing me back, though he never actually hurt me. Being knocked off balance was just what I needed. The loft and the people in the room disappeared in a white flash of anger. I saw only my partner's neck, and I wanted to choke it until his eyes bulged, until the son-of-a-bitch dropped lifeless to the floor. I flew at him in a rage and shoved him the width of the loft until I had him pinned against the opposite wall, one arm pushing on his chest while my forearm choked his neck.

"Good. Keep going," he managed to say.

That was not the response I'd expected, but I needed no encouragement to continue. I raged at him while pounding his legs with the bataka. I hit him again and again until I had to stop to catch my breath. I bent over, gasping, with my hands on my knees. It took some time for my trembling lips to stop quivering. When I regained some sense of self control, I was stone struck. What had I exposed? What kind of monster was I? I was a raging killer, and now all those people knew it. I grabbed my coat and hurried from the loft, too humiliated to return again.

I wanted to run from what I'd seen in myself that night—the horror I'd exposed to a whole room of staring people. Maybe that explained why I was about to move out of town. Or maybe it was simply because of what happened at work.

THIRTY

Big Apple

IT WAS NEVER MY DESIRE TO LEAVE WASHINGTON, but I lost my marketing job soon after that night at the loft. The Yom Kipper war of 1976 had ended and OPEC got even for our support of Israel by cutting the allotment of oil they supplied to America. Now I faced gas lines and station attendants had no choice but to ration what gas they had. Motorists had to shut off their engines and wait in line for hours in Washington's notorious summer humidity without the benefit of air conditioning.

The Washington Post's Help Wanted section—a daily fixture now at my kitchen table—was half its usual size because the lack of oil forced America's petroleum-dependent economy into recession. The banks pulled their home loan money, and the developer I worked for had no choice but to hang the yellowing CLOSED FOR BUSINESS sign in our building's marble lobby. I hated saying goodbye to Jim McMullin, my best boss ever. But he was out of work too.

It wasn't long before a single unemployment check was all I had left, though I would never tell anyone. So I took the first job that came along and joined a small advertising agency. I made half my former salary and instead of meeting daily with top architects and interior designers, I finalized ad schedules for car dealers. Still it was a job in hard times and I should have been thankful, though I wasn't.

Shortly after I took the job, the phone rang. I recognized the voice of a former advertising client and the longer we spoke, the more I felt my sense of importance returning. He had my full attention, especially when he gave the reason for his call. He'd learned of an opening for a really top job. I got increasingly excited—until he mentioned where the job was located.

"Michael," he said, "a chain of luxury resort hotels is conducting a search for a director of marketing, and you've got all the credentials they're looking for. They're headquartered in Manhattan."

"It's really nice that you thought of me," I said, "but Manhattan just isn't for me. It's too big and too far from my daughter. But I really appreciate your thoughtfulness."

"Just meet with them once," he urged. "Promise me you'll go for one meeting."

Hesitantly, I said I would.

I sat in the waiting room of Princess Hotels International's headquarters, thumbing a magazine and repeatedly checking my watch. I'd been kept waiting over an hour. I was plotting my escape when a well groomed woman wearing a tailored suit and a fashionable neck scarf approached. She shook my hand and led me down the hall to the vice president's office where she held my chair. I waited politely, watching the vice president work at his ornate mahogany desk. Mr. Jerry Ross didn't look up from his papers but continued writing. Minutes passed, and he was still making notes. I was angry.

Finally he looked up.

"What's your story, mate?" he asked flippantly.

"What's your problem, mate?" I shot back, annoyed.

I didn't care that my aggressive response would shorten the interview. I wanted to get the hell out of there and go home.

But the vice president loved that I took him on, and fifteen dreamlike minutes later, in a daze, I let Jerry—he said to call him Jerry—lead me from his office. He guided me through the corridors, introducing me to his associates as the new director of marketing. There would be no follow-up interviews, no meetings with human resources, no résumé checks, nothing. Just the job offer for a position I had no intention of taking in a city I hadn't planned to move to. I don't know what prompted me to accept his offer, but I said "yes" almost involuntarily after Jerry agreed to the last of my conditions. This one was non-negotiable: that no matter what business crisis arose, alternate weekends were sacrosanct so I could visit my daughter Lauren in D.C.

Driving back to D.C. after the interview, I fantasized about how Susan would react to my news. Our separation had lasted three months now and recently she'd turned me down when I proposed reconciling. But surely she wasn't serious. She couldn't want our separation to be final and the thought that I'd leave Washington would overwhelm her. She'd confess she really did love me and urge me to move back in, and the three of us would be a family again. That's precisely how it would go.

I called Susan with my news.

"Drop me a note with your New York address," she said.

I felt I'd made a mistake as soon I gave my two weeks' notice to the ad agency. An obsessive debate began. Did I have what it took to handle the more corporate environment? I didn't take direction gracefully from authorities and my lack of subtlety in an argument frequently got me in trouble. I wasn't good at office politics or fast on my feet, so what the hell was I thinking?

On the other hand, it was a really good job offer.

I torturously turned over the pros and cons like a pig on a spit.

It occurred to me that Dr. Bowman could help me, so I phoned him, luckily catching him between clients."

"One minute New York feels right to me," I said. "But the next it feels totally wrong. Moving would be a huge mistake wouldn't it? Would it? What should I do?"

"Michael," he began patiently, "how many times have we gone over this? So you tell me what's going on. I know you know the answer. You know exactly what you're doing."

"Well . . ." I said, clueless.

"Describe for me how your mom and dad handle decisions," instructed Dr. Bowman.

"Could you refresh my memory?" I said weakly.

"Remember what we said about choices? It was you who came up with the reason why they obsess over the simplest choices—why every decision creates debilitating debate? Can you recall your insight?"

"Because they're unsure of themselves?" I offered, choosing the obvious but aware I'd forgotten our important discovery.

"Because creating chaos is fundamental to your parents' dynamic," Dr. Bowman reminded emphatically. "Creating turmoil is the only way they know to vent their anxiety, so they dump it on everybody around them—especially on you and your siblings. And what did we learn about your mother? What does she do if forced to make a difficult choice? She shifts the focus to your father's doubts and second-guesses every decision he makes. Manipulating him makes her feel powerful. We've been all through this, right? So let me ask you, Michael, why do you feel compelled to repeat their pattern?"

"But what if I make the wrong choice?" I said, missing the point and still venting.

There was a brief pause at the other end as I heard Dr. Bowman sigh.

"Just remember what we said about decisions, Michael: that very few choices are matters of life and death. This one is not one of them. It's reversible. If you don't like New York, you can move back to Washington."

"True," I said flatly. "I guess I should try it."

A week later, with lamps and luggage crowding me in the front seat, I drove from D.C. heading north up I-95 for New York. By the time I neared New Brunswick, I was sure I'd made a terrible mistake. I still had thirty-six miles to go and already Manhattan willed my windshield. The clouds on top of staggered skyscrapers looked like fingers holding chess pieces—about to make the wrong move. And why again I was moving to the Big Apple?

I stopped the car at the New Brunswick tollbooth.

"Can I make a U-turn and return to Washington?" I asked the toll attendant.

The attendant motioned me through a break in the orange cones. Southbound now, I felt relieved until I started obsessing again.

My D.C. job is boring and what fool passes up a prestigious job in Manhattan? They don't come along every day you know.

At the next tollbooth, I made another U-turn and headed north again. Yes. Yes, this felt better. I could handle Manhattan. I was good at what I did. But when the city loomed in my windshield once more, all the doubts I'd corralled broke loose.

The Big Apple attracts the best. But suppose the most talented people are also the most ruthless? There's got to be a reason they make all those movies about small town dreamers who try Manhattan but wind up defeated and on a Greyhound headed back home.

I U-turned a third time, but as I turned the wheel I saw my eyes in the mirror. They confirmed there was nobody home.

Driving during a panic attack is probably not good, I thought, so I pulled off at the next rest area and sat obsessing, engaged in my own civil war, the north-bound against the south-bound, until my mind wasn't processing anything clearly.

It occurred to me that my Uncle Jacques lived in Manhattan and his advice was always sound. He would tell me what to do. So I called him and Jacques was mercifully patient while I stumbled through a confession of why I was staring at the no parking sign at an I-95 rest stop. Jacques's assessment was unclouded.

"What an asshole you are," he laughed. "Get back on the turnpike heading north. Take the Mid-Town-Tunnel and come up the Upper West Side. I'll cancel your hotel room 'cause you're staying with me tonight, and you'll start the new job in the morning."

Finding a parking space on the upper West Side was challenging but I circled Jacques' block repeatedly until I did. Jacques was waiting on the steps of his apartment building.

"Come on schmuck," he said warmly giving me a bear hug, "I'm buying you dinner."

turning calendar pages in search of a blank date. "How about the night of July 24?"

"Sure," I'd say. I could wait six weeks.

I met Elaine at a political rally for Jimmy Carter. She was a 1960s-style intellectual who wore no makeup and no bra. She wore a white, wrinkled, men's dress shirt, jeans and wire-rim glasses positioned on top of her forehead. We dated for a few months. One Saturday we drove north of Manhattan to Cold Springs, New York. I found a state park along the Hudson and pulled in. The afternoon was warm, and Elaine and I had a picnic. Elaine said she'd brought a surprise for dessert and opened her hand to reveal two transparent squares, like Scotch tape but with brown dots in the center.

"Acid," she said. "Just set it under your tongue."

I wasn't sure I wanted to try acid, but Elaine took her dot, so I slipped mine in my mouth as instructed. I couldn't taste the dot, but I felt it dissolve.

When I saw the bones of my hands, I knew acid was no ordinary high. A twig transformed into a snake, and everywhere I looked the forest was morphing. The tree branches silhouetted black against the afternoon sun moved up and down in the wind like pumping oil rig arms.

The park's brilliant hues pierced my eyes. I was a child freshly experiencing colors. The ground moss was a most brilliant green. I watched a clear drop of dew that hung from a leaf and in a flash of intuition I felt certain the leaf, like the moss, like the tree, like everything in the forest, was inseparable; part of a bigger, fluid whole. Separateness became an illusion. I was no longer *in* the forest. I *was* the forest. I *was* the twig. I *was* the moss.

In the silence of the wooded park, two deer stood in the distance. They paused from eating, and two heads rose and turned to watch me as I stared in awe of them. These graceful creatures with gentle, sensitive eyes were not afraid of me, and I felt protected by them. As they returned to chew on ferns, it struck me how out of place I felt in the forest. I wore clothes. The deer wore no clothes. They needed no disguise.

I headed back.

Elaine was waiting in the car. The moment I sat next to her, a whirlwind of energy tore through me—more energy than my body could handle. I felt a huge pressure in my chest and a surging through my veins, so I got out and asked Elaine to walk with me up and down the parking lot.

Should she drive me to a hospital? I wondered. *But the nurses? Won't they have to report me?* I pictured clipboard-carrying nurses on the phone with the police. I had to wait it out.

The trips around the parking lot helped. Energy still roared through my veins but I felt the worst was over and I wasn't so afraid they would rip me apart. I told Elaine perhaps I could stay seated now, so we returned to the car, where I dealt with alternating chills and hot flashes by blasting the heater and then the air conditioner. But the hallucinations continued relentlessly.

I became aware there was a third presence. It filled the car like a wet fog, saturated with disapproval, damp with malevolence. The fog enveloped me, penetrating like cold to the bone. It lingered, and then the damp presence crept forward, finally tracing the outline of a single pulsating magenta eye in the fog on my windshield. The eye scrutinized me, its glare stinging like razor cuts, until, as if some trial had concluded, it seemed to rest its case. It had hunted my cells for a kindred maliciousness and, finding merely weakness, dropped a corrosive net of disapproval over me. I was trapped, bound to it, perilously close to submitting to its judgment—a loathing only too familiar. I recognized the familial poison my poor cousins had imbibed, an overdose that disabled them for the remainder of their brief lives. I'd been able to spit much of it back out.

As if to increase its power over me, the eye on my windshield split like an amoeba. Two eyes became four, then eight until my entire windshield filled with rabid eyes. Their collective draw would surely have overwhelmed me were it not for a bolt of insight that let me to wriggle free.

The eyes are my own self-hatred. This is paranoia, I thought. *They're only mirroring what I think of myself, amplifying a hundred fold my own self-loathing. The hateful judgments that were tearing me apart—were coming from within.*

I got out of the car, hoping the fresh air would help. Elaine and I walked to the shore of the Hudson and wrapped ourselves in a blanket to spend the night.

Flashes of light appeared at the entrance to the park. A car entered, and as it pulled alongside our vehicle, I made out the white and black two-tone of a squad car. Clearly they saw us, because they flashed their high beams to have a better look. Elaine and I pretended to be asleep in our blanket. If the police came and asked us to move on, I'd surely go to jail. I was too far gone to fake it.

"Please, god," I prayed, "please make them go away."

I could feel the cops debating.

"Please," I prayed harder.

The engine started, and the patrol car slowly left the park.

Elaine and I rested until sunrise, when we drove back to Manhattan. Once again, the signs were clear. I had to face my loathing and root it out.

THIRTY-ONE

The Rack

The eyes in the windshield projected my own darkness, an anger turned inward that I'd only allowed myself to externalize once before, the night I erupted at the Washington Bioenergetic Institute. Then I was horrified to see how much rage I carried, and now those hate-filled eyes had reminded me again.

Where is all that anger coming from? I wondered. *It feels like the pit is bottomless. What kind of monster am I? Suppose someone gets close to me? What happens when they discover all my rage? Could my fear of discovery be the reason I hold back from women? Is that why I avoid the real thing and create fantasies—my Beowolf maidens? When will I be ready for real intimacy?*

I thought of Peggy's advice and how dead on she'd been. The Bioenergetic exercises put me in touch with my feelings, alright, but I hadn't expected such ferocity. What should I do with it? Should I work with a Bioenergetic therapist? The prospect of revealing my anger even to a therapist made me shudder.

Research led me to Manhattan's own Bioenergetics Institute, where the receptionist offered an appointment with Dr. Sarah Uretsky. Dr. Uretsky, she advised, had studied under the founder of Bioenergetic therapy, Dr. Alexander Lowen, who was in turn a student of Wilhelm Reich.

At the appointed hour, Dr. Uretsky ushered me into her office on Manhattan's 39th Street. The large loft space was carpeted, sparse and nearly empty. In the far corner below the lone window was a small, rolltop desk, two wooden chairs, a barrel-shaped wooden roller upholstered with cloth, a floor-to-ceiling mirror, a mattress and an umbrella stand that held warped tennis rackets and several well worn batakas.

Dr. Sarah Uretsky had a prominent nose and graying, neck-length hair. She was a large boned woman, but trim, and she moved gracefully. I guessed that she was in her mid-forties and Jewish. In fact she was in her sixties, Christian and a former dancer who had left Broadway to earn a PhD in Bioenergetics.

All business, she skipped pleasantries and directed me to a stiff wooden chair. I began with my standard first-session monologue, giving my family history and describing my previous therapies. Eager to show my sophistication, I referred to myself in the third person as if I were a doctor describing his patient.

Dr. Uretsky abruptly interrupted me.

"Take your clothes off," she said.

"My clothes?" I said surprised. "What? All of them?"

"You can leave your underwear on," she said.

"Why do you want me to take my clothes off?" I asked.

"So I can see your body. I want to see where you hold. How you breathe. Let's go!" She clapped her hands impatiently.

I did as she said and stood up. She circled me, studying, her hand on her chin. At one point she stopped and squeezed my jaw clinically, like a vet doing a pre-purchase inspection of a horse.

"A lot of holding," she said shaking her head. "Not much breathing here," her fingers ran across my abdomen. "It will be enough for today to get you breathing."

Sarah pointed me to the wooden roller upholstered in cloth.

"Lie with your back here," she tapped the top of the roller, "and stretch your arms and legs out horizontally . . . That's it . . . Yes, as far as you can."

I eased my back onto the roller, lying face parallel to the ceiling. Quickly the position started to hurt.

I didn't know they used the torture rack anymore, I thought.

I clenched my teeth, which brought Dr. Uretsky to my side. She shoved her thumbs into my jaw hinges until my mouth dropped open. Now the position hurt immensely, and I tried to get up.

"Stay with it," she urged.

I lowered myself back onto the roller again, but a minute later my pain turned to anger. I'd had quite enough of this sadistic nonsense.

I sprang off the roller, unaware that my fists were clenched, and glared at her, screaming, "This is fucking bullshit."

The force of it startled me, but I hoped I had intimated her.

"Good," she said, pleased, "Very good, Michael."

She handed me an old tennis racket.

"Come now," she said beckoning, me to the mattress. "I want you to do as I do."

She faced the bed, holding the tennis racket over her head, then swung in a downward arc until the racket head whacked the mattress. She lifted the racket up and then powerfully beat the mattress again, up and down, over and over.

"Now you," she handed me the racket.

Sarah stretched my arms back behind my head, gently pulling until they could go no further.

"Stretch as far back as you can before you swing." She pulled my arms a final time. "Keep your knees bent." She gently pushed on the backs of my knees to deepen the bend. "Good. Now swing the racket forward," she said, pushing as if to prime a pump.

I hit tentatively at first. But soon my body warmed and my anger kicked in as I swung harder and faster. Then the exercise ran on its own steam, and hate burned through my eyes. I forgot about Dr. Sarah Uretsky, I let go of all propriety, and I raged in a trance. I was conscious of nothing but the racket and the mattress, lifting and smashing, wanting to kill, again and again.

"Don't close your eyes," Sarah directed, "and let your voice out."

"Get your fucking hands off me, you bastard," I screamed, having no idea where that phrase came from or what it related to. I tapped into a furnace of fury, and I felt that I could scream forever. Several minutes later I was still hitting the bed powerfully when Sarah signaled me to hold up. I let the racket drop and stood silently, awed by the intensity of my fury. I felt my anger deepening into tears—but I quickly suppressed them

Sarah looked at me compassionately and gave me a moment. Then with one hand on my back, she gently but solidly pushed on my chest with the other, repeatedly reapplying the compression in a CPR-style movement. She paused to study my breathing, then began again.

"Good," she said pausing a moment later. "Now bend forward and touch the floor. No. No. Don't lock your knees, keep them bent."

She gently pummeled my back with her fists and then pummeled up and down my legs. Her drumming warmed my back as my legs tingled.

"How do you feel?" Sarah asked.

"Kind of weird." I paused to take better measure. "Actually I feel good."

"Your face is much more real," Sarah said.

I looked in the mirror. My locked grin was gone. My face was open, vulnerable, and my complexion had a hint of yellow, the way people look after they cry.

THIRTY-TWO

Divided We Fall

I'D NEVER HAD A VISE ATTACK IN THE MIDDLE OF THERAPY, but that's exactly what happened in my third session with Sarah. I was breezing on about something inconsequential when I began to feel agitated in my abdomen. That signaled a vise attack coming in the manic cycle, and, as if a clutch popped, my mind lurched into a higher gear. Out of habit, I prepared to divert Sarah's attention.

"So, Sarah," I said, "I see you still haven't mastered your answering machine," pointing to the red light blinking with waiting messages.

I changed my mind. I was no longer a child, and Sarah was not a parent or one of my school teachers who could send me away to St. Louis. I'd come to trust her.

"Sarah," I said with some urgency, "the attacks I told you about—the clamping vise—I'm having one now. My mind is speeding, and in a few minutes it's going to . . ."

"Stand up," Sarah interrupted.

I was relieved that she took charge.

"Touch the floor," she said, her fingers directing my back to bend over. "We need to ground you and get the energy out of your head. No, no. Don't lock your knees. Keep them bent."

Her fingers pushed my knees into a deeper bend. I strained to touch the floor while Sarah pummeled her fists up and down my legs and my spine.

"Hold that position," she said, seeing me start to tire.

The strain was intolerable and my legs trembled.

"Yes, that's it," said Sarah seeing my legs shake with energy.

My thighs felt on fire. All I could think about was how much I wanted to stand up, but I held the position.

When I did stand, my legs were hot and flowing with energy.

Sarah felt them. "Yes much better. How do you feel, Michael?"

The feeling of panic was gone. My scattered thoughts had regrouped. It was like seeing a film of a ball exploding and then running the film backward so the ball reassembles.

"What just happened?" I asked.

Sarah's reply was like something Peggy might have said. "Ideally, energy flows unobstructed through the body. But sometimes it gets blocked, and that causes imbalance. You feel out of sync. It happens during your vise attacks, Michael."

"Blocked by what?" I asked.

"By trauma, by memories. The body retains memories just as the mind does. Unreleased trauma forms blocks in the musculature that disrupt the flow of energy through the body. Just now your mind raced, and you felt overwhelmed. That happened because your legs, torso and neck were so tight, so blocked, the energy couldn't flow freely. It got trapped in your head, so to compensate your mind sped up, but it couldn't handle the load. The faster your thoughts raced, the more panicky you became. It's a vicious cycle, but you broke it by grounding yourself, which released the energy flow back to the legs."

What a strange new vocabulary this was. None of my previous therapists ever spoke of energy flow. Dr. VanDervort didn't. Dr. Bowman didn't. Half of me wanted to write it all off as nonsense, voodoo hocus-pocus. But it was hard to dismiss what just happened or the fact that for the first time, a vise attack had failed to run full course. Even more amazing, I felt calm and even peaceful. "Now I know what people are talking about when they say they feel 'centered,'" I told Sarah.

On the subway ride home, I thought about the frightening cycles of mania and depression that I'd suffered my entire life. With each attack I felt like I was going mad, and my family was riddled with relatives who had gone insane. If only I'd known about Sarah's grounding exercise. But as frightening as it was to feel that I was losing my mind, the consequences of failing to hide my vise attacks was worse. Failure meant I'd get sent away again.

So I honed my deception, and as the habit of deceiving others grew, I became Janus-faced. One face was that of a frightened child, surely losing his mind. I keep that face well hidden in the shadows. Others saw only my public face, the comedic mask, Mr. Master of Ceremonies.

The process confused me. The more time Mr. Master of Ceremonies spent on stage, the less I knew how I felt. I lived outside myself, peering in occasionally, curious to see if I felt anything. The split increased my isolation from others and from myself.

The habit of automatically sequestering my feelings solidified into a personality trait—a safe modus operandi. But that tactic failed me in the Bioenergetic positions. Glib comments lost their power to disguise when Sarah placed me on the roller or had me beat the mattress. Peggy was right—the Bioenergetic positions shattered my intellectual barrier; thus unblocked, my feelings gushed forth on their own. I felt sadness, fear, anger and frustration. My eyes were wide open, sometimes in a panic and sometimes exposing a fury so malignant that I sprang like a leopard from the roller to the mattress. On and on I raged with the tennis racket until, mercifully, my anger turned to sobs.

THIRTY-THREE

Mother Load

AFTER SIX MONTHS OF INDIVIDUAL THERAPY, Sarah invited me to her weekly group sessions. They started at 7:00 pm and often ran past midnight. We began the night with limbering-up exercises. Then each group member pantomimed his or her feelings through movement and sounds, but words were not allowed. A woman slithered across the loft hissing and moving her arms in a snakelike fashion. A man beat his chest gorilla-style, bellowing like Tarzan. A woman moved timidly across the floor with her arms crossed protectively over her breasts. Another man took steps, slumped over with a glue-like passivity, arms limp at his sides. Each mini-drama was a window to someone's state of mind.

Next we formed a circle and were invited to work on any issue we wanted. Some members were bursting to work. Others were emotionally flat, stuck and depressed, and they had to be prodded. Sarah showed us how to energize them by taunting them and shoving them around in the circle—whatever it took to get them going. We didn't taunt to hurt them; rather, it was a Bioenergetic technique to wake them out of their lethargy. That depression was the rage they had masochistically turned against themselves because it was safer. Now they could externalize it appropriately. Before long, even the most despondent among us would let loose on the partner that played a role intended to goad him—that of an offending mate, a disinterested parent or perhaps an insufferable boss.

Sarah orchestrated this work with uncanny instincts.

"Vince," she might whisper, "get in the center with Minerva and turn your back on her. No matter what she does, completely ignore her."

Vince ignored Minerva as if she didn't exist. Minerva, demanded to get his attention, tried to swing Vince around to face her. Vince held like stone with his back to her. Minerva tried every trick. She demanded. She pleaded. She came on to him. But Vince wouldn't respond. Infuriated, Minerva stormed to the mattress, took a tennis racket and let out screams that reflected years of accumulated disappointment.

There was time each group night for several of us to work, and while there was no formal agenda, themes arose spontaneously. Some nights we worked on our "victim," the all–too-human tendency to blame others for our own shortcomings. We worked on our fear of confrontation, our attempts to manipulate or to be passive-aggressive when we could be direct and more effective. Some members bravely brought up sexual issues—frigidity or impotence or their tendency to be infantile about their sexuality—and their work gave everyone permission to voice our own sexual uncertainties. We all had them.

Though only one person at a time stood in the center of the circle and worked on their issue, each of us could identify with their struggle. Though our personal stories varied, the underlying issues were universal. So it didn't matter who worked in the middle and who supported from the sidelines. The person in the center was working for all of us.

Our Bioenergetic tools of battle were dilapidated tennis rackets, old Jack Kramers or Pancho Gonzales's that had long ago lost strings and shape. By pounding the mattress with them, unexpected memories and powerful recollections arose that had lain dormant for years. Some women recalled molestation and stood stunned as pictures flooded in of the parent or relative who violated them. As children they were powerless, since no child could stand up to a depraved adult relative. But now as adults surrounded by supportive group members, they could tap into their rage and get it out. They'd grab a tennis racket, imagine their attacker's face on the mattress and furiously hit away, fighting back at last. They could recapture the strength the child had been forced to surrender.

Sexual abuse was more common than I imagined. I saw it so often in group that I could often recognize victims before they themselves knew. Women who were molested as children walked with an awkward, almost hesitant gait. Their faces looked like two separate faces that had merged; one was age-appropriate, but the second face, superimposed on the first, bore the expression of a child in shock. Beneath the child's startled eyes I saw a pool of panic, and beneath that a molten fury.

"How could you destroy your own flesh and blood?" I asked Sarah one session, "just to satisfy a sexual urge like an animal? Don't relatives care how totally it incapacitates a child?"

"What about you?" asked Sarah.

"What do you mean, what about me?" I replied surprised.

"You haven't talked much about your Mom's flirtatiousness," prodded Sarah. "She may not have molested you, but she surely was provocative."

"Maybe a little," I said.

I'd told Sarah about the sponge baths Mom gave me on sunny afternoons. She would lather me from head to toe, and when she reached my genitals, she would cradle my penis in her palm, raising it to wash underneath as the warm water tricked over it. I loved my baths, and Mom would laugh as she dried my penis softly with the towel, repeating the ritual with talcum powder.

"How about the way she teased you when you were older?" Sarah asked.

"It was confusing," I said. "Mom would tell Dad she loved him, but as soon as he left the room, she'd rest her head on my shoulder and whisper that Dad was a milquetoast. 'You Michael, you're my little man,' she would coo in my ear."

"It never went beyond teasing?" asked Sarah.

"You know, it was never about me. Even as a child I knew that on some level. I was her pawn, useful to hear her complaints that Dad didn't live up to her expectations."

"It confused you, though. It surely was provocative."

"Yeah," I admitted.

"What about your Dad? Were you able to talk to him about sex?"

"We had one awkward birds-and-bees talk. I didn't know which of us was more uncomfortable. He never told a dirty joke. Dad was way too much the moralist to joke about sex. He had to be a model of virtue for his son. You remember what he said about masturbation?" I asked.

"I don't," Sarah said.

"Dad visited me when I was at Lake Forest Academy. I masturbated a lot, but I felt guilty about it, so one day I tried to ask him if it was okay."

"You ever masturbate?" I had asked.

"I have," he said.

Silence.

"Well . . . Do you like it? Is it fun for you?" I asked.

"Son," Dad's voice acquired a familiar pomposity, "there are nobler things that a man can do with his time."

"God forbid he should enjoy it!" Sarah kidded.

"Well," I said, "in all fairness, there was a ton of morality to go around in the Bible Belt. They taught boys that sex and love were unrelated. You were only supposed to love a virgin. A girl who let you do anything before marriage was a slut. So there was plenty of guilt to go around for boys and for girls. It seems comical in light of what we accept today, but back then we took it seriously."

"So you were taught that sex is dirty?" asked Sarah.

"You bet," I said. "Why do you think boys called it the 'dirty deed'? It wasn't supposed to be pleasurable. One position was accepted—standard missionary—and the only moral reason to have sex was to procreate."

"Okay, Michael. Enough talking. Let's get to work." Sarah handed me a racket and pointed to the mattress.

I beat the mattress, tentatively at first but soon my pace quickened and I felt fire in my eyes.

"Get your hands off of me," I screamed at the mattress. There was that phrase again. It often came up when I worked, but I hadn't a clue why.

Sarah tried hypnosis to discover its origin but it didn't help. Then one night I had a dream. Or was it a memory? I don't know.

It was one of those dreams where you are asleep, but you are aware that you are dreaming. In the dream I was at our home in the woods in Montague, Michigan. The year must have been 1951. Montague was a village on the shores of White Lake with only a drug store, a grocery store and the old Park Movie Theatre. The surrounding area was forest.

Mom, Dad, Jill, Randy and I lived on a hundred secluded acres, and our nearest neighbors were a mile away. When Mom traveled, she left my brother, sister and me in the care of either a nanny or a handyman. Most of the staff was Cuban like Josefina, the people who returned with Mom from her frequent vacations in Havana. Typically the Cubans worked for us for a couple of years and then moved on. They were handsome, big boned men and women with creamy skin and bright white teeth. Our nannies wore heavily starched white uniforms that scratched when they hugged us.

In the dream, Mom had left me in the care of a new handyman, McDalio. He came to us about a year before Josefina, and he was related to one of my former nannies. At twenty-two, he was the youngest Cuban Mom had ever employed. Unlike the others, McDalio wasn't handsome, and he was skeleton-thin. His pants were grease-stained with an excess of belt looped around the buckle. He wore a flannel shirt, usually with the tail hanging out, in both winter and summer. His face had patches of wiry beard stubble, and his hair was always oily. But the two things I remember most about his appearance were his teeth and his voice. Some of McDalio's teeth were white, some were solid gold, and there was a gold frame around his big front tooth. He laughed without cause in a squeaky voice like Tiny Tim's. When he came near, I always shoved my fists down my pant pockets.

"I don't like him," my sister Jill whispered when she met him.

We raised a couple dozen chickens in Montague, and my favorite chore was to gather the eggs. I pulled open a wire fence to enter the wooden chicken coop. It didn't have electricity but enough light came through the planks to see shapes once my eyes adjusted to the dark. Our chickens roosted in straw nests on double-decker bleachers and every morning I gathered their white and tan eggs and carefully set them in my galvanized bucket. Sometimes a nest was empty except for the eggs, but other times I had to snatch the eggs from beneath a nesting chicken. Although I was afraid the hens would peck my eyes, they never did. Either they didn't mind me taking their eggs or they forgot why I came. Chickens aren't like dogs. Dogs get to know you, but you're always a stranger to a chicken, and when I entered the coop they'd cluck hysterically and flap and scatter. I'd sit with them a while. A few would ignore me. Others watched me with robotic head movements. In my dream the chickens had quieted and I was in my own private world. It was dark, safe and peaceful in the coop.

The creak of the coop door jarred my thoughts as it opened in a three-phase movement. I was the only one who ever went in the coop, so this was odd. A chicken rose, clucked, flapped, and scattered as a head appeared silhouetted in plank light. My breath stopped. It was McDalio. Why was he in my coop? Did he bring a message from Mom? But why didn't he just yell it in?

McDalio's gold teeth materialized in the dim light when he sat down on the bench. I pushed my fists into my pocket. His breath spilled over me, rancid from garlic and beer. I arose to leave but McDalio yanked me back on the bench. I thought about yelling, but who would hear me? Mom, Jill and Randy were gone and there were no neighbors within shouting distance. McDalio, still grinning, unbuttoned my jeans and yanked at my zipper until my pants fell down.

"Get your hands off me, McDalio," I demanded, pulling them back up.

But when McDalio's grin turned into a menacing glare, I let go of my pants. The look on his face terrified me. Why was it familiar? His scratchy, grease-smelly hand covered my mouth. The other hand touched me below, and his rough fingers began to circle round and round. I eyed the door but saw McDalio's eyes grow mean again. I'd seen that look, and I froze. McDalio's hand stopped circling, and his head dropped below the bench. His beard stubble scratched my thighs, and then his wet mouth was on me. I gagged. He looked up with dripping teeth.

I knew instantly where to hide and retreated to a familiar safe room deep inside. In my safe room I had power to generate fantasies and the force to alter this scene. I created a long handgun with six loaded chambers. McDalio didn't know the gun was in my hand. I cocked the hammer and the click broke the silence of the coop. I lowered the barrel into McDalio's greasy scalp. He looked puzzled as his surprise turned to fear. My finger squeezed and the barrel flashed, blowing the side of McDalio's scalp away like the melted side of a candle.

But the sting of his tongue returned to snatch away my imaginary victory. I waited, watching scattered chicken feathers on the bench, filling my nostrils with the scent of dry straw. McDalio finished and rose. Through the dark his finger came at me, warning me. Floor planks squeaked to signal his exit as he dissolved into the darkness. A chicken clucked and fell silent. I didn't move and stayed shielded by the dark except for thin lines of sunlight that intruded through the slats.

There was nothing I could do. There was no one to tell, and no way to get McDalio punished. Dad was away a business trip. Mom would never believe me. Instead, she would warn me about my overactive imagination and assure me that McDalio wouldn't do such a thing.

I passed through the coop door into the blinding sunlight, checking to the right and left before I carefully made my way back to my room.

Sarah listened to the story of my dream.

"This was a dream? Or it was real?" She asked.

"I honestly don't know," I said. "The memory feels real, and it would explain why the phrase, 'Get your hands off me' keeps coming up when I hit with the tennis racket."

"It would," said Sarah thoughtfully. "But how did you feel afterward with this guy around the house?"

"I can't remember. I have a sense that I steered clear of him and that he didn't stay with us long. I recall feeling really alone with what happened—like shouting at a crowd but no one hears you. I knew in my gut that if I said something, I wouldn't be believed. That was the worst of it really. For sure, Mom would tell me to stop making things up. My sister Jill would believe me, and we confided a lot, but I wouldn't have said anything about something like this. She was just a kid—three years my junior—so it was best to let go of the whole thing.

"Was there another incident? Was McDalio with your family long?" Sarah asked.

"Not that I know of. I don't know for sure this one was real. I do know he wasn't with us long," I said. "I confirmed that because I called Mom after I had the dream, not to say anything but to ask if she remembered McDalio."

"Vaguely," she said. "He didn't last very long. I remember he didn't work out and Dad had to fire him."

"Can you recall what he did to get fired?" I asked.

"I think Dad found out that he had a girl over to the house and he lied when Dad confronted him about it."

"Do you know who the girl was?" I asked.

"No. Wait a minute, maybe it wasn't a girl," she said. "I think it was another man."

THIRTY-FOUR

The Grin

After my dream of the chicken coop, other painful recollections came knocking at my consciousness. I ignored them by keeping in motion, perusing an uninterrupted chain of activities. Jogging around the Central Park reservoir kept my mind focused on my running. Wandering the aisles of electronics stores and visiting car dealer showrooms were frequent distractions. But work was the best distraction, and I'd been a workaholic for years. It wasn't something that I carefully planned as a tactic of avoidance. Planning implies a level of consciousness not yet characteristic of my choices, but it was a routine that worked and I was a creature of routine. I preferred to stay at my computer long after my office building's corridors had emptied. I worked until the early hours, often walking home when the only sign of life on Manhattan streets was a speeding gypsy cab or a traffic signal's sequence from green to yellow to red.

At our next session, Sarah urged me to take a very different course of action.

"As a little boy, you instinctively sensed the limits of what you could handle and repressed what you couldn't. But you're stronger now. You're capable of taking in painful recollections without fearing they will overwhelm you." Sarah looked softly into my eyes.

"Now I want you to go for it," she rose from her chair and took my hand. "I don't want you to hide from a single memory, Michael."

"I will try," I promised.

Most therapists know what's going on within their patient's psyche—why a patient operates as he or she does. But the most effective therapists couple that knowledge with an instinctive sense of when their patient is ready to see what the therapist knows. They also know when the patient is not ready because if they aren't ready, the therapist's insight won't be heard. This sense of timing is an art. There are no formulas for it. Sarah correctly sensed that I was ready when she urged me to go deeper. She also knew that I was motivated, ready to reverse my lifelong pattern of repression.

My first efforts to examine recollections were painstakingly deliberate. When I sensed I was uncomfortable about some thought, but I wasn't quite sure what troubled me, I restrained the temptation to get in motion and ignore it. I forced myself to stop and go over what I'd been thinking, like a child taking a time-out.

What was I thinking that left me feeling anxious? What was I trying to avoid? Did someone upset me? What was difficult to accept?

Slowly I began to unravel layers of the onion, examining each memory until I felt I understood its unsettling components. Details filled in, turning hazy watercolor memories into sharp photographs.

I was surprised by how many painful moments were memories of adults who wanted to break me—authorities who relished crushing a young boy's spirit. Often I recalled a hurtful comment from a teacher whose position of authority lent credibility to his or her low opinion of me, an opinion I assumed must be correct since the professor was the authority.

I thought of my mean professors as *spirit killers,* and their cruelty bewildered me the way *phonies* astonished Holden Caulfield.

Why would a professor get pleasure from being unkind? I wondered.

I concluded that these professors had themselves been badly

treated as young men, and they responded vengefully, thinking it the job of each generation to pass their own affronts on to the next.

My linguistics teacher at Lake Forest Academy was a spirit killer. Professor Homer Demetrius would stand at the blackboard, turn and eye his prey, awaiting the perfect moment to pounce and claw the spirit out of a bright, young student. He would take every occasion, use any cheap trick, leap on any innocent slip of a student's tongue to dash a boy's pride and relish the humiliation.

Yet I imagine that as a young man Demetrius wasn't the cruel person he'd become. I pictured him in his own student days as a sensitive man who read voraciously and talked excitedly about the book he was reading. I imagined him hurrying over to a classmate to share a particularly wonderful paragraph. But by the time they made Demetrius a full professor, he had changed. Little by little his teachers broke him, and piece by piece he succumbed to the bureaucrats, the nitpickers and the pompous ones who approached life's complexity with total certitude about every issue. Because he lacked my stubborn will, Demetrius surrendered to his tormenters, and as he adapted their world view, his sweet nature soured. In class he became haughty, quick to bully the gentlest students. I hated how he picked on anemic students, and impulsively I challenged him anytime I saw an opening. Because I did, Professor Demetrius despised me, but I never buckled under his withering glare. On occasion I even drew first blood, as I did the day Professor Demetrius brutally mocked a fellow student who didn't have the answer to some obscure linguistics question. After Demetrius finished ridiculing the poor fellow, I raised my hand.

"Pardon me Professor Demetrius, but why would anyone need to know that? In fact, why need to know any linguistics since it's of no practical value? I haven't seen a single classified ad offering employment for a trained linguist, sir," I said sarcastically.

Professor Demetrius leered at me and responded quickly without measuring his words.

"Linguistics is one of the hoops I had to jump through to get my degree, Grossman," he sneered, "and now I get to make you jump."

"A high-minded teaching philosophy," I scoffed.

"Grossman, you are a loser, and you always will be," snarled Professor Demetrius.

His words stung but I had a comeback. "And how much weight should one place on the opinion of a linguist?"

Memories of more spirit killers returned—pictures of Dr. Cronick, Headmaster Finius Monahan and others. Their faces formed in rows in my mind as if they were assembling for a class portrait. Because each of them had frightened me, I'd copped a cocky attitude with them, just as I had with my father when he towered threateningly over me. It wasn't the smartest way to handle authorities. It surely wasn't smooth.

I'd become too reactive, on constant watch for disrespect, at times misinterpreting an authorities' intent. I needed to better understand why without warning my role as Mr. Master of Ceremonies turned into an imitation of Malcom X. What was happening? Was there a way to damp down my opposition that wouldn't leave me feeling like a wastebasket for some authorities' bad energy?

Sarah and I discussed my rebelliousness in our next session.

"I understand where you're coming from," she said. "As a child you would have been crushed if it weren't for that iron will of yours. But you're an adult now, Michael, and blind opposition to every authority isn't working anymore, is it? You're 'acting out.'"

"So I'm supposed to just cave in?" I asked sarcastically.

"How about opening your eyes and seeing if the authority in question is out to hurt you, instead of automatically copping an attitude?" suggested Sarah.

I shrugged.

"You turn a lot of people away whom you could be letting in." Sarah took my hand. "You're so busy being oppositional that you miss the friendship and warmth that surrounds you. You even miss out on what the members in group try to give you."

"I don't oppose them." I argued.

"Yes you do. You even oppose me, Michael and I'm here for

you completely. But if I say something is black, I can count on you to argue that it's white."

"Not always," I said defensively.

"Always," Sarah said. "There are times when it's useful to play devil's advocate, but you do it thoughtlessly."

It hurt to have Sarah criticize me, but she was right. For years I distrusted people in positions of power, and I relied on my defiance to limit their control. At least now I understood why I acted that way. My willful opposition prevented my parents from breaking my spirit. But my rebelliousness had outgrown its usefulness. It was no longer appropriate but a predictable opposition that got in my way wherever I went, especially at my place of work. My colleagues knew I'd have something contrary to say about anything they proposed, and it was tiring. I hated the looks they passed when I entered the conference room. Clearly work was the wrong venue for battling old ghosts.

Sarah was right. I had to deal with my rebelliousness. But if I wasn't going to be oppositional and cocky, how was I supposed to act? It was exhausting to be combative, and I wanted to be liked. But what would happen if I allowed that desire to come to the fore? I vowed to give it a try. I would squelch my oppositional posture, even if it risked being susceptible to another's control.

Having made that decision, it was startling how quickly my yearning for acceptance bubbled to the surface. What I really wanted was to enter the conference room and see faces that liked me. Overnight, I wanted my associates' approval more than I feared their dominance.

But what will it take to make them like me? I wondered.

I needed a way to make them aware that I'd changed, but it had to be subtle. I figured the most startling way to draw attention to the new me was to keep quiet during staff meetings, a change of behavior everyone would notice. So I gagged my annoying instinct to be combative during meetings and stopped challenging my bosses' suggestions. I resisted being contrary for months, attending meetings with a silence that baffled my colleagues.

When enough time had passed that I'd clearly signaled the arrival of a new me, I spoke up again. But now instead of challenging my colleagues, I seconded their ideas. I provided additional arguments in favor of their proposals. It was only a matter of months before I knew their preferences so well that I could mirror their positions, determined to say whatever it took to please them.

What amazed me was how quickly their opinion of me changed. People I'd consistently annoyed were warming to me, and oh, how I basked in their approval. If my malleability won them over, it was a small price to pay. How quickly I stifled my habit of opposing. How automatically I began to mimic styles and shift positions until that became my new modus operandi.

Before long my social style and convictions morphed to suit my audience. Talking to the mechanics at my service station, I no longer had to think about going macho. Puffing my shoulders up and making my voice a little gruffer came automatically. The mechanics called me a regular guy, not like those damn yuppies in the neighborhood. In the company of theatergoers, without forethought now, I elevated my pinkie finger as I commented on the play.

"That's a clever observation," they said.

After a second drink at the bar after work, I could even stomach agreeing with the bigot on the barstool.

"You're damn right, my friend. The world's amuck with fucking liberals," I nodded.

My change of tactics—the shift from rebellion to appeasement—may have looked to some like a transformation, but it wasn't. It was merely a change of costume, a new variation on an old fear-inspired role, Mr. Master of Ceremonies. At the core there was no difference between the two roles—the former played by a frightened fraternity pledge whose manic dialog carried him through another dreaded social event. My new script, as fear-driven as the first, proved equally unsatisfying.

I was still searching for a core of balance, real transformation. I was feeling doomed, as if my human contacts would never be satisfactory because I could never get the balance right. Would I always ride the pendulum to unsatisfying extremes? Though it was buried, I felt a native kindness for others and even a passion to protect them. Would I ever be able to share it? Would I always have to water it down by filtering it though layers of protective roles? I wasn't so sure that being liked was the lesser evil. Suppressing my honest opinions sickened my conscience. I felt ashamed when I nodded in agreement to please the bigot at the bar, though I'd forget it in an hour. Did it even matter that the people I accommodated were themselves formed of fads and fashions that would all change tomorrow? I was tiring of being a mirror on a gaily colored carousel, flashing bright reflections of the images I circled.

My new tactic hadn't made me any happier. Yes, I was better liked, but at too high a cost. Saying what others wanted was isolating me from myself, and it felt as if my core was shrinking in the distant horizon. Accommodating everyone was making me angrier so that I needed thicker walls to contain my bubbling rage. At least my old rebelliousness gave me a chance to vent. Now my anger built without release. I held my locked grin so tightly that I couldn't respond comfortably in any social situation, and I had to examine sentences before I let the words out, least, unchecked, who knows what I'd say? As my discomfort grew, I needed longer periods of silence—time away from people—to regenerate the energy required for the next act.

No, acquiescence wasn't the answer either. People liked me more, but every time I nodded "yes" when my heart said "no," my jaw locked tighter. Each time I muzzled what I really thought, I gave away one more piece of myself. I was fading, growing paler with each charade.

One person that my acquiescing didn't please was Sarah, and she quickly let me know it.

We were talking about how often Mom traveled when I was a child, and Sarah asked how I thought Mom's absence affected me.

"It didn't make much difference to me," I said.

"Do you really mean that?" Sarah asked. "You didn't care that Josefina was more the Mom than your own Mom was?"

"It was okay with me," I said grinning.

Sarah looked impatient.

"What in God's name do you really think?" she demanded. "The woman was gone half your childhood. No feelings at all about that Michael? None whatsoever?"

"It wasn't her fault," I said. "Running was how Mom coped. She had her own issues to deal with. You know my grandmother was cold as ice. No wonder Mom ran."

"You didn't answer my question," Sarah demanded. "I asked how *you*, I Michael Grossman, how *you* felt. How was it growing up in a home without a mother around?"

"I never thought about it," I said too quickly.

Sarah scowled. I hurried to say something she wanted to hear.

"I . . . I suppose I didn't like it. I'm sure I didn't like it."

Clearly that didn't satisfy Sarah.

"What the hell do you want me to say?" I asked.

She was silent.

I sat grinning.

She pointed to my tight, locked, nervous grin, always in place now regardless of the subject.

"That grin," she motioned, "for god's sake, let go of your jaw."

Sarah rose from her chair and stood behind me, powerfully forcing her thumbs into my locked jaw hinges. She drove her thumbs deep into the hinges until my jaw released and dropped down. I was unaware of how tight I'd been clenching.

"Stand up Michael," said Sarah. "Okay. Breathe into your belly and see what feelings come up."

None did.

Sarah said our time was up.

In the next group session, Sarah called on me.

"Michael, stand in the center," she said.

I stood in the circle, grinning and unsure what to do with my arms. If I crossed them I'd look defensive; if I let them hang loose, I'd feel too vulnerable. My mind raced to prepare for what was coming. Surely Sarah would bring up Mom's frequent travels. I'd say that I was angry at Mom and that would get me off the hook.

Sarah whispered instructions to several in the circle and the group began to taunt me.

"What an asshole you are," said one of the members as he shoved me in the chest.

"A momma's boy," another pushed me from behind.

I took their jibes unfazed. I grinned and let them shove me, knowing I could hold out longer than they could. One after another belittled and shoved me. At last my eyes narrowed and my grin dissolved. I forgot about handling them and charged.

"Fuck you," I screamed as I beat the chest of the nearest of them with my bataka.

I turned around in the circle to warn them all.

"I'll crush you. Every damn one of you."

"You, Michael? Not wonderful Michael?" one of them taunted.

"Why, Michael would never hurt a flea," said another sarcastically.

"You little shits," I screamed. "I'll pound you bastards into the floor and I'll squash you." I symbolically twisted my heel into the rug.

I wasn't grinning now.

I raged in their faces. My anger didn't abate until finally, out of breath, I had to stop. Panting, with my hands on my knees, I kept my eyes on the carpet and weighed my impulse to run from the loft. I couldn't look at them. The image I so carefully crafted—Michael the sensitive, nice, oh-so-concerned person—had dissolved. The Michael they'd seen was horrible. I had to avoid their eyes.

When I did look up, I saw to my surprise that they were smiling and warm to me. One of the guys massaged my back. Another gave me a gentle hug that immediately softened my battle-postured chest. My anger dissolved into a deep core of sadness, and it was all I could do to hold back my tears. I so wanted to let them go.

"That was the most real we've ever seen you," said someone in the circle.

In time I understood why my rage didn't disgust them. I saw that each member in the group had a similar, well-cloaked anger. If we didn't fear it so we would direct that anger at the real culprits—the spirit killers—but we were too afraid of both them and our anger.

It was safer to turn it on ourselves, and it became depression. Each member considered his or her personal anger to be uniquely horrible, a shame only he or she had to hide. Concealing it like an awful secret played havoc with our self-esteem.

As the weeks passed, every group member exposed his or her dark side, and seeing their anger made it easier to accept my own. Every member had a secret monster like mine—the raging beast I'd exposed. Seeing theirs, mine didn't seem so awful, and I no longer felt that I was irreparably broken. I was human, which meant that I had anger. But it wasn't my only emotion. I was also capable of a deep and gentle caring for the members of the group.

The angriest group member, Pamela, had an emotional range with two options. Either she smiled unctuously or she flew into an unprovoked tantrum. She'd flip from grin to scowl following the beat of her own unfathomable rhythm. Pamela toyed with her anger in therapy for years, but she kept it in tight rein and never showed anything deeper than a tantrum, the way a singer gives voice from the throat but not from deep within the belly. Then one night in group, Pamela let her monster loose. She sprang at us with nails extended, dying to claw our eyes out. As she circled us, she let out a piercing shriek that stung my ears. My breath seized, her rage was so terrifying. Her energy was demonic and endless, and I was afraid this would end only when Pamela was dragged off to a hospital. But Sarah calmly worked with her, patiently telling her to keep breathing while she gently massaged her forehead. Somehow Sarah kept Pamela from going over the edge until finally the high-pitched shrieking dropped to an anguished moan and then to choking sobs as tears came in waves and rode the rhythm of her breath. We took turns rocking Pamela in our arms like a baby until finally she lay on the floor exhausted and the room fell silent. What bravery Pamela showed us.

As Pamela worked, the world outside the loft window had transitioned through sunset to a black evening bright with polar stars. When Pamela arose, she was calmer than I'd ever seen her. Her face was open, and her eyes were radiant.

"Thank god," someone said.

* * *

In time we saw that we'd hidden our anger because getting angry at another involved the terrifying possibility that a parent—our critical caregiver—might be unworthy and might actually deserve our fury. It was less threatening to idealize the parent and turn our anger inward against our self, to assume we were the problem. But by getting angry in the safe environment of the group, we chipped away at an awful secret, our closely held belief that anyone so angry must be unimaginably horrible. Exposing our monsters—safely showing our rage to people who understood—enabled each of us to accept what we most feared. One by one we tore off our monster masks, only to find there was no phantom too awful to behold. We were people, just people, flawed as humans are, struggling with the universal difficulty we all have—to love ourselves.

"Hiding your dark emotions cripples you," Sarah said. "Posturing, pretending that you don't have moments of greed, selfishness, lust, intolerance, only prevents you from moving beyond those feelings to the real sweetness I see in each of you."

Sarah had it right again. Accepting our dark emotions freed us to discover the gentler voice within us. When Sarah felt we understood this, she shifted the focus of our work. We worked less on our anger and more on getting to know our essential, spiritual selves. We trained to listen for our voice and to trust it. At first I wasn't sure there even was a voice. If it was there at all, it was halting, uncertain, a whisper. But the voice grew louder, and in time I knew it unmistakably as my voice.

Now to seek its deepest levels. But for that, I had to remove the barrier blocking the way. The barrier was a sense of worthlessness coupled with neediness that sent me hunting outside myself for an answer that always lay within.

I want so badly to feel worthy and cared for and important and special, I thought.

Those feelings were the foundation I needed to move beyond myself and care more deeply for others.

I hadn't chosen the wrong goal. Learning to love is the end game for therapy. But I bought into the popular notion that I needed the symbols of worthiness, the things we buy that say we are someone. I assumed purchases could relieve the emptiness I felt.

I needed to learn that like my anger, my obsessive hunger to acquire was getting in my way.

THIRTY-FIVE

The Importance of Stuff

THERE WAS A HOLE IN MY BEING, like when a cartoon figure gets shot and then walks around with a circle cut out of his center. I tried everything, believing another gadget—a new car, a new home—could fill the void.

The hole had been there from my earliest recollections, and I'd learned by example how to fill it: you bought stuff. Of course, it took money if you wanted what Dad called "the good things in life." So I wanted to make money. But the status that came with money was of less importance to me, perhaps because I'd been born into wealth. Maybe if I'd come to America through Ellis Island, I'd have felt differently. Sure, I could get miffed at a condescending, Armani-clad shop clerk who talked at my tattered blue jeans rather than to me, and I wasn't above relishing the clerk's deflated pretensions when I handed him my embossed card with an Upper East Side Manhattan delivery address. But something more cardinal than status drove me to work as hard as I did, even at the cost of my health. Something primal drove me to skip vacations and even to ignore my poor body's plea for a bathroom break.

Hold it a bit longer. Finish the spreadsheet first, I demanded of my bladder.

Sarah helped me discover why I felt each new purchase would supply the missing piece. The clues we unearthed pointed to painfully awkward moments when my parents felt duty-bound to hug their children and to the ways they avoided that unpleasantness. Why hug a child when a toy will suffice? So my sister Jill, brother Randy and I learned to focus our energies on acquiring the substitutes for parental warmth—on getting stuff. We waited for the perfect moment to raise the curtain on the seasoned performances that got us stuff. If Mom and Dad were leaving on a trip, we knew exactly what to do.

First came tears, then the mournful reminders, "You always leave us." Finally their chance for redemption, "If you really love me, you'll buy me a . . ."

The rules for getting stuff were set when I turned ten in 1952. I'd read about a new state-of-the-art product from General Electric called a clock radio. Its technical capabilities amazed me. With a clock radio it wasn't necessary to awake to a jarring bell alarm. You just set the wake-up time, and gentle music ushered in your day. At night Bing Crosby crooned you to sleep, until at the appointed time, the clock radio turned itself off. Its design was futuristic, made of plastic instead of wood, with a bright copper strip to frame the speaker.

I told Dad all the things a clock radio could do, reminding him that my birthday was coming soon. I reminded him over and over until he threw up his hands and promised I could have the radio. I phoned Dad daily as my birthday neared. His secretary put me through.

"What does Mr. Con Artist want this time?" Dad asked.

"Imagine, Dad. Just nine days and I'll be ten," I said, pleased with my subtlety.

The birthday came. The clock radio didn't.

"It's on order," muttered Dad.

With each day that passed, getting that radio became more important. I was obsessed with it. There was my life—and there was my life if only I had a clock radio.

One day when I called, Dad said, "The radio came in. I'll bring it home tonight."

I waited for hours at the front door, but Dad arrived carrying only his briefcase.

"I forgot it, Mr. Con Artist," he said, "You think it's the only thing I have to remember? I'm trying to make a living so you can eat."

I reminded him for days, but repeatedly it slipped his mind. Disappointed after a month, I gave up and stopped calling him. I didn't matter anymore.

So Dad brought the clock radio home.

A miniature steam engine was the next only-thing-that-mattered, then an electric train, a microscope, a tricycle, a bicycle, and finally a motor scooter. For weeks I'd think only about each successive toy, but the gifts never lived up to my expectations. The excitement of tearing at the wrapping paper was followed by an inevitable letdown, and when each new toy didn't do the impossible, I tossed it on the growing pile of my disappointments.

When I turned fourteen, I got a motor scooter driver's license, and Dad promised me a scooter. Months after I was told it would arrive, the big, green Grossman's Department Store delivery truck pulled into our driveway. The driver dropped a ramp and wheeled down an Italian Lambretta motor scooter. It was spectacular in gray and maroon two-tone paint with a tan leather seat. It had a dashboard with a clock, a lockable glove compartment and even a continental kit with a whitewall tire.

Dad said he'd have the first ride, though he'd never driven a motor scooter. He over-throttled and jerked the clutch, and the front wheel rose up. I stood in the middle of the road and watched him ride away, tilting from side to side, growing smaller. I was pretty sure Dad didn't know how to turn the scooter and sure enough, when he tried, down he went. I ran up and made sure he wasn't hurt. But Dad's mood had turned. He glared at me in dead silence as we pushed the motor scooter home. A circle of sweat grew on his shirt under the hot sun. I didn't mention the dent.

When I turned sixteen, I took out my savings, and Dad split the cost of a used car with me. We went to the car lot where Dad had found a sensible, low mileage Chevy. But in the back row of the car lot I saw a green Lincoln. I kept taking Dad back to it until he gave up and I drove off the lot raising and lowering the Lincoln's power windows and changing stations with the radio's power tuner.

I quickly tired of the Lincoln and traded it in on a Triumph TR3 convertible. Then I bought a Pontiac Catalina convertible, a Corvette, a Citron, a Ford, an MG and an Alpha. I spent my weekends at used car lots turning "car crazy" into an addictive obsession.

Years later in a session, Sarah and I talked of a dream that suggested how powerfully I'd identified myself with my cars. I had the dream in my late teens. The recurrent nightmare always opened as I took a newly purchased used car to my local garage. The mechanic would yell from under the hood and tell me to try again to start the engine. I'd crank and crank, but the car wouldn't start. In a variation of that dream, the car did start, but it sounded like the pistons would come through the hood. In a third version, the car started, but the engine shook, sputtered, carb-flamed and died. I knew enough to put my hand to the tailpipe and smell for oil before I bought a used car, but in my dreams, the car puffed blue smoke and filled the garage with the stench of petroleum.

Each version of the dream ended the same way. An unshaven mechanic, never sympathetic, would beckon me under the hood. He'd point his big steel wrench to one problem after another, shaking his head at each flaw.

"The thing's a total wreck," he'd say, "Can't be fixed."

I'd awake agitated. The car was broken. I was broken, and the mechanic said I couldn't be fixed.

"So what do you make of the dream?" Sarah asked rhetorically.

"Well, my fear was unfounded. I wasn't irreparably broken," I said. "But you can't buy what I was looking for—only I didn't know that yet. They don't make a car with the performance specs I had in mind. Or did I just go to the wrong mechanic?"

Sarah smiled.

THIRTY-SIX

My Mother's Child

SOME PICTURES STAY WITH YOU like the afterimage on a TV screen—memories of Mom endlessly primping at her mirror or Dad gesturing through a cloud of cigar smoke from behind his desk. They make my intestine twist and the anger they bring feels bottomless. *Will I ever be finished with my parents?* I wondered, imagining my future therapy, seeing a tottering old man pushing his walker into Sarah's office.

I described Mom's modus operandi one night in the group.

"Here's what running an errand with her was like," I said . . .

"You have the most exquisite eyes," said Mom, smiling at the supermarket cashier.

The cashier beamed.

She told the receptionist at the doctor's office, "What a wonderful smile you have. And those eyes, my god you have the most exquisite eyes."

She told the pharmacist, "Your skin, oh, what wonderful creamy skin you have. And those eyes! Exquisite."

She put an arm around a clerk at the shoe store.

"Michael, have you ever met this wonderful woman? Meet my friend Clara." (Mom had introduced me to Clara a dozen times.) "This is the woman I'm always telling you about." (Mom never mentioned Clara outside her presence.) "She's one of my very favorite people. And Michael, have you ever seen such exquisite eyes!"

"The woman's a broken record," I told the group.

"My Dad's just as insincere" said another member. "If you support the right to life, he tells you so does he. If you are pro-abortion, he is too. The guy says anything he thinks will please you."

"Not George," said a third member. "My Dad assumes everyone is his intellectual inferior."

Sarah listened, but strangely tonight she wasn't interested in our characterizations. She seemed impatient, skipped the warm-up exercises and beckoned us to gather around her. What she said surprised us.

"It's time," she said, "to stop focusing on your parents—on what you did or didn't get from them. When are you going to face the real enemy? It's not your parents, though I appreciate that you see them more clearly now and acknowledge their shortcomings. But you're preoccupied with them. Are you aware of how enmeshed you are in them, how much energy you put into disapproving of them? You bring up their flaws repeatedly, but why do you think your reaction is so visceral? Yes, they were your parents, but did it ever occur to you that something else is also at work? Could it be that the things you don't like about them—that they were manipulative or narcissistic or arrogant—that these are the same traits you dislike in yourself?"

I looked around the circle, glad to see that my fellow group members looked as puzzled as I was.

"Blaming your parents is easier than talking about your own imperfections," said Sarah.

Where is this coming from? I wondered.

"I don't understand," someone said.

"You don't want to," Sarah said. "You don't want to see that your parents are reflections of who you are."

"Don't you mean that the other way around?" asked another.

"I mean exactly what I said," replied Sarah sharply. "Before we are born into each new incarnation—we select our parents for this life, and we choose carefully."

I let a puff of air go through my lips.

This was farfetched, I thought. *If Sarah believes in reincarnation, fine. Half the world believes in it. But prenatally choosing our parents? I don't think so.*

"No way would I have picked mine," I muttered defiantly.

"The parents you choose," Sarah continued undaunted, "mirror the character issues you're here to work on this time around."

A hand waved. "What kind of issues? Can you give an example?"

"You give me an example," Sarah challenged. "Take someone you think of as needy—someone greedy for attention, for love, for security. Greed is the core issue he or she came to life to work on. At birth, what kind of parents might such a soul choose?"

"Acquisitive, money-hungry parents?" someone offered.

"Good," Sarah said. "In that case what happens as the child grows up? The greed he sees in his parents helps him see his own greed so that he can work on it. Let's take another example. Take a passive individual. What kind of parents might he or she pick? Judy?"

"Parents who get pushed around?" Judy offered.

"Good," said Sarah, "Yes that would help the child reflect on his own passivity."

Bill raised his hand. "So we pick parents with the same issues that we have?"

"Sometimes," said Sarah. "But it's not quite that simple. Parents don't necessarily mirror our own issues. Sometime their characters differ, but always in ways that help us see our own issues more clearly. Take that person with passivity issues. Besides passive parents, what other kind of parents might a passive child choose at birth?"

"Well," said Debby, "the passive child could pick a controlling parent. To survive, he would have to learn to assert himself—at least enough to break the parent's dominance."

"That's right," Sarah said. "To survive, he'd have to become an independent person in his own right."

"So parents are like bad examples?" Asked Bill.

"I'd put it differently," Sarah said. "I'd say that our parents are tied to our personal karma. They reflect who you are and prompt what you need to work on to grow healthier.

Come on, I thought, avoiding Sarah's eyes. *Reincarnation, maybe, but the idea that we choose our parents, and pick ones with similar issues? That's crazy. Can you imagine an unborn child looking for parents with particular character flaws? Ludicrous. Look at me. Was I anything like my parents? Of course not. How many times did I swear, "I'll never grow up to be like them." If they're the ones I picked, I must have been looking for polar opposites. Dad was religious. Not me. They were both into status. I could care less. My social-climbing mom was an embarrassment. I could see her ordering the fancy china set out if someone important was coming to visit. I'd shuffle into the living room in a torn shirt and muddy shoes—precisely to show the guest that I wasn't a thing like her. So while generally Sarah was pretty sharp, she was just wrong this time.*

"Okay, let's go to work," said Sarah, interrupting my thoughts,

The members of the group tightened the circle as Sarah waited for us to settle.

"I'd like you to close your eyes, get quiet and go within," she said. "Breathe deeply and let yourself get quiet. Good. Now picture the parent that first comes to mind. What kind of person do you see? How does that person make you feel? How do you relate to him or her? Then ask yourself, "Why did I choose this particular person to be my parent?"

I shut my eyes, but the best I could do was to get a picture of Mom preening in her mirror. How could Sarah suggest I was anything like Mom? I was scheduled for a session with Sarah tomorrow and I couldn't wait to tell her how wrong she was.

I was early for my session. Sarah's patient came out, and we awkwardly eyed each other. It's funny how people act in a therapist's waiting room. Patients pretend they don't see each other and they rarely speak, as if talking would expose the obvious—that we were in therapy.

I entered Sarah's office and took my seat to wait while she finished an entry in her calendar. I wasted no time when she looked up. "You are totally off, Sarah. I am nothing like Dad or Mom. I couldn't be any more different if I tried," I said.

"That's my point," she said. "Can you see how hard you try to be different from them? If you really were different, you wouldn't have to work so hard at it. You're enmeshed in them whereas if you had separated from them—had become your own person—they wouldn't come up so often. Yet every session returns to them as this one has."

"I only bring them up to give you history," I said. "That doesn't prove I'm like them."

"What I see is how bound to them you are," said Sarah, "and it seems to me that all your efforts to be different tie you to them more tightly."

Sarah paused so I could digest this.

I tried, but my thoughts drifted. My eyes fell on my badly scuffed loafers, and I remembered something from when I was fourteen . . .

Mom was at her makeup table when I entered her bathroom. I nearly gagged from her overpowering perfume. The black silk dress she wore highlighted her Kabuki makeup—eggshell white with red rouge. A pearl necklace sagged from the weight of an emerald clasp.

"You're not going to dinner looking like that," she said eyeing my scuffed loafers, tattered jeans and untucked flannel shirt.

"I'm fine," I said. "It's what I wear."

"Not to my dinner party, it isn't. Get upstairs and find a pair of pressed slacks and an ironed shirt. And change those god awful loafers."

"Who cares?" I protested.

"Everyone. Do you want people to think we're a bunch of vagabonds?" She imperiously shooed me out the door.

It was delicious that my attire annoyed Mom, though I felt a little uncomfortable arriving at the party inappropriately dressed.

I felt an urge to whisper to the guests, "I could dress better if I'd wanted. I do know the difference. But my clothes say I'm not at all like her."

I kept staring at my scuffed loafers.

"Michael?" Sarah interrupted my memory. "Are you still with us?"

Her question brought me back, and I described the memory.

"There you have it!" said Sarah clapping her hands. "You've made my point exactly. Do you see how enmeshed you are? Even the clothes you selected were based on what she would think. Tell me this. Did you give any thought at all to how Michael Grossman might want to dress for the party—to Michael's own taste in clothing?"

"I guess not," I admitted.

"Because you're that bound to her," said Sarah rising and handing me a tennis racket. "Let's see if we can't separate Michael from Mother."

Sarah went to the mattress in the corner of the room.

"I want you to imagine two faces here," she said patting the mattress. "Imagine your Mom's face here," she said tapping the left mattress corner, "and put your own face—that of little Michael as a child—here on the right."

Sarah stood at the opposing end of the mattress and began to beckon seductively, mimicking Mom's familiar tactic.

"Come to me, my special little man," teased Sarah. "It's you I want, not your crazy father."

I'm not falling for it, I said to myself. *It will be different this time. I'm an adult with years of therapy and I won't be easily fooled. I'll protect little Michael no matter what she does.*

Sarah kept motioning, enticing, smiling and finally pleading for me.

I watched the way a cat watches its mistress pour milk, "*What if she really means it?*"

I ignored her pleas but I couldn't help wondering how it would feel if just for once she put her arms around me and held me to her tight.

What if she's changed, I thought.

"You know I can't trust your father, Michael." Sarah knew just the right words. "He's out of control. The man is crazy. Unreliable. You are the only one I'm sure of. That's why you are so special to me. You, Michael. Mommy's Little Man."

Sarah's outstretched arms implored me.

Trap. It's a trap, the adult in me warned.

Still, I debated.

She looks so different, doesn't she? What if she really wants me this time? Would she put her arms around me and make everything safe for once and for all?

A Mona Lisa smile crept onto Sarah's face.

A rush of yearning crumbled my resolve.

"Mommy!" I reached for her.

Instantly, Sarah turned her back on me, mimicking Mom's pattern and continuing her role.

"Herman! Michael didn't shovel the walk today," she said. "You told him to shovel the walk. Do something about him, can't you, Herman?"

It shocked me. The same old Jack had popped out of the same old box, yet I was surprised.

What was Einstein's definition of insanity? I thought. *Doing the same thing over and over again but expecting a different result.*

Sarah continued to play Mom perfectly.

"Herman, are you are going to stand there and let him get away with it, Herman? I need help with him, Herman."

Suddenly, standing at the mattress, I was neither Michael the little boy nor Michael the adult. Unexpectedly my role transformed, and I became my mother. As I arched the tennis racket high, my feelings became her feelings. A powerful contempt came over me for my son Michael—that ugly little boy whose face was on the mattress.

He wasn't good enough. He isn't worth my time. If only I could choke the life out of him.

The crack of my racket echoed in the loft as I smashed the boy's face repeatedly.

"Words," said Sarah. "Open your eyes and let your voice out."

"You piece of shit," I screamed at the little boy. I wanted to eradicate him, my pathetic offspring, and I beat his image again and again.

Spent finally, I stopped to catch my breath. The room was silent, and I was done with my role-playing. I was myself again, but Sarah gave me a moment to collect myself.

"I really hate her," I said on the edge of sobbing.

"Because you felt her hatred for you. You were something she used," said Sarah.

"I hated her because I wanted a mother," I said holding back my sobs. "All I wanted was to be held."

I waited on the edge of tears for Sarah to comfort me.

"Are you sincere?" Sarah asked.

Her question took me by surprise.

"Do you ever manipulate people?" she asked.

What is this about? I wondered. *Why is Sarah being unkind to me at such a vulnerable moment? Whose side is she on?*

Furious, I started to grin at her.

"That grin of yours. How sincere is that?" Sarah asked.

I tried to fathom where Sarah was going with this. But she was the one person in the world I trusted, and whatever she was doing, I was sure she had my best interests in mind. So I squelched an impulse to become defensive and stayed open for whatever was coming next.

We sat together in silence.

I drifted once more, this time recalling a recent encounter with an old acquaintance.

"Where are you, Michael?" Sarah asked.

I described the memory of the recent meeting.

"I ran into someone recently who reminded me of Mom." I said.

"Yes?" Sarah prompted.

"A girl I used to work with. Michelle Clamente. I hadn't seen Michelle since my advertising days years ago. But I recognized her coming out of my local grocery store, and I hailed her.

"'It's so good to see you,' said Michelle. 'I'm eager to know how you are. We have to have dinner and catch up. How about next Wednesday night? Is that good?' 'Sure,' I said . . ."

Michelle had been so enthusiastic about seeing me that, when I called on the following Wednesday, it seemed odd she'd forgotten the dinner date entirely. But she quickly regained her composure.

"No. No. Of course," she said. "Tonight. Yes. The London House at eight."

Even before our drinks came, Michelle, who I'd only known casually, shared her most private thoughts.

"Did you know I'm gay?" she asked.

"What a wonderful thing," I said too enthusiastically.

Could I sense how happy she was to be out of the closet? Did I know her first husband was abusive and impotent and that she left him for her partner? Her sex life was so much better now.

A pleasant two hour dinner sped by, and we hugged outside the restaurant.

Michelle insisted, "You have to meet my partner. I'll call Monday to set a date."

What a nice thing, I thought walking home. *Michelle was so easy to talk to.*

I sat silently.

"And . . ." prompted Sarah.

"Sorry, Sarah," I said coming out of my thoughts. "And I never heard from her. Not that Monday or the following Monday, not ever again."

"I see," said Sarah. "And what do you make of that?"

"She was toying with me, the way Mom always toyed with me. I left the restaurant feeling this big connection to her, and poof, she disappeared. It all meant nothing to her."

"And?" Sarah said, still prompting.

"Yes, well I do the same thing. You know I do. I've done it to you and to the members of the group. I act like I'm close to people but never follow through. I say we must get together, but I never call. That's what my mother does to everyone."

"Why Michael?" Sarah asked emphatically. "Try to tell me why you and your mother do that—what does it get you?"

"I don't think what Mom does and what I do are exactly the same, though the effect on the people we hurt is identical. But our motivation is different."

"How so?" asked Sarah.

"Well, Mom manipulates because she wants something from people. She feels entitled because she thinks she never got enough. The world owes her, and goddamnit, she'll get her due one way or another. I'm more like Michelle. I manipulate people, but I think Michelle and I do it for different reasons."

"How is it different?" Sarah repeated the question.

"Look at Michelle. It's not like she wanted something from me. I can't offer her anything."

"So why did she pretend to be so intimate?" Sarah prompted.

"I think it has to do with fear—with a powerful feeling we both have—that we aren't adequate—not good enough. That's how we feel in front of other people. I think Michelle is terribly uncomfortable and as frightened of people as I am. She comes off as self-assured and professional, but I think she's actually shy and lacking in self-confidence—embarrassed about herself. Part of it is self-loathing. She's afraid that people will judge her with as much loathing as she judges herself."

"So she does what?" Sarah prompted.

"She feigns intimacy because it discourages people from judging her. Boy do I know how that works. If the other person feels they are really special to Michelle, guess what? They won't stop to judge her. They are too busy feeling flattered. As for me, I concentrate intently on pleasing people, but I do it to distract them so they won't look too closely at me. I feign intimacy and keep the jokes rolling because that's what it takes to get me through a social encounter unscathed."

"Are you that afraid of what others will see in you?" Sarah asked.

"I'm petrified. I'm afraid they'll see right through me and know that I'm angry and aloof and inadequate. So I pump up the Mr. Master of Ceremonies balloon, and as long as I do it well enough, my secret is safe."

"It must be a fearful world, Michael, if everyone in it is out to judge you. But at least you do see that you're projecting—ascribing your own fear to others."

"Remember my experience in the park? It's the angry eyes again, Sarah. I externalize my own self-loathing and project my fear of being inadequate onto others. I assume it's what they think of me. No wonder being around people exhausts me. I have to be on constant guard. Socializing in my world means I'll be dragged out of my comfortable hiding place into that precarious world, where a whole lot can go wrong and not a lot of good happens."

"This is important, Michael," Sarah said. "I want you to work on this.

I clung to the subway strap on my way home. Billboards were a blur in my window as I reviewed our session. Like Michelle and, yes, like Mom too, I worked people. I feigned intimacy automatically, only to vanish, leaving them to wonder what had happened to me. My performance was involuntary, a protective shield deployed unconsciously because social encounters pushed me to the edge of the cliff. The only traction, the only holding rail, was to grab my audience's attention—a skillful performance that left me in charge. The trick was to play off their humor, their politics, their fashions and to mimic their style. I stayed in control as long as it was I who choreographed the exchange and orchestrated the conversation, keeping others focused on anything but me. I made sure they didn't have enough time to study me, and by limiting their penetration, I survived the encounter. But I had to talk energetically enough to lead them from topic to topic. Succeed, and they wouldn't notice how porous I was. They wouldn't see how much power they had to make me morph shapes because I lacked the substance to maintain my borders. The alternative, to let them really see me, wasn't an option. If I let that happen, I was theirs to mold, and human nature finds the chance to mold irresistible. They'd swallow me like a morsel.

My solution was to operate simultaneously as two personas. One was painfully shy and reclusively private, while the public persona was the antithesis—Mr. Master of Ceremonies—who said flattering or funny or intimate things. That persona appeared to be so interested as it watched mouths without listening. Its job was to sustain conversation until a "leave-them-laughing" line permitted a showman's exit.

But my charade left me split in two, and over time the gap widened between the gentle, sub-rosa interior and the over-energized public face. As the split between essence and appearance widened, the chasm grew harder to bridge.

I picked up with that theme in my next session.

"Okay, Michael," Sarah said. "So if we get beneath your grin, who's there?"

"Sarah, I've been rebelling or accommodating or joking so long that I hardly know anymore. As a kid my rebellion kept them from breaking me, but I annoyed a lot of people. When I got older and couldn't take people's disapproval anymore, I tried to be popular. That left me even lonelier. My roles aren't working for me."

"Good," Sarah said approvingly as she came over. She touched my shoulder and looked confidently in my eyes. "Actually, Michael, you are not in a bad place at all."

It didn't feel that way.

"Stand up," said Sarah. "Get on your feet and move across the room. Dramatize the real Michael."

I tried to imagine who I really was, but nothing came to me.

"Okay, take your seat," Sarah said.

I awaited new instructions.

"I want you to pray."

That felt awkward, but I was facing the only person I trusted.

"Get quiet now," she said, "and seek the help of Spirit. Go within and ask, 'Spirit, who am I? Who am I really?' Listen for the answer."

I sat upright in my chair, feet flat, eyes closed. I felt my body quiet as I listened for a voice. The silence of the room was pleasing and in time a soft white energy lit in my mind. But I didn't get a message, and no banner danced across the screen with the answer.

In the next group session, Sarah told me to stand in the center of the circle.

"Ask them," she urged. "Ask the group who you are."

"Who am I?" Turning to each one in the circle. "How do you see me?"

I stood relaxed and smiling, confident I'd get pat-on-the-back, touchy-feely feedback. But their response wasn't at all what I expected. No one smiled, and they didn't mince words.

"You pretend to be one of us, but you hold yourself apart," someone said. "You're insincere."

"You keep your distance from us," echoed another, "and you never let yourself be vulnerable."

"You're aloof," said a third. "You think you're better than us."

I was shaken. I worked so hard for so many group sessions to carefully craft an impression of Michael the kindly, Michael the concerned. I put my arms around them and looked kindly at them. Yet they saw past all that to my manipulativeness and narcissism. Worse, they saw the reverse side of my low self esteem: my secret arrogance, the part of me that held myself out to be superior to them. I'd been especially careful to hide that, and now I felt stripped naked.

Wasn't I superior? Wasn't superiority the birthright Grandfather Isaac bequeathed to each of the four "I" cousins? Though I would never say so out loud to the group members, hadn't I surpassed them in the accepted measures of success? I made more money, and didn't I have a midtown window office? The title on my embossed business card said "important." The doormen rushing to hold my elevator acknowledged my status.

But like a tenuously stacked tower of playing cards, my secret arrogance collapsed when brushed even slightly. The mildest criticism could deflate me and stronger criticisms, like the group members' comments, left me unraveled.

Nor was the irony lost on me that if I was so superior, why was I so desperate for their approval? Why, even as I held them at arm's length, was I silently screaming for their attention? I might as well have carried a neon sign that flashed, "Notice me. Notice me." If an hour passed and no one in the circle mentioned me, I sulked. My mood teetered on their notice. I schemed to interrupt and say something when someone else took the center of our circle. If I made them laugh, I was delighted. If I impressed them with some insight, my chest barreled with pride.

"That's a really good point," someone noted.

"I never thought of it that way," said another.

I pretended not to notice the compliment, but my god, how delicious it was. What did I care if my insight was right or wrong? That wasn't the point. What mattered was that the spotlight was back on me.

Yet all along they'd known my game, and when I asked for the truth, they gave it to me.

I couldn't get out of that loft fast enough when the meeting ended.

I had a vise attack that night. It swept over my consciousness and bound my energy, dragging me under the water's surface. I clawed to return to the surface for air, but I only slid deeper into the lonely water, dropping toward the bottom. As I sank, the beams of light overhead grew dim.

In the darker regions of the water I saw her. Mom was preening, carefully applying lip gloss with a shell for her mirror.

So I had chosen her carefully.

THIRTY-SEVEN

Fear Itself

"YOU KNOW, SARAH," I said at our next session, "no matter what subject we work on, I find the same underlying emotion. It's like an onion. On the surface I think I'm dealing with my narcissism or my anger or the isolation I feel. But peel the layer away and there it is again."

"There what is?" asked Sarah.

"My terror. My raw fear. I'm way too scared, way too much of the time. I feel this layer of anxiety behind my eyes and in my gut. I don't trust the ground under my feet. I'm on guard around other people because I assume they are judging me."

My anxiety wasn't linked to a specific situation. Rather it was latent and pervasive suggesting the clinical term "free floating anxiety." It was a subterranean chorus of "what-ifs" that looped in my brain.

I just coughed. What if it's cancer? Why didn't my boss smile? What if he's going to fire me? What if the bite on my leg is Lyme disease? What if the stock market crashes? What if I look like some known criminal and no one believes I'm not him? What if I go blind or deaf or have a heart attack? What if I get hit by falling debris from a skyscraper? What if . . . ?

I did the best I could to face my fears head on. Given a choice, I asked for the bad news first. But I still felt afraid, and I felt cowardly. So I rode motorcycles, flew airplanes and boated in questionable seas. I accepted jobs I wasn't trained to do. I kept testing myself, pushing, but it never mattered that I succeeded. I kept running scared.

"What do you fear?" Asked Sarah. Can you go back to its origin?"

"Dad scared me. I think some part of him liked making me feel unsafe, a little unsure of myself. He had a bully's desire to intimidate that gave him power, and he wasn't above scaring Randy or me if it fed his machismo. He did it up to the day I wrestled him down. After that, he kept his distance."

"That was a turning point, wasn't it?" Sarah noted.

"But he sure did have a bully streak, and his need to feel manly would ignite it. I remember the day my brother Randy got the brunt of it."

"When was that?" Sarah asked.

"It's an almost comical story if you ignore what it did to Randy. But I know for sure Randy wasn't laughing. He still talks about that day."

"Tell me," she urged.

"Dad was friendly with an old guy named Sonny Sinclair, a local flying legend in Muskegon. The guy was ninety-two, yet Sonny could still pass the pilot's medical exam. Anyway, Dad had always dreamed of getting his pilot's license and started flying lessons, but he couldn't pass the medical exam due to his high blood pressure. So he decided Randy and I should learn, and he took us for a lesson. Years later I actually got my pilot's license and advanced licenses as well."

"He took both you and Randy for the lesson?" Sarah asked. "How old was Randy?"

"Randy was nine and I was fifteen. Dad drove us for our first lesson, and Sonny Sinclair was waiting to greet us, standing by a small blue Cessna at the Muskegon airport. He wore a green military flight suit, and a pair of green Dave Clark headphones hung around his neck.

"Sonny swung open the cockpit door and directed Randy to take the pilot's seat on the left while Sonny took the co-pilot position. I sat in back. Dad stayed behind on the tarmac. I rather liked the takeoff, watching the ground drop away as we gained altitude, heading out over Lake Michigan. The flight was smooth, and I loved seeing the city of Muskegon laid out below us like a map. But a strange look came over Sonny's face when we leveled off at five thousand feet. He let out a 'Yeehaaw,' pulled hard on the yoke, and the front of the plane lurched vertically and shook violently. The plane stalled, meaning it fell in a stomach-twisting dive while the ground out the cockpit window grew bigger. Finally Sonny yanked the yoke toward his chest and brought the plane back to level flight. I searched my seat pocket for a paper bag while Randy, his face the color of spring leaves, had a death grip on his seat frame.

"We climbed a second time to five thousand feet when Sonny reached over and set Randy's hands on the yoke.

"'She's yours, kid,' he said, resting back with his hands cupped behind his head.

"Randy's eyes were white with dwarfed pupils.

"'I don't know what to do,' Randy pleaded.

"'Hell, boy, just fly the ol' girl.'

"The plane twisted on its axis, and Randy squeezed the yoke as hard as he could. Nothing happened.

"'Pull her out of it, boy,' bellowed Sonny. 'Full left rudder.'

Randy hadn't a clue what Sonny meant by the rudder. He turned helplessly to Sonny, whose eyes spun on their own axis.

"'Like this, boy,' said Sonny, twisting his yoke counterclockwise and simultaneously slamming the left rudder pedal. The metal cabin creaked, rotated and dropped into another steep bank.

"'Take me back!' screamed Randy.

"'Hell, all ya gotta do is just steady her, son,' said Sonny, correcting the yoke position.

"'Back!' screamed Randy above the growing engine roar. 'Please, sir. Oh god, please!' he begged.

"Sonny took over, brought the plane in and greased the landing.

Even before touchdown, Randy tried to bolt from the cockpit, restrained by Sonny's arm until the plane halted and the prop stopped. Randy crawled down from the cockpit and staggered away, refusing to talk to Sonny or Dad."

"And?" Sarah prompted.

"I suspect a lot more of that kind of bullying went on than I can even begin to remember. You know how much I've blanked out. But it's no wonder Randy grew up fearful, and surely I did. And I think as a boy Dad himself experienced the same uncorralled fear. And I think most of Isaac's descendants ran scared. Dad was frightened, and beneath his pompous, erudite exterior he was unsure of himself. I saw the fear in the riddled disorientation on the frantic faces of my spacey aunts. Cousins Ian, Ira and Irwin knew the fear only too well. We were a family of mice in a maze, cornered, scared and in a frenzy about which way to go. Our smallest choices mushroomed into life and death decisions, each one requiring obsessive debate. Shopping for a new home or considering a job offer sent each of us into a seesaw of tortured arguments supporting first one side and then the other. All of us recycled the pros and cons long after our exhausted friends tired of helping us.

I dealt with my terror in either of two contradictory fashions. Either I'd be extremely cautious and deliberate obsessively for days, or I'd make a reckless, impulsive decision on the spot. The importance of the choice didn't matter, and I could take either course depending on my mood. I'd asked Susan to marry me on an impulse. I might anguish for weeks over which of two laptops to buy.

Sometimes my mood favored the status quo. *Stay in the rut you're in. Leave well enough alone. Change is risky. The devil you know is the safer choice. Yes, you are miserable in your job, but a new job will surely be worse.*

A more anxious state of mind could lead to a spur-of the-moment decision—just to get the choice over with. When my mind glowed from debate, often the only thing that mattered was to cool it down quickly. Any decision would cool it. Any decision at all would get the meter needle out of the red zone, release the pressure and prevent my mind from blowing.

Nine, eight, seven . . . pick one or the other . . . six, five, four . . . choose any one—it doesn't matter . . . three, two . . . for god's sake choose now!"

My work with Sarah brought me to the edge of my fear. I stood and peered down into the valley where my primal distrust had settled. The ground under my feet might open and swallow me at any moment. I trusted no one. Human goodwill was the devil's ploy. Women want what they can get. Physicians care more for their egos than their patients. Teachers want to make students jump through hoops. Authorities will crush you when they can.

Distrust also meant that I mustn't ask for help. Why owe someone? Why rely on anyone? It was better to balance the globe on my own shoulders because I knew I wouldn't drop it. Besides, whom could I hand it to? My relatives? My cousins? My parents? Dr. Cronick or Dr. Razar? They all had their own agendas.

I learned to distrust as a child, but as a child what choice did I have except to rely on my parents? I could choose an allegiance with either an explosive father or a narcissistic mother, and while it wasn't a clear choice, the accord with Mom seemed the lesser evil. Her narcissism meant that there would be very little nourishment, and her seductiveness confused me, but the treaty gave me safe passage around the minefield surrounding my Dad. So I made a pact with the devil.

Sarah helped me see what that alliance cost. It turned my world view to suspicion and deeply rooted cynicism. I doubted human intentions. Everyone wants something.

"So what's happening to me?" I asked Sarah as our session neared the end. "I'm more fearful than ever."

Sarah came and sat next to me and quietly cupped my cheeks in her hands.

"You aren't more fearful," said Sarah, looking into my eyes. "But at last you are acknowledging your terror. You can see now how afraid you are to trust another. It may not feel like it, Michael, but you are in a very good place. An important place. This is the place and the way it feels when you are ready to open up to love."

THIRTY-EIGHT

Broken Patterns

SHORTLY AFTER MY SESSION WITH SARAH, a friend asked if I was up for a blind date.

"You'll like Susan," he said.

"What's she like?" I asked.

"Really sweet," he said.

I didn't trust sweet.

"What's she look like?" I asked.

"Cute," he said. "Blonde."

"What's she do?"

"She's a psychiatric social worker," he said. "She works at the state mental facility in Queens."

"My first wife was a psychiatric social worker, and her name was Susan," I said. "I might have a thing for Susan Psychiatric Social Workers."

A week later I met Susan, my friend and his date at Mortimers, a casual Upper East Side bistro. As promised, Susan was an attractive blonde, about five-feet-four with a nice body. I was surprisingly at ease with her even during lulls in the less-than-riveting dinner conversation. Over blue point oysters and pink cosmopolitans, Susan chronicled her day. We learned she awoke early because her pillow was lumpy and we were supposed to rejoice that Bloomies got her preferred facial cream in.

I changed the subject. "Looks like the president blew it today with his attempt to rescue the hostages in out embassy in Iran. The helicopters crashed in the desert and never made it to Tehran."

"They should make Rosalynn the commander-in-chief," said my friend.

"Rosalynn's a great first lady, isn't she?" his date agreed.

Susan had nothing to say.

After dessert, when Susan had finished her second glass of port, we rose to say our goodbyes.

"Nice to meet you," I said to Susan mechanically.

I stood in the street and scouted for a cab.

Susan started for her car and then turned back to me as an afterthought. "If you want a lift, I'll drop you off."

She'd driven in from Long Island and had her car.

"But I'm on the West Side," I said. "It's out of your way."

"No matter," she said. "Glad to do it."

Manhattan residents don't get rides home from restaurants. You cab home or you take the subway, because even if a companion has a car, a cross-town lift can take a driver forty-five minutes out of the way. Susan's offer was remarkably considerate.

When we reached my apartment, I considered asking her up, but I was ambivalent and sensed she was too. I waved goodbye a second time as her Oldsmobile sped away.

At our next session, Sarah asked, "Are you dating at all?"

"I had a date last Saturday, but she's not my type," I said.

"What is your type?"

"As if you didn't know."

"Humor me."

"Well . . . Intellectual women turn me on. As long as they're good looking."

"Yes . . . ?" prodded Sarah.

"And I like them a little standoffish," I joked.

"And of course withholding."

"Yeah, withholding ups their appeal. If they are unapproachable, I'll like them even better. Unapproachable must mean they are better," I smiled at Sarah. "Dating is such a game. If I show a woman I'm attracted to her too soon, she'll lose interest, and if she seems disinterested, that's a turn on for me. It's important that I find the perfect lose-lose situation, don't you think?"

Sarah smiled. "And these women remind you of . . . ?"

"Gee, I can't imagine," I said.

Sarah laughed and then grew serious and leaned closer.

"Michael, all of us gravitate to familiar patterns in relationships. But what is familiar isn't necessarily what's healthy. Rosalind toyed with you. One minute she was close. You were her 'little man.' A minute later she turned her back on you and betrayed you to your father. Inconsistency is the only 'love' you've known from a woman. It's the model you look for. But you also know it doesn't work, and it prevents you from having the kind of intimate relationship you want so badly. So what do you think you should do about it?"

"My head says you're right, Sarah, but ice queens turn me on." I said.

"The question was, what do you want to do about it?" Sarah repeated.

"Join the priesthood?"

Sarah looked impatient.

"I'm attracted to women who don't have a capacity or desire to be intimate," I said.

"Recognizing that is good," said Sarah. "But what's next?"

I shrugged.

"Don't discount action," Sarah hinted. "Sometimes you have to take a step, to do something just to break your pattern. What would that mean in your case?"

"Perhaps dating someone who doesn't fit my mold?"

Sarah nodded in approval.

"Fine," I said. "Take Susan, the girl I just went out with. She doesn't fit the pattern. She's warm. She's approachable. But her availability is a turn off. It's pretty screwed up."

"Are you attracted to her?" Sarah asked.

"Yes, but I don't feel any urgency about the attraction," I said. "If I date an ice queen, I become obsessed quickly. I bring her gifts and hold doors and offer to move furniture. Whatever it takes to get her to like me."

"Yet your relationships with 'ice queens,' as you call them, never work out," said Sarah.

"So tell me," I said, "how am I supposed to know if a woman is right for me when I can't trust my own instincts?"

"Are there things about Susan that you don't like?" Asked Sarah.

"Well, she babbles, and she's probably too social for me," I said. "She's more into fashion and jewelry than politics or philosophy."

Sarah said nothing.

"Yet she isn't superficial," I continued, "From the little I know of her, she's exceptionally giving. I overheard her change her entire weekend plans without hesitation when her secretary called to say she needed a ride to a funeral. And she has a gay friend who is dying of AIDS, and she sits with him every day at the hospital."

"Then what's the but?" Sarah questioned.

"Well there's something off about her giving. She's almost too nice. Trying too hard. There's a 'goody two shoes' quality to her."

Sarah said nothing.

"This is worse than due diligence Sarah," I said. "Suppose I just ask her out and see where it goes?"

"I think so," said Sarah, "but stay conscious. Be aware of how she is different from the women you usually date."

That night I called Susan, and we talked for nearly an hour. Her wit was lightening quick. If I teased her, her comeback was immediate and edgy. Friends, she admitted, said her tongue was so sharp her lips must be bloody. Yet I felt no meanness to her teasing.

I learned Susan was a social worker who for twenty years had headed up a psychiatric hospital ward for New York State. But she was tired of her job and debilitated by the bureaucracy.

"Why not look for something new?" I asked.

"I really hadn't thought about it," she said passively.

At the end of the call, she invited me to dinner.

"Come over Saturday and I'll cook for you," she said. "My butcher has terrific steaks, and I wrap them in strips of bacon."

The following Saturday I hopped the Long Island railroad and watched as apartment buildings with laundry strung on fire escapes gave way to brick townhouses with well manicured lawns. Susan was standing on the platform when I stepped off the train. She gave me a warm hug.

"Damn it," I said turning as the train pulled out. "I left my backpack with my wallet in the overhead bin."

She turned for a pay phone and called the railroad.

"We can wait," she reported, hanging up the receiver. "Your train will return in thirty-five minutes."

When the train did pull in, I jumped through the doors and ran from car to car to find my backpack. I assumed the train would pull out while I searched and planned to get off at the next station and cab back to Susan's apartment. My backpack was in the bin where I left it, but the train had not moved. So I hurried out the door. The train hadn't moved because Susan was standing on the tracks in front of the engine with her palm outstretched like a cop.

What a curious contradiction she is, I thought. This was the same woman who was too passive to leave a boring job.

About six months later Susan and I had dinner at a Cuban diner. The place was a dive, but the food was authentic, and at any hour, day or night, rows of taxis double-parked out front on Broadway as cabbies dashed in for takeout. The cuisine was a Manhattan oddity: One side of the menu featured Cuban specialties; the other side, Chinese.

Over fried bananas, string pork and moist black beans we turned to the subject of our old flames. Sipping sangria, Susan mentioned that her former boyfriend was moving back to New York. I didn't like the wistful way that she spoke of him.

"We should live together," I said. The words were unplanned and came out unexpectedly.

"Are you really ready?" Asked Susan.

"Yes," I said.

"Okay," she said.

My God, what did I just do? I thought.

I didn't sleep that night. I lay awake thinking over my impulsive offer.

I acted hastily. I'm really not ready. My apartment is too small. Susan has a cat, and I'm allergic to cats. Is she ready to stop dating other people? Am I? What if she isn't who I think she is? I have to tell her we need more time. We could wait six months, and after that, if it still felt right, we could talk more about it. I'm going to call her and suggest it in the morning.

But I never got around to calling Susan in the morning. I postponed calling her later that day and I continued delaying until moving day arrived, and with it Susan and her cat, her suitcases and a carload of neatly taped brown boxes. As planned, Susan arrived on a Friday that was my scheduled weekend with Lauren in Washington—and we'd discussed that I'd be leaving as soon as I helped get her boxes moved in. I carried her belongings up, gave her a hug and a key, and left.

"See you Sunday," I said, heading for my garage.

I didn't tell my daughter Lauren about Susan. Sunday afternoon found me heading back North along Interstate 95 toward Manhattan. I must have something karmic with I-95, because the closer I got to New York, the more unsure I felt about living with Susan.

It was a mistake. We'd acted too hastily. Why didn't I think about it first?

By the time I reached the Trenton toll booth, I'd achieved a meltdown. Susan had to go.

Sometime after midnight, I shoved my suitcase past the door to our apartment. Sensitively, Susan had packed her things away so that the apartment appeared unchanged.

She sat up in bed, "Hi honey. How was the weekend with Lauren?"

My eyes were the size of eggs. "This is a mistake," I blurted out.

Susan rolled her eyes. Did I detect amusement?

"We'll deal with it in the morning," she said turning back to sleep.

By morning I was fine again, and Susan never mentioned it. It occurred to me that I rather liked being handled.

Susan seems to know me and she accepts me for who I am.

Or so I thought.

THIRTY-NINE

State of the Union

By the winter of 1980, Susan and I had lived together for two years. On Friday nights when I didn't visit Lauren, it was our habit to leave Manhattan and drive north to my Ludlow, Vermont cottage. Including Susan and me, the car now carried five—Max, the dog that Susan rescued from the streets in Queens, and two stray cats that Susan found on the subway. We'd reach Ludlow about two in the morning, when I'd set about reopening the freezing cottage. First I lit a fire in the Vermont Castings stove that stood on a raised platform in the living room. Susan, Max and the two cats headed upstairs to bundle in bed under a heavy quilt while the house warmed. As they slept, I headed for the basement crawl space to repair the water pipes, which regularly splintered from the cold.

Besides the wood stove, the cottage had electric baseboard heat, but because it cost so much, I turned the heat off when we left on Sundays and drained the water from the pipes that were also wrapped with electric heat tapes. My frugality was pound foolish, because even using heat tapes, I always found several pipes split or frozen on our arrival. Through many a cold Friday night I elbowed my way along the basement crawl space, replacing split pipes with bright new copper tubes, fluxing the ends and heating the couplings until the solder sucked in to form its shiny seal.

By morning the house had water again and while my gang still slept, I'd head to Sweet Surrender, the local bakery, for my morning ritual of donuts and coffee. Friends proclaimed it a three, four or five donut morning based on how wild my eyes looked after a sleepless night followed by massive doses of coffee and sugar.

One Saturday I was especially jumpy from my caffeine fix. Susan was washing dishes in the kitchen.

"Who's your true man," I said playfully.

"You," Susan said half-heartedly.

"Gee, don't knock me down with enthusiasm," I said.

Susan continued to sponge the dishes.

"You're my woman," I said, playfully putting an arm around her waist.

She ignored the gesture.

"Best man you ever had?" I tested.

"Umm," she muttered.

Her indifference was unsettling, and I felt my intestines tighten with a familiar panic that dated back to worries about my first wife. And even earlier.

What's going on here, I wondered. *Why is she growing cool to me?*

"Wan'na get married?" I blurted out.

My words startled both of us. I'd said them without a moment's forethought as if they burst suddenly from ruptured piping.

Susan turned to face me with a quizzical look.

"No kidding," I said.

"Why fix what isn't broken?" She asked.

What's bothering her, I worried. *Is she unhappy with me? Does she wish she wasn't with me?* I had to know, so I pressed on.

"It's time to quit fooling around," I said "This play-house relationship is for kids. Either we should get married or we should split up."

"Why? What's wrong with it the way it is?" Susan said.

"We're too old to play house. We ought to make a commitment or hang it up."

I was kidding at first when I suggested marriage, but her sudden coolness turned my playful suggestion into a cause celebre. I had to be sure she wasn't thinking of leaving, and her disinterest was all the motivation I needed to keep cajoling and threatening her until later that weekend she reluctantly said she would marry me rather than see us split up.

A few Saturdays later I was sipping coffee at Sweet Surrender when our plumber, Al Lestrano, pulled up a stool.

"Hey," he said, "still fixing the pipes like I showed you?"

"Yeah, thanks, Al." I shook his calloused hand. "That flux works like a charm. Cold work at night though isn't it?"

"Better'n what I go through in mud season," said Al.

"I suppose," I said. "Say, Susan and I want to get married, and I need a rabbi or a priest. Know anybody you like who could do it?"

"I could marry you guys," he said.

"You?"

"I'm a justice of the peace, so I have the power to marry people." said Al.

"Ever married anyone?" I asked.

"Nope."

"Great. Susan and I will be your first."

In August of 1982, Mom, Susan's parents and about twenty friends crowded for the ceremony in a bright sunroom off the rear of our Ludlow cottage. The room had a Woodstock feel with walls of blonde pine, a beamed pinewood ceiling and a big circular, stained-glass window. Rays of sunlight fell on the bundles of local flowers our friends had gathered.

Susan had thought more seriously about what we doing than I, and I learned later how reluctant she'd been to go ahead with the ceremony. She had locked herself in the bathroom and was refusing to come out. Her girlfriends pleaded with her.

"People came a long way," they coaxed.

"Nothing but death is final," said another.

"You can always undo it later," said another.

Eventually they coaxed her into the guest-filled room and to my side. Unaware of what had occurred, I told everyone to make a circle and to hold hands. I said a prayer and turned the ceremony over to Al.

Uncertain, Al turned back to me for direction.

"Just marry us," I said. "Whatever you say will be fine."

Al chose the only words he knew.

"Do you, Michael, promise to love, honor and obey this woman?"

"I do."

The ceremony proceeded traditionally until Al asked, "And do you, Michael, promise to give Susan all your worldly possessions?"

"No way," I said firmly.

"I beg your pardon," Susan demanded.

We got through the ceremony.

At around six that evening our group assembled for the wedding dinner in an atmosphere fit for a movie set. Dark, antique cherry walls framed the massive stone fireplace in the lobby of The Great Stone Ridge Inn & Hotel. Suits of armor with shields and drawn swords stood in the adjacent rooms. The bridal suite had a four-poster bed with a white net canopy. On the dressers were flowers in vases on crocheted doilies, and in the center of the adjoining bathroom was a four-foot wide, double-deep porcelain tub on lion claw legs.

Dinner was in the main dining room where we seated our guests at tables arranged in a U-shape so we could all be together.

"Don't you think you've had enough," I whispered when Susan beckoned for another bottle of champagne.

"Not nearly enough," she said, unrestrained in her misgivings.

The more she drank, the more critical she became.

"Do you always have to talk with food in your mouth?" she asked.

"Why did I have to make all the arrangements?" she demanded.

"You're so selfish," she noted.

Her voice grew louder, and our guests turned, some amused and others anxious about our bickering.

"Could you lower your voice," I whispered. "Can't this wait until we're back in our room?"

It was a tactical blunder, because while my request didn't restrain Susan at the dinner table, it gave her permission to continue haranguing me back in the bridal suite. She ranted on through an endless night, proceeding through a list of my shortcomings, stopping only for her mouth to suck any last drops she could pull from a lipstick-stained champagne bottle she held like a trumpet.

"Why didn't you wear the black shoes I set out for you?" she demanded. "My friends think the way you dress is embarrassing."

"Why do you change every decision I make?" she asked.

"Can't you hang your own clothes up? What am I, the maid?" she continued.

Susan supported each charge against me with an impressive recall of detail.

"You haven't changed an iota from your behavior on Memorial Day in 1979, when you made my parents and me sit all day in a hot car while you searched for some stupid computer jack. It's always all about Michael—whatever precious Michael wants. I agree to ride with you for one simple errand and you turn it into a trip to the cleaners, the bank, Home Depot and the UPS center. I'm a prisoner in your car."

I pictured a pneumatic drill-hammer in place of her mouth.

Maybe if I capitulate, her harangue will end, I thought.

"I'll try to be more aware of it," I said. "Perhaps I could tell you the stops I'm planning to make before we leave?"

"You say you will, but you won't. You never keep your promises," she added.

Capitulation didn't work. I'd try logic.

"I had to stop at the bank for cash so we could eat at Palmers," I said. "You wanted to eat at Palmers, and they don't take credit cards. I had to pick up my dry cleaning to wear the blue shirt you said you wanted me to wear. And it was your package we sent by UPS. I'm trying to please you, but you won't see it."

Susan's mouth rippled through the bottom of the champagne bottle.

"We didn't get the chandelier I wanted either. Who says you get to make all the decisions?" she slurred.

It was a groom's worst nightmare. I lifted the bride's veil to find a red-eyed harpy.

Marriage created a subtle change in our relationship, as when plates shifting miles beneath the earth cause rumblings at its surface. Formalizing the relationship altered Susan's perception of me. I was her husband now, and as a child she'd been taught what that meant. Daily she'd listened to her mother's friends complain about men and mutter that a wife was an indentured position. Husbands, they said, were irritants that left creases in the couch cushions and wrinkles in the bedspread. I became a splash of wine on Susan's freshly ironed tablecloth.

If I took cheese from the refrigerator, Susan's hawkish eyes followed waiting to sponge any crumb that should fall. She hurried my damp shower towel to the washing machine, and if I dropped a Kleenex in the wastebasket, she rushed to empty it as if hoping to eradicate any trace of me. I tried to help around the house but she wouldn't have it. It fit her new script better to do it all and then complain that I was useless. Soon I stopped trying to help, knowing that standing aside minimized the friction but noting also that standing aside increased the growing distance between us. My own growing coolness had an unintended effect. Susan found it appealing, and the more standoffish I was, the more attractive she found me. But when I warmed to her again, she quickly lost interest. I felt like I was being spun around. While dizzying, it had a vague familiarity.

Months passed with the two of us seated as if in opposite cars on a Ferris wheel. It was clear that so positioned, we could never meet.

FORTY

Susan

SUSAN'S BIOLOGICAL PARENTS PUT HER UP FOR ADOPTION at her birth in 1950. A couple named David and Elaine wanted a child, and after completing the required paperwork, they brought Susan home to their modest ranch house in Cheektowaga, New York, a suburb of Buffalo.

Susan was four when the doctors had grave news. They advised David and Elaine that Elaine had an incurable liver disease and gave her at best a year to live. Elaine didn't tell Susan immediately, but Susan was suspicious of the rows of brown medicine vials on her Mom's dresser. She wondered why her mom spent so much time at clinics and hospitals. At family gatherings, the whispering about Elaine's condition grew so conspicuous that Elaine decided it was time for her daughter to know the truth. With the mother's eyes filled with tears, Elaine confirmed Susan's worst fear. Susan took the news stone-faced and without a tear. Following her natural instinct, she put the matter out of her mind and pretended everything was just fine. But pretending became harder when her relatives came to visit. They insisted on pulling Susan aside to remind her of mother's condition.

"Just a matter of time," they insisted. "Be extra good to your mom. She won't be here long."

Susan tried as hard as she could to be extra, extra good.

Though Elaine grew progressively weaker, the disease moved slower than expected, and she confounded the doctors and relatives by staying alive for ten more years. That bought her a precious decade to prepare her adopted daughter for the inevitable. As if to compensate her daughter for the coming loss, when Elaine felt up to it she took Susan shopping. They bought anything Susan showed an interest in. If she liked a red dress, her mother gathered it off the rack along with its twin in blue, and then they looked for matching hats.

When Susan was fourteen and Elaine thirty-nine, Elaine went to the hospital for the last time. Her death was mercifully quick. The following week Susan, her father David, and the relatives gathered for Elaine's interment, tearfully encircling the casket to hold hands as a priest led them in prayer. Susan dropped her hands, crossed her arms and scowled.

In the months that followed, Susan's father took for granted that the household chores would get done, and Susan did them as if her life depended on it. When school let out, she hurried home to vacuum the carpet, take a cloth to the windows and prepare her father's dinner. She was her Dad's "good little girl" if his house sparkled and dinner was on the table when he pulled in the driveway. Susan made a nightly point of listing each chore as she served his dinner.

"Look what I've accomplished after school," she'd say. "I washed the china and vacuumed upstairs. I did the laundry and put on fresh bed sheets, and is your steak done enough?

Her father's nod of approval meant that for the moment Susan could relax.

After a proper time of mourning, Susan's father went on a blind date and met Paula, an attractive, proper Catholic woman from a large Italian family. The two began to date several times a week, then almost nightly, and soon it no longer mattered to David that Susan had prepared his dinner. He was at his favorite restaurant with Paula. Susan cleaned harder and tried to come up with tempting dishes for her dad, but she'd fallen off his radar. She spent many evenings alone, decorated by herself on Christmas Eve, placing gifts under the tree for her father in an empty living room. David married Paula, and Susan's fears that she'd be entirely forgotten proved unfounded. Fortunately for Susan, Paula very much liked her stepdaughter. The two teamed up to do the housekeeping, though as time went on they reversed their roles. Susan mothered Paula, guiding the inexperienced stepmother in the care and feeding of her father. A year later, Paula gave birth to Susan's half brother, Edward and it was agreed that Susan's bedroom would become Edward's nursery, while Susan would get a smaller room. An unspoken caste system developed, and it was simply assumed that the birth child outranked Susan. Even Paula's four sisters, Susan's new aunts, assumed the hierarchy was the expected natural order. The four aunts added provisions in their wills for Edward, though none for Susan.

When she was fourteen, Susan went to summer camp. It was a lonely time for her. After lunch in the big dining hall, she would gather with her campmates for mail distribution. Names were called, but there were no letters for her. After several weeks at camp, she called her dad and pleaded with him to bring her home. He agreed to get her that afternoon, and Susan tugged her plaid suitcase down the long dirt road to await his arrival under the camp's entrance sign. Hours passed, but she never saw her parents. The camp director convinced them not to come. "She has to learn to tough it out. It's all part of growing up," he insisted.

At sixteen, Susan graduated Cheektowaga High with honors. Several colleges accepted her, and she chose Syracuse University, only two hours from home. But in four years of college no one visited her. No one came for her graduation, so Susan skipped the ceremonies too. She went on to get her Masters in Social Work at Adelphi University, and no one came to that graduation either.

MSW in hand, she looked for a job as a social worker, but in 1970 the job market was lean. She and her college boyfriend, newly accepted to the New York State Bar, settled for more menial jobs—she scooping ice cream and he helping a local caterer. At night they sent out resumes. They married a year later and moved into her husband's prominent Long Island family home.

* * *

Susan had two preoccupations, cleaning and shopping, and she did both with a frenzied sense of urgency. Friends nicknamed her Cinderella when she refused to come have a drink with them until she finished her obsessive cleaning. She became agitated if a picture frame wasn't level or if she found a dark garment in the white clothes hamper. Her husband urged her to relax about the housecleaning. But she couldn't, and when he returned home at night, Susan insisted on listing each completed chore—a childhood ritual obsessively replayed.

Her second passion, shopping, led her to the malls, and almost daily she returned home with a new treasure. Her excessive credit card balances irritated her new husband, but he decided it was easier to pay the bills than to confront the issue.

Over time a brittle tension developed between the two, and the marriage soured. Susan ignored that they'd grown remote, preferring instead to concentrate on her perfectly set dinner table, rearranging the plates and trying alternate floral arrangements until her world seemed as pretty as the magazine pictures she'd dog-eared. But it was not pretty, and in the third year of their marriage, the couple separated and then divorced. Susan began to doubt that she would ever have the secure, picture-perfect family she'd often imagined.

She moved into a small rental apartment and found a social work position at the State of New York's Creedmoor Psychiatric Center, a mammoth sprawling facility. Staff called Creedmoor "the mother ship" because from a huge central campus location, like a giant octopus, it fed paperwork to a handful of satellite offices. Before long, Creedmoor promoted Susan to head up its Astoria Queens office. She directed a team of therapists who adored her because she'd roll up her sleeves and clean toilets with them if that's what it took to get them ready for a state inspection—an unusual attitude that created Susan's fiercely loyal staff.

After work and in her spare time, Susan decorated and then redecorated her new apartment, determined to create a prefect home. Decor became her consuming focus as the apartment filled with curtains, china, doilies and antiques. She lay carpet and changed the wall colors, and then she changed the colors again.

Credit cards paid for the decorating and redecorating as Susan tried to create the family picture that drove her. In her mind, as long as she had credit cards, she had money. The annoying spending limits on cards were easily circumvented. When she maxed out one card, she picked from the stack of credit card offers that arrived daily and she applied for another, shifting balances like a three-card monte game. She opened each new line of credit just in time to cover her growing debt, ignoring soaring balances and usurious interest rates. Frosty martinis after work helped put out of her mind the nuisance calls that began to come from collection agencies. Vodka kept her debt invisible. Susan saw nothing more than the porcelain ballerina or the china butter dish that she clutched tightly as she moved through the checkout line at the local clearance center.

Holidays were another excuse to redecorate, and Christmas provided Susan an opportunity to display her most impressive collection. She unboxed the battery-operated Santa that swayed to an Elvis tune, the mechanical Santa typing Christmas lists, the Santa circling on an airplane, Santas in cars and in trees, electric reindeer in flight and ceramic Christmas villages with homes, churches, banks and railroads. She decorated multiple Christmas trees with treasured ornaments saved from her childhood.

Credit cards in hand, she rang up Easter Bunny trees and strings of heart-shaped Valentine lights, glowing Fourth of July flags, blinking peppers for Cinco de Mayo. She accumulated Halloween villages with haunted houses and lightning sounds, dimly-lit cemeteries, and witches riding broomsticks. The green flags flew on St. Patrick's Day. Every closet brimmed with crates full of decorations, as if to complete a child's fantasy world, her escape from an otherwise untenable reality.

Friends teased that Susan had a holiday disorder. What she didn't have was a choice. She shopped compulsively, and if her search along aisles of knickknacks produced nothing thrilling, she withered like a plant that had gone too long without water.

FORTY-ONE

Couple on the Couch

IN 1996, WE'D BEEN MARRIED FOR FIFTEEN YEARS. We had almost separated twice, coming so close that after one high pitched battle, Susan met with a divorce attorney.

I hated the thought of failing in a second marriage. I imagined the looks I'd see when I told family and friends—the "didn't I tell you so" glances they'd exchange while acting supportive but writing me off as flawed.

I urged Susan to join me in couple's therapy.

"We could see Sarah together," I urged. "Have we really given this a chance? Surely we can work it out?"

My plea has a familiar ring, I thought. *Isn't this the same argument—perhaps the very words I'd used in the hope of keeping my first marriage going?*

Susan agreed to see Sarah with me.

We entered Sarah's large, sparse loft and apprehensively took our seats, each anxious to plead our case. Susan spoke first, wasting no time as she started a list my faults. She ticked off fifteen years of them, barely pausing for breath, while I sat grinning, jaws locked, with my face turned away from her to hide my anger.

Sarah interrupted Susan some twenty items into her list.

"So why do you stay with him?" Sarah asked. "You didn't get a baby. You say the sex is no good. You don't seem to like him. So tell me, Susan, why do you stay?"

Susan expected Sarah to advocate for togetherness, so the question caught her off guard. I was unnerved by it too.

"Well, I, I'm not sure . . . He didn't always . . . usually he . . ." Her voice lost its machine gun cadence.

Sarah asked her once again, "Why don't you leave him?"

I shifted in my wooden chair, uneasy about Sarah's line of questioning.

Why is Sarah painting Susan into a corner? I wondered. *After all Susan's complaints, what choice does she have but to announce that she's leaving me? What's more, Sarah is acting like that's what she recommends. Will Susan ask for a divorce right in front of Sarah? Or will she wait until the ride home?*

I felt beaten as the session ended, as if the jury had found me guilty and sentencing was imminent. Susan and I silently gathered our coats and left the loft. On the way home our cab got caught in heavy traffic, and we sat wordlessly in the back seat. Happy-go-lucky reggae music streamed incongruously from the front as the taxi driver's knit cap bobbed to the beat above the partition. I said nothing. Why should I facilitate my own execution? Susan cleared her throat.

Here it comes, I thought.

"We need to stop at D'Agostinos for radishes and pork chops," she reminded me.

By our third session, Susan was still working through her list, but I could look at her again.

"He's my father all over again," Susan told Sarah. "He lets me down like my father did. Neither of them can keep a promise."

"We agreed you and Michael would discuss that issue at home. Did you?" Sarah asked.

"For Christ sake," I interrupted, "one time sixteen years ago, before we were married, I told her I wished I could take her to the Seychelles. It wasn't a promise. It wasn't a binding contract. It was a casual goddamn comment—a wish I said aloud—but I've heard about it now for sixteen years. How come she never brings up all the things I do for her? You know why you never hear about them? Because she's the god damn queen of victims, that's why."

"What about that Susan?" Sarah asked. "Is it easier for you to assume Michael always lets you down?"

"He *is* just like my father," Susan protested.

"That's a safe position for you, isn't it," Sarah said. "You don't risk a thing."

"Why should I trust him? The man never comes through," said Susan.

"If you really believe that, then I ask you again, Susan, why stay? Isn't it obvious you'd be happier out of the relationship?"

Susan face went blank. We both said nothing for a few minutes until Sarah said it was time to stop.

As the cab sped through heavy uptown traffic, Susan announced she was finished with Sarah.

"Why?" I asked, surprised.

"I don't like her style," she said. "She's too pushy."

"Isn't that what we wanted?" I asked.

"You see her all you want, Michael, but I'm done," Susan said.

In our next session, Sarah was annoyed when I told her of Susan's decision.

"You can't do the work for her, Michael. How are you going to get anywhere coming to couples therapy alone?"

"She's trying," I said lamely.

"Is the woman meeting your needs, or are you settling?" Sarah asked.

"I'm not going to quit."

"Because it scares you to death," Sarah's voice rose. "You're terrified of being alone."

"Until I'm sure I've cleaned up my own act—that for once in my life I've been totally there for a woman—I'm not leaving," I said.

"Because you're scared," Sarah insisted. "And I repeat. You can't do the work for two."

"For god's sake, Sarah. If I leave Susan, I'll always think that I caused the split. I'll worry that no woman could stand me for long, and I'll have the same issues with the next woman and the next. I can't keep doing this."

"The two of you pass like ships in the night. You never connect, which tells me a lot. I'm not telling you to leave, Michael," said Sarah. "I'm telling you you're scared out of your wits. You are afraid of being left, and we both know where that comes from—from a boy whose mother teased, betrayed and left him on a daily basis. But you aren't a child anymore. You're an adult, and I suggest that if you stay with Susan, at least open your eyes and see what the hell is going on between the two of you. Wake up, man. You say you want to be open to the woman. Great. If she responds to your openness, mazel tov. But if she doesn't, at what point do you consider the possibility that you are wasting your time?"

I stared blankly at Sarah with my arms crossed. I eyed my watch. I couldn't wait to escape the loft.

Sarah stared back at me, drumming her fingers impatiently. At ten to the hour she stood up, ending the session. That was the point at which she always took out her black notebook to confirm our next appointment. But as I left the loft, I realized she'd forgotten to do it.

FORTY-TWO

No Man's Land

OUR MARRIAGE CONTINUED in a state of mutual deterrence.

The prevailing tension took me back to my first marriage. If there was any difference, this time I was conscious of how angry we were—something I couldn't acknowledge before. The first time around, we heaped our anger in a pile in the center of the room. It was obvious to both of us that the heap was there. But it seemed safer to tiptoe around it than to mention it. Neither my first wife nor I dared acknowledge the pile, heaped high with our disappointments, because acknowledging it might force the issue. The safer course was a self-imposed obliviousness, a form of blindness that fell automatically and was like the blank stares of Grandfather Isaac's daughters, my aunts. Denial let my first wife's barbs ricochet off my consciousness, and while her insults left me feeling kicked in the stomach, they slipped away so quickly that I left the room knowing only that something bad had happened. But I wasn't sure what, or why I felt so unhappy. On rare occasions when we did confront each other, our responses lacked proportion. She jaywalked. I dropped the A-bomb. Her escalation followed mine until a mildest criticism sent both of us climbing a Himalayan peak. We were kids playing an adult's game. We thought it was a game about winning, and we chiseled, cheated and chipped away at the marriage until there was no choice but to call the game.

In my next session I told Sarah how worried I was about my second marriage.

"Will it end up like my first? Will I end up like my cousins'?"

"Meaning what?" Sarah look puzzled.

"Ira, Ian, Irwin . . . None of them could sustain a relationship. Not one of them could be emotionally intimate. They all died alone. I'm the only one who ever married, even though my first marriage didn't make it. So what does it say if this one fails too?"

"It says that you try again," Sarah said.

"I don't want to try again," I said bristling. "I want to get it right this time. I want to be a better husband in the marriage I'm in now. I don't want to end up like them."

"Your cousins were damaged," Sarah said. "They weren't capable of intimacy, but you are making progress and you can love. Maybe you aren't quite there yet, but you have the capacity."

"So why do I hold back on my more tender feelings?" I asked.

"You know when you will?" Sarah asked.

She had my full attention.

"You will give wholeheartedly to a woman as soon as you love yourself. That's when you will feel safe—and when you'll feel loved also."

"So how is that going to happen?" I asked

"You're getting there," Sarah said. "Adults with your background have to do a kind of self-parenting."

"What the hell does that mean?" I asked.

"Think about how you helped raise Lauren. You give to a child, you nurture her, and over time a reserve builds in the child, a reserve of love, a pool of having-been-given-to, if you will. Then along comes a day when the child begins to love you back. But accumulating that reservoir has to come first. And you are building one for yourself in here. We're building it together. You can be insincere. You can be narcissistic, Michael, but more and more I see you giving back. And you're doing it wholeheartedly."

"Maybe," I said hopefully.

FORTY-THREE

Finding Michael

THE STATUS QUO PREVAILED THROUGH 1998, our seventeenth year of marriage. Susan and I remained hunkered down in opposing trenches, too fearful to confront—too insecure to leave.

Susan huddled with friends to relish her martyrdom. Tongues wagged in consolation as she proceeded down the impressively long list of my transgressions.

"Is it true?"

"The bastard!"

"He did that?"

"I don't know why I put up with him," Susan sighed.

Her Greek chorus condemned me in delicious unison.

"He's the cross you bear," they nodded sympathetically.

In sessions, Sarah continued to question the marriage, guiding me deeper into my sadness until I had to acknowledge, however tentatively, that my relationship with Susan might have to end. At first I stubbornly resisted, knowing a second failure would lead to deeper loneliness. But in time it was clear even to me that I could handle it.

That was a pivotal point, because when I seriously considered leaving Susan, the unexpected happened. I'd always described my fear of leaving as my fear of being left. I shed that passivity now. I realized my fear of being left wasn't as bad as the oppressive feeling of aloneness I felt when the two of us were together.

Prepared to leave but still hopeful, I decided to confront Susan every time she cut me with a mean-spirited judgment. My candid confrontations were mechanical at first, but soon a new directness replaced our stealth fighting below the radar. I discovered that my fear of being direct—the risk that I'd be abandoned if I was—depended on a myth. I'd presumed there was security in being a couple when in fact both of us were already alone.

When my first marriage ended and I went through months of despair, I'd turned to fantasy—to my Beowolf bar maidens—and I was tempted to summon them again. But I understood how dangerous those sirens were, and I couldn't let myself drift onto their rocks or be lured by their distractions from issues I had to deal with. Instead I forced myself to stand and tell Susan how much she hurt me. Then I asked her for what I needed, and what I wanted became clearer. I wanted a mate without a scorecard who loved me for who I was. I wanted to feel those important waves of contact when I looked into her eyes and to feel we were together in a way that couldn't be shared with others.

I was determined to try a final time to reach her. I knew a difficult candor was my only hope.

It took forced concentration to keep me alert during our exchanges. I had to quash my habit of becoming oblivious to her as a means of avoiding unpleasant friction. Instead I had to grab hold of my thoughts, shake them and demand that my mind focus on everything Susan said, her smallest gestures. I could not let a single judgment drop unnoticed or ignore one manipulative act without responding. I had a choice. Either throw the grenade back or watch it go off in my face.

My efforts may seem more like battle tactics than acts of love, or like the tedious parlay during international diplomatic negotiations. But I hoped to break seventeen years of destructive habit and find love with the woman I'd chosen. That required a mature, deliberate effort, not the expectation of a magic infatuation or faith there'd be an explosion of testosterone.

So I watched carefully, trusting in our capacity for love but at the same time knowing we both needed to change. I'd chosen a powerfully manipulative mate. I knew her tactics. How many times had I seen her wait until we were in a crowded elevator and then put me down, assuming there would be no retribution. Now I wouldn't let her comment pass. I insisted that we discuss it on the spot, even as the people in the elevator turned to stare. It was an unpleasant effort. Clearly the elevator onlookers saw me as a bully and Susan as an innocent victim. But I ignored their discomfort and my own so that I could deal with the issue in real time. Dealing got easier, and before long, the sack of discontents each of us carried slowly emptied.

Paradoxically, the more persistently I challenged Susan, the more open to her I became. I found myself really wanting to know what upset her, and as my interest grew so did my ability to hear her complaints without freezing up in defensive deafness. I took her concerns seriously. I didn't care a bit about dish towels, but I knew it upset Susan when I mindlessly flung a towel on the counter, so I retrieved it and hung it carefully on its bar. I liked to eat at home, while Susan loved restaurants, so I made a point to eat out more often. These were small things, surely not the stuff of romance novels. They were the dull, sundry aspects of everyday life—tedious, yet powerfully consequential.

Progress came in spurts with predictable setbacks.

In a session with Sarah, I described a recent unpleasant evening when Susan couldn't resist playing her old game. She'd asked me to buy her a particular piece of jewelry, and I told her I wouldn't. So the following night, she asked for it again—this time slyly, innocently asking in front of a crowd of friends while remarking that she didn't have a lot of jewelry. It would be a win-win situation for her, she assumed. Either she'd get the jewelry or I'd come off as the bad guy.

"So you said what?" Sarah asked.

I said, "No, you can't have it, Susan . . . as you know very well since we discussed this just last night. You do remember our discussion, don't you, Susan? When I explained why we can't afford it? Your recent credit card expenses, Susan?"

I paused.

"And Susan said . . . ?" Sarah prompted.

"She shrugged her shoulders and rolled her eyes at her friends."

"So you keep taking it, Michael. Why? Are you that afraid to leave her?"

"I used to be, Sarah, but I no longer am," I said. "I could leave tomorrow. I'm not staying because I'm scared."

"Then why?"

"I believe we will reach each other," I said quietly.

"And when is this supposed to happen?" Sarah asked sarcastically.

I shrugged.

That further annoyed Sarah.

"Then what do you expect from me?" she said.

I shrugged again.

Sarah and I had a dozen such exchanges. She saw me as weak. I felt she hadn't seen a change in me. On the other hand, I trusted Sarah and knew her instincts were reliable. Was I staying married only because I was weak?

Without intent, my efforts to respond to Susan more directly started a chain of transformations that changed how I acted with everyone. To come from a real place for her, I had to first explore my own character and what I needed from her. With that exploration, the sense grew that I had a right to what I wanted, that I was worthy of it. My sense of worthiness left me less willing to acquiesce to others by reflecting a character I knew they'd prefer. I wasn't willing to shuffle through my deck of pleasing personalities. How strange that felt. Someone who'd habitually reflected light began to generate his own.

The more clearly I saw myself, the more certain I was that the raw ingredients of my nature had always been there, including a native empathy for others and more confidence than I imagined possible. Giving others my honest opinion, without first scanning to know theirs, became my new habit. I offered it without acquiescence and without expectation, respectfully and devoid of rebelliousness. When asked at the bar if I heard the one about the black or the fag, I no longer feigned weak amusement, masking my discomfort with a limp smile. I said the joke wasn't funny. I said so without rancor. My candor came tentatively in the beginning, and I would clench my stomach, ready for battles that never came, because when I spoke genuinely, people could hear me. When I pursued an argument, I found intermediate levels of expression whereas before I knew of only two: passive silence or nuclear blast.

That's when it dawned on me. Mr. Master of Ceremonies was on his deathbed.

As I corkscrewed inward, becoming more familiar with my core, I was at the same time drawn outside myself, listening to others and feeling concerned for them. The reservoir Sarah described was filling, and the reserve I built up meant I could care for others, not as a finishing school technique but from the native compassion I felt for anyone seeking the way through their own psychological maze, yearning to find the way home.

FORTY-FOUR

Contact

THOUGH SUSAN AND I HAD BEEN MARRIED FOR NINETEEN YEARS, it wasn't until the millennium year that we became a couple. I wasn't expecting anything unusual on the humid, summer afternoon when I came into our bedroom to check on dinner plans.

Susan was sitting at the corner of the mattress staring at the floor. She looked anxious, and her skin was pale, so I didn't bother her about dinner.

"What's wrong?" I asked gently.

She looked up slowly, not fully present, appearing bewildered. There was red in the whites of her eyes. They finally held on me as if I'd just come into focus.

"Michael, Dad called earlier. He told me that Mom lost her balance and fell in the living room this afternoon." Susan spoke deliberately, like a foreigner struggling with the language. "She fell on the coffee table and broke her arm. Something's wrong with her balance, and she has headaches, Dad says. He took her to the hospital."

I sat next to Susan on the bed, and wiped her eyes with a tissue. "What did they say?"

"The doctor asked Mom to move her finger to her nose. She missed it repeatedly. He wants her to have a MRI of the brain," said Susan looking worried.

"How long has she had the headaches?" I asked.

"She can't recall, Michael. She's so confused. She can't sleep because she's terrified and Dad and Edward are wrecks. They haven't a clue what to do. I'm flying home next Monday to take Mom for the MRI."

"Can't they do it sooner than Monday?" I asked.

"She has to wait for an MRI machine that is open-faced. Mom's too claustrophobic for the tunnel ones," Susan said.

"Does the doctor think it's a tumor?" I asked.

Susan looked tortured.

"They don't know, but it may be," said Susan, resting her forehead on her palm.

"If it's a tumor, it's not necessarily malignant, right?" I asked.

"Even if it is, they might be able to remove it with a laser."

"Then let's not assume the worse."

"The dizziness could also be her new blood pressure medication," Susan said hopefully. "They put her on beta-blockers a few weeks ago."

She fell silent. Her face looked weary and her eyes were vacant for a moment. Then her presence returned.

"Michael, I can't stop thinking about Elaine's funeral. I'm seeing it over and over like a terrible daydream."

"Please tell me" I said.

Susan said nothing.

"What do you see?" I prodded gently.

"I'm a little girl, back when Mom died. I'm at her funeral in my good wool coat, standing next to Dad and my relatives. The sun is out, but my coat isn't keeping me warm, and I'm shivering. Mom's casket is huge. It's on this ugly pulley machine with ropes and wheels that squeak as the men lower it. I'm so unhappy. I try to call to her, but nothing will come out. My uncles are crying, and Dad's wiping his eyes with that disgusting handkerchief he always carries. I want to cry too, but the air won't pass in my throat. The casket goes lower and lower into the hole until I can only see the top of it. A moment later I can't see it at all . . . and Mom's gone. There is just this big hole in the lawn. The men come with shovels and start to fill her grave. I can hear every shovelful of dirt slide across Mom's casket. Each thud feels like they're hammering my head."

I took her hand.

Susan turned to me, pleading, "What if Paula has a tumor, Michael? What if I lose her too?"

Her face looked older than her years. As I gently brought her to my chest, she began to sob.

"Mom's dizziness . . ." she paused to catch her sobbing breath. She looked up at me and continued, ". . . her dizziness and her headaches. It feels just like it did with Elaine. All I wanted was to have my mom, but the relatives kept insisting she was going to die, as if I wasn't supposed to want her to live. When Mom stayed alive for so long, I prayed that my uncles were wrong. But then she died, and I was left with him—with Dad," Her face turned bitter. "He forgot I was even there. I was just a little girl, Michael, but he . . ." She left her sentence unfinished and began to cry.

I rocked her back and forth as her sobs came on choked breath. I don't recall time passing, only that I held her in my arms, tenderly rubbing her back and holding her to me until her sobs softened and turned to silent tears.

She looked at me with wet eyes.

"I know I'm difficult, Michael, but don't you leave me too," she pleaded.

"It won't happen," I promised.

I cupped her chin in my hands as tears flowed down my palms.

"Let it come, Susan," I urged. "For god's sake, let all of it out."

Susan's sobs grew quickly into a terrifying wail and then to the most primal of screams, a child's gut wrenching call for help, so penetrable that my chest felt crushed.

"I want my mommy," she cried pounding her fists on my back. "All I want is my goddamn mommy."

"I know you do, honey," I whispered. "I know you do."

I held her until her wailing softened. She was content to stay rocking in my arms. In time she lay still as I held her, and slowly her eyes closed. I gently lifted her into bed, carefully setting a blanket on her. I sat back on the bed corner and saw that the light outside our bedroom window had faded with the falling of night. The moon, ice-white earlier, had become an orange harvest moon.

After a while Susan stirred, and I switched on the bed lamp to be sure she was okay. She opened her eyes briefly, and I saw that the drawn edges were gone from her face. Her skin had a hint of yellow, and her wet eyes were open and unprotected like those of a child. She tried to force a smile, but I smoothed her cheek with my fingers as if to say it wasn't necessary. Soon she fell asleep again. I turned off the light and slipped into bed alongside my wife.

When Susan awoke in the morning, I stiffened my shoulders, unconsciously preparing for the usual tension. It wasn't there, but I didn't notice its absence at first. That realization that the vibration in the room had changed didn't come like a firebolt. I wasn't expecting any change, nor was I drawn magnetically to notice it, nor spellbound by it. Rather my awareness that Susan was different dawned gradually, subtly. I noticed it first in the tiny sequences of her arms as she sat up in bed and stretched, the kind of stretch that follows a really good night's sleep. Her outstretched arms lacked their usual protectiveness, their attempt to distance me, and at the top of her stretch, she smiled warmly. As she dressed, I had the sense that she was glad to have me in the room, and it occurred to me that while I might not be the man in her pictures, for a brief but potentially sustainable moment, she'd opened up to me last night and realized that I was safe—and that I might offer even more than safety.

The events of the previous night didn't cause the change. Nor did it come because doctors soon determined that Paula's dizziness wasn't life-threatening. Transformation came from years of effort—the work Susan did on her own and my sessions with Sarah and the therapists that preceded her. While that night wasn't the cause, it was the catalyst, and it marked a turning point.

The change in Susan, in us, while inconsistent, was undeniable. Susan confirmed it in casual moments when I least expected it. I'd be napping on a lazy weekend afternoon and sense her presence at my eyelids. I'd open my eyes and find her smiling at me, and she'd stroke my forehead and whisper, "Do you know I love you?"

Or in a cab she'd turn, and when our eyes met she would say, "How lucky I am."

She didn't say it every day. There were days when I encountered her old indifference, even days when Susan cut me with an outdated judgment. There were also days when her affection was mechanical, as if re-cropping a digitized picture to include me again.

But undeniably we had moments of real connection now.

Trusting Susan made it easier for me to open to my group members and my friends. I could look people in the eye without fearing that they would discover I was aloof or that they'd see my monster and dismiss me. With a carefully chosen few, I dared share a tender eye-to-eye communication, a contact I couldn't risk previously. I could reveal myself without marshalling defenses, and I began to relax from my exhausting hyper vigilance.

I even asked for help to shoulder my globe.

FORTY-FIVE

The Beginning

TWO MORE YEARS PASSED. In the fall of 2002, I turned to Susan.

"We don't even know if we're legally married," I said over coffee.

"I know," she said. "Do you think Al the plumber ever filed the marriage papers?"

"Who knows? But we have a long weekend coming up. We'll get to Vermont on Thursday night, so let's go to Town Hall Friday morning and find out."

"Sure," she said. "After twenty-one years, I think we're married with or without the papers. But it would be nice to be official. All these years and we never bothered to pick up the marriage certificate."

"We had mixed feelings didn't we?" I said. "Let's find out Friday."

I don't recall a lot of things about the year 2002. I can't remember if Vermont's winter was especially rough so that the pipes in the crawl space required more repairs than usual. I don't remember my donut count at the bakery that Friday morning or if the coffee was freshly brewed or stale from sitting too long. I can't even remember if the weather that Friday was gray or sunny, dry or snowy. All I remember is the sense of excitement I felt as Susan and I approached the charcoal, red brick building with the sign LUDLOW TOWN HALL.

We walked down the wide-planked corridor along gray wood walls to the town clerk's office. In the center of the room was a black bank vault with gold antique lettering. A tall oak table bowed under the weight of uneven stacks of files, and the mammoth computer printer it held seemed at odds with the turn-of-the-century decor.

We approached a girl standing behind the full-length counter. She wore granny glasses that rested at the end of her nose.

"Can you see if we have a marriage certificate, please?" I asked.

Bored by our request, she tore off a scrap of paper and handed us her pen.

"Name. Address where you lived when you married," she said mechanically. "The year you married, too."

I said nothing but looked her hard in the eye and waited.

"Please," she added as an afterthought.

With that information, she entered the black vault, returning minutes later with a large blue ledger. She wet her index finger every few pages until her finger finally stopped. "I Michael Grossman and Susan Doeing Mandel," she read looking up, "411 West End Avenue, New York City, 10024?"

"That's us," I said.

"It's here. You can get a copy for seven dollars," she said.

I slapped two five dollar bills on the counter, but Susan handed one back to me, pulling a five from her purse.

"My half," she smiled happily.

The clerk handed us our marriage certificate. We studied it a moment. I didn't expect to feel so proud.

"Best seven bucks I ever spent," I said nodding to the clerk.

"Nice you feel that way," she said. "Not everyone does."

I thought about that as we left Town Hall. That was exactly how I felt. I squeezed Susan's hand, and she returned the pressure. It was only a small moment, nothing monumental, but how good I felt. I took a breath of the crisp Ludlow air and enjoyed the fall morning. I hoped Susan and I would always feel this way, but if we didn't, one thing was certain. We'd passed the point where we could accept the former state of our marriage as safe or satisfactory. If we didn't love each other tomorrow as we did today, if we really were ships missing each other in the night as Sarah once suggested, then at least we were strong enough now to go our separate ways. That chilling thought stirred an ancient fear—that I'd lie on my deathbed feeling isolated and uninvolved, that I'd die alone like my cousins, having fallen to Isaac's curse. Yet I wasn't like my cousins, and I did not expect their fate.

Not that my escape from my history is perfect. I still have tenuous moments and fragile days when I make choices that don't reflect the best in me. I have moments of untethered anguish when I still sense Isaac's influence or hear my father admonishing me in a wind that once blew hard enough to bend the heaviest branches. In those moments, fewer now than ever, what used to be an almost biblical presence now lacks force. The voices are mere echoes from my past, wind whisperings without the power to drive a vise attack or send me off my core.

As Susan and I walked home from Town Hall, we passed a farmer's field with rows of pale yellow pumpkins. The field brought to mind our vacation in the French wine country. We visited several vineyards, some little known, a few quite famous. The vineyards permitted us to sample their wares and swirl the rich juice round our glasses. Our tour took us past rows of wooden fences with gnarled black vines bearing clusters of infant grapes that appeared to hang tenuously, yet they held firm even in the relentless sun, the winter cold and stormy days when the rain blew them nearly horizontal. The wine masters worked tirelessly to bring them to harvest. Still, despite hours of care under their protective eyes, a successful crop was never a certainty but rather a mystery precariously linked to soil conditions and unforeseeable climatic events. In some years, perfect conditions coalesced and gave birth to wonderfully rich wines. Other years, the same vines, tended just as carefully, bore a weaker juice. Science offers a partial explanation, but some of it is divine mystery.

My own survival is similarly providential. It is due in part to my toil but also due to something inexplicable that falls to the realm of a blessing. But identifying the cause of my good fortune isn't essential. More important are the gifts themselves, insights offered during years of sessions, tiny wisdoms with the power to banish demons, a hundred acts of love that held me together in the face of the psychological terrors that haunt us all, each in our different way.

The gift-givers, my therapists themselves, are my heroes. Sometimes I think of them as diligent professionals and sometimes as karmic angels. Whatever their true nature, they led me in harmonic succession along the damp walls of my dark labyrinth to the light of my core. Having found that core, I can stay present and know in every moment how I really feel. It is in that core that my love grows, along with my passion for the precious moments that remain in a life. In that core I experience the peace that is now my natural state. It is the state of mind I automatically return to, the way bent fibers reform to their native shape, or the way a pond calms after the ripples fade from a tossed stone.

Epilogue

WHEN A STORY IS DONE, it ought to be finished, and yet we have epilogues because stories don't finish. We have sequels because new things happen to old characters, so our picture of them keeps shifting. Doubtless you see your parents today very differently from your childhood image of them. What's more, your parents' good friends and relatives see them differently than you do. Perhaps there is no absolute reality to character—only kaleidoscopic perceptions that depend on who's turning the instrument. It would be different if we emerged from the womb like finished marble statues.

So we need updates, and it wouldn't feel right to leave this story without a mention of an unexpected turn in my relationship with my mother. After all, some might come away with the impression that Rosalind was the villain in my book—if psychological memoirs have villains. I don't think they ought to, since such labels freeze frame a moving picture.

In 2002, Mom had an unnecessary heart bypass operation. I say unnecessary because while the two doctors on duty convinced me she would suffer a heart attack without an immediate bypass operation, after that surgery her family doctor called me to say that what happened at the hospital was a sham. He said the week before he had given Mom a complete workup and that, absolutely, she did not need the bypass. He implied the surgery was performed to enrich the surgeons, a claim a doctor doesn't make lightly, so I give his accusation special credence.

The surgery had an immediate effect on Mom's memory, precipitating her Alzheimer's disease. The result was that a year after the surgery, my brother Randy, sister Jill and I gathered with Mom for a family meeting at which we asked her to move from her home in Tucson to an assisted living facility and later to a memory impaired unit. As part of that difficult transition, we asked Mom to choose among Michigan, California or Rhode Island, so that one of us three kids could look after her. We assumed she would choose to live in Michigan with my wonderfully capable sister Jill, but to all our surprise, Mom chose to move to Rhode Island, where I live.

I'd drawn the short straw.

In the beginning, the move was awful, and my relationship with mother went further downhill—if that were possible. As the dementia set in, Mom's worst character traits became exaggerated. As happens with many seniors and their adult children, she fought me about giving up her car. She battled me at every step when it came to the selection of the assisted living facility itself, asking why couldn't she rent a private house instead of being "abandoned" in a single room like a "jail." We picked the finest independent living facility available in the state, yet on the day of the move Mom stood in the handsome lobby of her new home yelling to be sure all the staff and residents would hear, "How could you move me into a crummy dump like this? Do you kids really hate me that much?"

Months of sundowning followed the move—the midnight calls when Mom awakened my wife Susan or me to accuse me of stealing her jewelry and her funds. She would hide her jewelry and then insist the staff was stealing from her—persisting even after the missing items reappeared. Her after-midnight phone calls often included bitter accusations that I hated her, insults, cries that she hated me followed by abrupt hang-ups, all of which she denied in the morning. Only my obligation to a parent, and not a good parent at that, kept me motivated to carry on with the rounds of trips to physicians, pharmacies, dentists, eye doctors and dry cleaners and her frequent visits to emergency rooms, as Susan and I did the hundred chores every son or daughter or daughter-in-law who has become a caregiver knows so well.

And then it ended. At perhaps the lowest point in my relationship with my mother, Susan and I witnessed a most unexpected transformation. In some, Alzheimer's brings out a person's worst traits. But in others these dissolve, leaving only the patient's native virtues. In Mom's case, mercifully, the latter scenario held true.

Today when I check in on her, the face of the woman I battled for so long bursts into a rich, brilliant smile the moment she sees me. She comes running in labored steps, arms outstretched to hug me, thanking me so much for visiting, reminding me how proud she is of me, and repeating over and over that she loves me so much.

Of course at first when this began, I held close to my old doubts and suspicions, and to be honest I'm still not sure who inhabits Mom's body and soul. I also don't care. I am thrilled to hug her right back, tell her that I too have missed her since our last visit and mean it honestly. While repetition is usually the bane of an Alzheimer's caregiver, I don't mind a bit when Mom tells me over and over again of her pride and affection for me.

It is important to note that I have not forgotten who she was. Remembering the old Rosalind is imperative, because for years I repressed that picture, ignoring the damage I did to myself by denying it—living unconsciously in part because of my refusal to see my parents clearly. So as not to lose those precious gains, I frequently remind myself whom I am dealing with.

And yet I also honor her transformation. Mom changed for the better, a mercy for my brother Randy, my sister Jill, my wife Susan and me. Like my therapy, this similarly falls to the realm of a blessing—and maybe it's something even more ethereal—something karmic.

Mom is now ninety-two. Presuming she will die before me, when her time comes I will feel that someone important is gone from my life. I will miss her—something I'd have bet the house I'd never feel. I will be able to stand before her remaining friends, before my family and relatives, and deliver a eulogy that comes from my heart, without clever sidestepping, and I will send her off with real tears in my eyes.

Life's funny, isn't it? Just when you know you have to give up on it, it turns around and bathes you in its goodness.

About the Author

I Michael Grossman is the author of *Coming to Terms with Aging: the Secret to Meaningful Time,* from RDR Books. Grossman has also written numerous newspaper commentaries, consumer and trade articles on topics ranging from ecology, ethics, travel marketing, flying, and bank marketing to applied ergonomics. Among the publications in which his works have appeared are *Advertising Age, Ergo Solutions, The CLIA Cruise Industry Annual Report, The American Banker* and *Plane and Pilot*. Grossman has appeared on national radio and TV shows including Arthur Frommer's Travel Channel show and NBC-TV's New York City affiliate.

Born in Muskegon, Michigan, Grossman currently resides in Rhode Island with his wife, three dogs and a cat.